THROUGH HITLER'S BACK DOOR

*SOE Operations in Hungary,
Slovakia, Romania
and Bulgaria 1939–1945*

by
Alan Ogden

Pen & Sword
MILITARY

ISBN 978 1 84884 248 9

The right of Alan Ogden to be identified as Author of this Work has been
asserted by him in accordance with the Copyright,
Designs and Patents Act 1988.

A CIP catalogue record for this book is available from the British Library.

Typeset in Stempel Garamond by
Phoenix Typesetting, Auldgirth, Dumfriesshire

Printed and bound in England by
CPI Antony Rowe, Chippenham, Wiltshire

Pen & Sword Books Ltd incorporates the Imprints of Pen & Sword Aviation,
Pen & Sword Maritime, Pen & Sword Military, Wharncliffe Local History,
Pen & Sword Select, Pen & Sword Military Classics and Leo Cooper.

For a complete list of Pen & Sword titles please contact
PEN & SWORD BOOKS LIMITED
47 Church Street, Barnsley, South Yorkshire, S70 2AS, England
E-mail: enquiries@pen-and-sword.co.uk
Website: www.pen-and-sword.co.uk

Polliciti Meliora

As one who, gazing at a vista
Of beauty, sees the clouds close in,
And turns his back in sorrow, hearing
The thunderclouds begin,

So we, whose life was all before us,
Our hearts with sunlight filled,
Left in the hills our books and flowers,
Descended and were killed.

Write on the stones no words of sadness –
Only the gladness due,
That we, who asked the most of living,
Knew how to give it, too.

Major Frank Thompson (c.1942)

Published with the kind permission of Dorothy Thompson

Contents

Maps

Preface

Historically the business of modern war had been conducted by politicians, diplomats and soldiers, but when on 1 July 1940 the British cabinet approved Winston Churchill's idea for a single sabotage organization called the Special Operations Executive (SOE), an incremental cast of businessmen, bankers, academics, engineers, journalists and adventurers materialized out of nowhere to 'set Europe blaze' and rid it of the Nazi scourge. Nowhere was this more evident than in SOE's Eastern Europe activities, where the line-up of operatives included oilmen, miners, civil servants, chartered accountants, business executives, journalists and a clutch of professional soldiers. The end results of some of their endeavours to set these distant parts of Europe 'ablaze' are still mired in controversy.

Basil Davidson was one such operative. Formerly a journalist, he describes SOE thus in his wartime memoir, *Special Operations Europe*:

> Distrusted by the War Office and deplored by the old pros of secret intelligence, SOE was all the same an extremely English organisation: no other country's rulers, I should think, could ever have evolved it. It was, in short, a triumph of deliberate amateurism. Its uppermost ranks were filled, at this stage almost to a man, by senior businessmen and bankers or others aspiring to be such when the war was over. Now this might be anything but amateurish in terms of economic warfare; if you wanted to know what to do about Romania's oil wells, then call in the men who had managed or financed them. But it was wonderfully amateurish in terms of political warfare. For SOE.'s chief aim and job, more and more after 1940, was promoting armed resistance, a work which took SOE straight into the middle of politics: and politics of a special kind. This was the politics of upheaval and protest, of subversion of conservative order, even of revolution: the kind of politics, in

vi

short, that was rightly held in horror by senior businessmen and bankers. They knew absolutely nothing about such matters, having previously regarded them as the business of the police. Now, quite suddenly, they had to act – in other countries of course – against every good conservative habit and belief.

When Hugh Dalton was given the task of running SOE by Churchill in July 1940, he first had to set out the scope of its activities. In *The Fateful Years*, he recalls:

As to its scope, 'sabotage' was a simple idea. It meant smashing things up. 'Subversion' was a more complex conception. It meant the weakening, by whatever 'covert' means, of the enemy's will and power to make war, and the strengthening of the will and power of his opponents, including in particular guerrilla and resistance movements.

'Subversion' was indeed to prove a challenging and controversial concept, and in several instances put SOE on a collision course with the FO and the SIS. Whereas its activities in Bulgaria were limited to formulating and supporting a Partisan resistance movement, SOE's ambitious agenda in Hungary and Romania was nothing less than 'regime change', with the aim of extracting unconditional surrender from both countries and their irrevocable withdrawal from the Axis side.

The political structures of these south-east European countries were complex and relatively fragile. Bulgaria had been free from Ottoman rule and occupation for just over fifty years; Slovakia had severed its ties with the Czech Lands of Bohemia and Moravia only after the German annexation of its twin sister in 1940 (and, of course, Czechoslovakia, formerly part of Austria-Hungary, had only come into being in 1918); Hungary, given free reign by her Habsburg King and Emperor in 1867 after over 300 years of involuntary servitude to Vienna, found her territories reduced by nearly 60 per cent in 1918 as a defeated member of the Triple Alliance; and Romania, under the suzerainty of the Ottomans until 1878, nearly doubled in size when awarded Transylvania at the Treaty of

Trianon. They all had one thing in common – chronic territorial insecurity.

Anthony Hope's *Prisoner of Zenda*, published in 1894, revolved around the fictional state of Ruritania, where the court heaved with intrigue, and plotters abounded. Such fiction seamlessly merged with fact in many instances in the inter-war Balkans where several prime ministers were shot, kings assassinated or abdicated, elections regularly rigged and colonels carried out *coups d'état*. It was all very un-British, far removed from Walter Bagehot's *The English Constitution*. So to this end, I have sketched out the individual political landscapes in the key periods up to the outbreak of the Second World War in order to convey the vivid contrast between British and Balkan political traditions and practices.

Romania, Bulgaria, Hungary and Slovakia were all German allies, though their commitment to the war effort of the Third Reich varied. All had made the decision to throw their lot in with the Axis, unlike the other countries of Europe which had either been forcibly occupied by the Nazis or remained neutral. So any SOE operation mounted within their borders was in enemy rather than enemy-occupied territory, heavily policed by military forces and gendarmerie and populated with suspicious peasants, ever fearful of giving assistance to 'resistors', if not downright hostile. Furthermore all these states had well-developed and experienced security services, usually supplemented by Gestapo and Abwehr units. This was a far cry from the other Balkan states like Yugoslavia, where a reservoir of defeated soldiers had taken to the hills in large numbers to plot their revenge on the invading Germans and Italians, or occupied Greece, where the appalling famine of 1941/2, together with the ferocity of German response to sporadic acts of resistance, had radicalized much of the population.

This is a story about the courage of individuals in the face of overwhelming odds. Whatever rights or wrongs can be laid at the door of policy makers and desk-bound decision makers, nothing can detract from the astonishing determination to stay the course shown by all those members of SOE who parachuted into these Fascist outposts of Fortress Europe. Hunger, ill-health, lack of hygiene, exhaustion, cold and treachery all combined to make life behind enemy lines as insufferable as it was dangerous. For weeks on end, the SOE missions moved continually at night, chased by enemy troops and their paramilitary forces, betrayed by local villagers, awaiting air drops that never came and listening out on their W/Ts for orders that were rarely specific. Wearing British Army uniform and carrying ID was no guarantee that the rules of war would be applied if they were captured, for in October 1942 Hitler had issued his notorious *Kommandobeheehl*, the general order that decreed that all commandos captured behind German lines would be 'slaughtered to the last man'.[1]

Furthermore the rules of engagement for Axis forces in Partisan warfare were far removed from the Articles of the Hague Conventions. For example, detachments of the German 1st Mountain Division received the following guidelines for one of their first operations in Greece in late 1943: 'All armed men are basically to be shot on the spot. Villages from where shots have been fired, or where armed men have been encountered, are to be destroyed, and the male population of these villages to be shot.' The distinction between 'armed men' and British liaison officers was to prove tenuous.

That said, SOE did push the boundaries out and the distinction between soldier and spy was blurred on more than one occasion. One officer who was infiltrated into Hungary recorded that 'my own civilian identity document was a certificate in German with original stamps stating that I was an Italian working in the aircraft factory in Poland in the capacity of interpreter, and that I had lost my papers in an air raid. This was an exact replica of an original document.' Fortunately for him, he was captured wearing uniform. Another recounts how, dressed in civilian clothes, he sat around in cafes in occupied southern Hungary, making notes of passing German units and their insignia.

A further complication to the subversive activities of SOE in these countries was the fact that they had all been effectively conceded by the Western Allies to Russia; not surprisingly therefore, operations in the Soviet 'sphere of influence' were to prove diabolically difficult.

Had it not been for the RAF, there would have been no SOE operations in Eastern Europe and the Balkans. The pilots and aircrew of Bomber Command were equally courageous as the men and women they dropped. Flying at night across enemy territory in large, relatively slow aircraft with only the illumination of the moon and dead reckoning to guide them, dodging belts of ack-ack and night fighters, they had to identify 'pinpoints' in remote mountainous areas before they could safely discharge their human cargoes. It was easy to get lost and run out of fuel as happened on the first run of the AUTONOMOUS Mission to Romania. It was equally easy to crash into the side of a mountain in atrocious weather conditions. Miraculously, most crews returned from these hazardous operations,[2] and I am only too conscious that I have failed to do them justice in this short account.

If the Bulgarian Partisans and their SOE mentors never achieved the quantum effect of the Yugoslavian Partisans under Tito, this does not diminish in any way their fortitude and courage. In the course of researching this book, my friend Maxim Behar in Sofia arranged for me to visit the archives of the Historical Museum. His secretary, 24-year-old Tatyana, made all the necessary arrangements and when I arrived, she asked me whether she could help since her family had been involved with the Partisan movement. Unfortunately there was no time to go and see her grandmother near Petrich but later Tatyana sent me details of what had happened. Her grandfather's brother, Asen Stoyanov, had been living with a Partisan *cheta* in the hills when he fell sick. On return to his village, a neighbour had called the police – presumably incentivized by a reward – who immediately surrounded the house. Rather than surrender, Asen retreated to the top floor and blew himself up with a hand grenade. 'That's why Granny still lives in a single-storey house,' Tatyana told me. Her grandmother's brother, Velin Vaklinov, also a Partisan, had been apprehended by the Gendarmerie and summarily strung up from a tree, upside down. His father became speechless for months on end, mortified, perplexed and angry about the ignominious death of his beloved son. Finally, Tatyana informed me that the village schoolteacher, a woman called Elena Georgieva, had been shot as a Partisan. The well-tended graves of all three can be seen to this day in Krasava village. I was impressed and relieved that a granddaughter had kept the flame of her Partisan grandparents burning so brightly.

Alan Ogden
London

Notes to Preface

1. The full text reads: 'From now on, all enemies on commando missions, even if they are in uniform, armed or unarmed, in battle or in flight, are to be slaughtered to the last man.

   If it should be necessary initially to spare one man or two, for interrogation, then they are to be shot immediately after that is completed.

   In case of non-compliance with this order, I shall bring to trial before a court-martial any commander or other officer who has failed to carry out his duty in instructing his troops about this order, or who has acted contrary to it.'

2. In support of the Yugoslav resistance, 11,632 flights took off, of which 8,640 successfully completed their mission. Only eighteen aircraft were lost.

Acknowledgements

The germ of *Through Hitler's Back Door* lies in the Commonwealth War Cemetery on the road to Ploieşti in Romania when I stopped over eleven years ago and came across the headstone of Captain David Russell MC, Scots Guards, standing somewhat out of place in a graveyard predominantly of young airmen shot down in the course of bombing the Axis-controlled oil refineries. Later on, with the help of Major Julian Lawrie and the Scots Guards Regimental archivist, I was able to piece together Russell's story for their regimental magazine, and the late Colonel Oliver Lindsay kindly agreed to publish a shorter version in the *Household Division Magazine*. It was during the course of this research that I came across the names of others who had been involved with SOE in Romania and so I decided to expand the story to include SOE operations in all the countries which were Axis allies in Eastern Europe.

Sadly, nearly all of the participants in SOE are no longer with us; some were killed in action, others have passed on. It was a particular shame for me to miss Kenneth Scott (CLARIDGES) who died in September 2008. However, it was also a great joy to be able to talk to Ivor Porter, the surviving member of AUTONOMOUS; his memory and wit are still remarkably keen. Griselda Cuthbert, the niece of David Russell of the RANJI mission, most kindly contacted me to discuss his personal papers which she had inherited from his sister's estate.

Fortunately I was able to locate John Sehmer's son, Jamie, and John Coates's partner, Frances Cooley, who were unstinting in their help and enabled me to build a much better picture of the respective individuals. Frances kindly put me in touch with Claerwen Howie who, as the official biographer of her late father-in-law, has an unrivalled knowledge of his wartime activities in Hungary. The Sound Archive at the Imperial War Museum was also a rich source of memoirs, particularly in respect of Basil Davidson, Henry Threlfall, John Coates and Guy Micklethwaite.

Much of the Bulgarian and Hungarian material in *Through Hitler's Back Door* comes from the HS (SOE) series of files in the National Archives (HS4 – Eastern Europe; HS5 – The Balkans; HS9 – Personnel). The staff there have invariably been commendably efficient and courteous. The library of the Royal Geographical Society proved invaluable in its treasure-trove of contemporary maps, allowing me to plot accurately the infiltration and exfiltration routes of the missions. Finally, I would like to thank Ian Trenowden of the Special Forces Club, Associate Professor Tzvetana Kjosseva of the Bulgarian National Museum of History and the Imperial War Museum for allowing me access to their photographic archives.

Throughout compiling this account, I have received encouragement from many people and would particularly like to thank Professor Dennis Deletant of SSEES, Professor Martin Conradi for his introduction to Frank Thompson's family, Professor M.R.D. Foot who gave the green light to my publishers, and to Brigadier Henry Wilson of Pen & Sword for his enthusiasm and help throughout.

Glossary

A Force A Force was a special services unit created in 1940 by General Wavell to organize by every available means the deception of the enemy High Command. The mission of its N section was to train soldiers in escape and evasion techniques. From September 1941 until the end of the war it was led by Lieutenant Colonel Tony Simonds, but it was subsumed by MI9 when the latter established its own ME section in Cairo under Lieutenant Colonel Dudley Clarke.

Abwehr *Amt Ausland/Abwehr im Oberkommando der Wehrmacht*, a German intelligence organization reporting to OKW. Headed by Admiral Canaris, the Abwehr was organized into three sections: foreign intelligence, sabotage and counter-intelligence. Its main role was intelligence gathering, although it had its own special forces unit, the *Brandenburgers*. Invariably it found itself in competition with the SS.

Andartes Greek guerrilla fighters.

BANU The Bulgarian People's Agrarian Union.

Blind drop Agents parachuting into hostile territory without a reception committee to meet them.

BLO British Liaison Officer.

BMM British Military Mission.

BW The Black Watch, a Scottish infantry regiment.

CFI Czech Forces of the Interior, the name given to the rebel Slovak Army units which took part in the Slovak National Uprising. Later known as the

First Czechoslovak Army, a name symbolic of the promised reunification of Czechoslovakia after the war.

Cheta   The word *cheta*, a small military unit no more than thirty strong, is derived from the Turkish word '*çete*', meaning gang or band of brigands.

Chetnik   In 1941, Yugoslav resistance forces consisted of two factions: the communist-led Partisans and the Chetniks. Based in the Serbian lands, the *chetniks*, or 'Yugoslav Army in the Fatherland', were a Royalist movement led by Colonel Draza Mihailović. Initially supported by Britain with military missions and arms, the *chetniks* were abandoned in late 1943 in favour of Tito's Partisans.

CNR   Romanian National Council, an SOE-sponsored exile group in London.

CPB   Communist Party of Bulgaria. Also known as BKP and BRP (Bulgarian Workers Party).

DCM   Distinguished Conduct Medal awarded to NCOs and ORs for outstanding bravery.

D/F   Direction finding, a technique to identify the location of wireless transmissions.

Drive   see Sweep.

DSO   Distinguished Service Order, a medal awarded to officers for outstanding bravery.

EAM   the Communist-dominated Greek National Liberation Front.

EDES   *Ethnikos Dimokratikos Ellinikos Syndesmos*, a right-wing Greek Republican party under Colonel Zervas. Sworn foes of ELAS.

ELAS   The Greek People's Liberation Army or *Ellinikos Lad'kos Apeleftherotikos Stratos* (abbreviated to ELAS) was the military arm of the National

	Liberation Front (EAM) during the period of the Greek Resistance until February 1945.
FO	The British Foreign Office.
Force 133, 226 and 399	Force 133 was the cover name for SOE's organization in Cairo from 1941 to 1946; Force 226 was the name for its Yugoslavia operations until June 1944 when all its Adriatic special forces missions were coordinated out of Bari by Force 399.
FS	Field Security.
HM	His Majesty's.
HMGs	Heavy machine guns
HMG	His Majesty's Government, a sobriquet for the British Government.
HQ	Headquarters.
IGC	Intergovernmental consultations on migration, asylum and refugees; part of the League of Nations.
IMRO	Internal Macedonian Revolutionary Organisation.
ISLD	see SIS.
JANL	Yugoslav Army.
Kontračeta	Anti-partisan units composed of pro-Bulgarian Macedonians, who were organized and equipped by the Bulgarian police in the period between 1942 and 1944.
LAC	Leading Aircraftman.
LOB	A pool of officers 'left out of battle'.
LMGs	Light machine guns e.g. a Bren gun.
LRDG	Long Range Desert Group, a British reconnaissance and intelligence-gathering unit in North Africa.
LUP	Lying-up point, a camouflaged position in enemy territory. Also called a 'hide'.

MC	Military Cross awarded to officers for bravery.
ME	Middle East.
ME 76	Codeword for SOE Hungarian Section.
MEF	Middle East Forces, a British Army Theatre of Operations Command.
MG	Machine gun.
MI9	A department of the British Military Intelligence Directorate, MI9 was set up in 1940 tasked to assist Allied servicemen stranded in Nazi-occupied Europe to return home. These consisted mainly of soldiers who had found themselves cut off after the Dunkirk evacuation and airmen who had been shot down or who had crash landed behind enemy lines. As the war progressed, it expanded its coverage to include all theatres of the conflict where British servicemen were involved.
Moon period	The week either side of a full moon when there was sufficient light for night flying operations.
MSR	Main Supply Route.
MTB	Motor Torpedo Boat.
N Section	see A Force.
NCO	Non-commissioned officer.
NID	Britain's Naval Intelligence Division.
OC	Officer commanding.
OCTU	Officer Cadet Training Unit.
Odred	Slavic word for detachment or unit.
OF	The Bulgarian Fatherland Front.
OKW	The *Oberkommando der Wehrmacht* served as the military general staff for the Third Reich, co-ordinating the efforts of the Army, Navy and Air Force (Heer, Kriegsmarine, and Luftwaffe). In practice, it translated Hitler's ideas into military

orders and issued them to the three services. As the war progressed the OKW found itself exercising increasing amounts of direct-command authority over military units, particularly in the West.

ORs   Other Ranks i.e. all those other than officers and NCOs.

OSS   The Office of Strategic Services was the approximate US counterpart of Britain's SIS and SOE with which it cooperated throughout the Second World War and its immediate aftermath. The OSS was created by Presidential Military Order on 13 June 1942 and it functioned as the principal US intelligence organization in all operational theatres. Its primary function was to obtain information about enemy nations and to sabotage their war potential and morale.

OTC   Officer Training Corps.

PICME   Political Warfare Executive Middle East. See PWE.

Pinpoint   a map reference indicating the area to drop men and materials. Manned by a reception committee, pre-agreed signals would be used to indicate whether it was safe to drop.

POW   Prisoner of war.

PWE   Formed in August 1941, the Political Warfare Executive was a secret department created to produce and disseminate both white and black propaganda, with the aim of damaging enemy morale and sustaining the morale of the occupied countries. Reporting to the Foreign Office, the staff came mostly from SO1, which up until then had been the propaganda arm of SOE. As PWE was a secret department, it used the cover name Political Intelligence Department (PID). The main forms of propaganda were delivered by radio broadcasts and printed postcards, leaflets and documents. PWE created a number of clandestine radio stations.

RAF	Royal Air Force.
RDA	Royal Dutch Army. A group of Dutch officers, who had escaped from POW camps in Poland, assisted SOE/MI9 in Budapest from 1943 to 1945.
RE	Royal Engineers.
RMAS	Royal Military Academy Sandhurst.
RSHA	The *Reichssicherheitshauptamt* (Reich Security Head Office) was a subordinate organization of the SS, created by Heinrich Himmler in September 1939 through the merger of the *Sicherheitsdienst* (SD or Security Agency), the *Geheime Staatspolizei* (Gestapo or Secret State Police) and the *Kriminalpolizei* (Criminal Police).
SACMED	Supreme Allied Command Mediterranean.
SAS	Special Air Service Regiment (SAS) founded by David Stirling in 1940 in North Africa.
Section D	Formed in 1938, Section D was an integral though distinct branch of SIS, under the command of Major Laurence Grand RE. Tasked to cause trouble in German-occupied Europe, it was later merged with SO2 of SOE.
SD	*Sicherheitsdienst* or Security Agency.
SG	Scots Guards, a Brigade of Guards infantry regiment.
SIG	Special Interrogation Group, a small unit of German-speaking soldiers attached to the SAS.
SIME	British Security Intelligence Middle East.
SIS	Founded in 1909 as a joint initiative of the Admiralty and the War Office to control secret intelligence operations in the UK and overseas, during the 1920s SIS established a close operational relationship with the FO through providing Passport Control officers within embassies, based on a system developed during the First World

	War by British Army Intelligence. This provided its operatives with a degree of cover and diplomatic immunity. SOE operations were overtly offensive in the occupied countries, which clashed with the more discreet approach of SIS, leading to a significant level of friction between the two services. Despite these difficulties SIS nevertheless conducted substantial and successful operations in both occupied Europe, and in the Middle East and Far East where it operated under the cover name 'Interservice Liaison Department' (ISLD).
SMGs	Sub-machine guns e.g. a Sten gun.
SNU	Slovak National Uprising.
SOE	The Special Operations Executive was formed in 1940 out of a collection of other agencies such as MI(R), a branch of the War Office's Military Intelligence Directorate, Section D of SIS, the Independent Companies (later Commandos) and the propaganda section at Electra House. Responsible for propaganda (SO1) and subversion (SO2), SOE reported initially to Dr Hugh Dalton, Minister of Economic Warfare, and then Lord Selborne.
SOPs	Standard Operating Procedures were drawn up to cover routine in the field, especially security.
STAVKA	the Supreme Main Command of the USSR (*Stavka Verkhovnogo Glavnokomandovaniya*).
Sweep	an anti-Partisan tactic involving the advance of a large number of troops through a Partisan-held area with the intention of 'driving' the Partisans into ambushes.
Wehrmacht	Germany's armed forces.
WO	British War Office.
W/T	Wireless transmitter and receiver.

Part One

Hungary and Slovakia

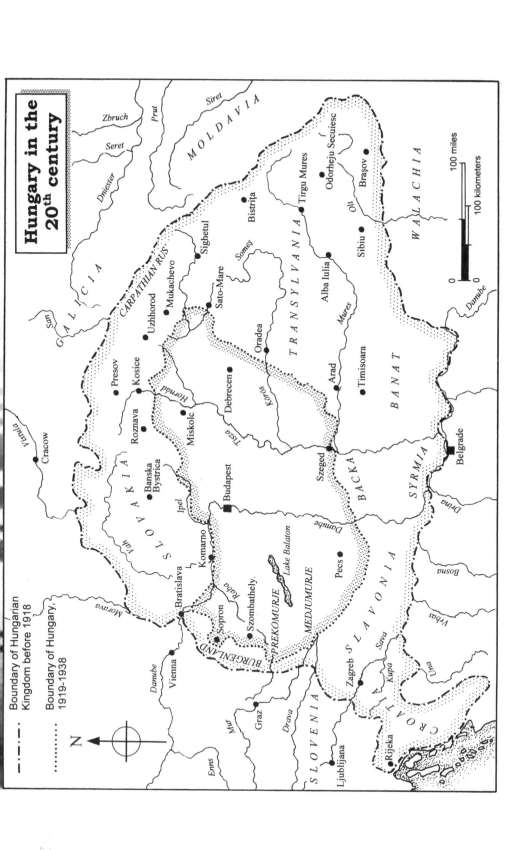

Hungary in the 20th century

N

Boundary of Hungarian
Kingdom before 1918

Boundary of Hungary,
1919–1938

100 miles

100 kilometers

GALICIA

MOLDAVIA

WALACHIA

TRANSYLVANIA

BANAT

SLOVAKIA

CARPATHIAN RUS'

SYRMIA

BACKA

SLAVONIA

SLOVENIA

CROATIA

BURGENLAND

PREKOMURJE

MEDJUMURJE

Zbruch

Prut

Seret

Siret

Dniester

San

Vistula

Cracow

Presov

Kosice

Roznava

Banska
Bystrica

Miskolc

Uzhhorod

Mukachevo

Sighetul

Sato-Mare

Bistrița

Somes

Oradea

Debrecen

Tisza

Körös

Mures

Alba Iulia

Arad

Timisoara

Sibiu

Tirgu Mures

Odorheju Secuiesc

Brașov

Olt

Szeged

Belgrade

Budapest

Ipel

Hornád

Váh

Komarno

Bratislava

Morava

Rába

Sopron

Szombathely.

Lake Balaton

Pecs

Danube

Drina

Bosna

Vrbas

Una

Kupa

Sava

Zagreb

Rijeka

Ljubljana

Graz

Vienna

Danube

Enns

Mur

Drava

Seret

Siret

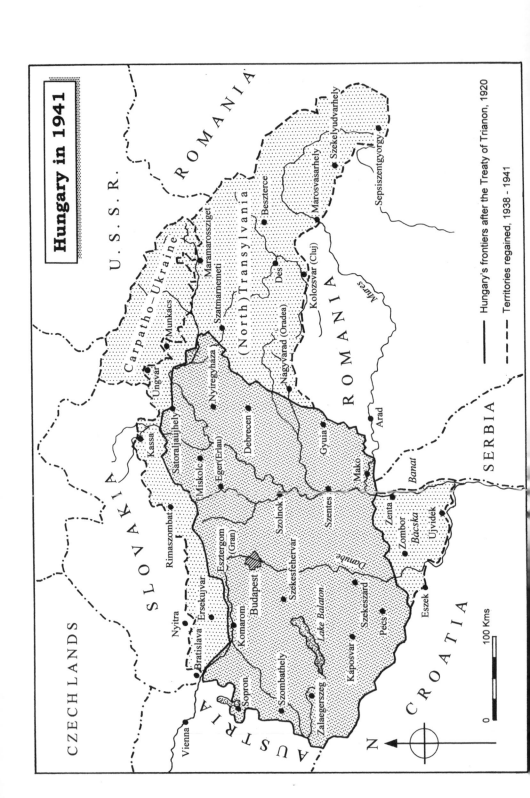

Hungary in 1941

CZECH LANDS

U.S.S.R.

ROMANIA

SLOVAKIA

Carpatho–Ukraine

(North)Transylvania

ROMANIA

SERBIA

AUSTRIA

CROATIA

Vienna
Bratislava
Nyitra
Ersekujvar
Komarom
Sopron
Szombathely
Zalaegerszeg
Lake Balaton
Kaposvar
Szekszard
Pécs
Eszek
Szekesfehervar
Budapest
Esztergom (Gran)
Szolnok
Szentes
Danube
Szeged
Zombor
Zenta
Bacska
Ujvidek
Mako
Gyula
Debrecen
Eger (Erlau)
Miskolc
Satoraljaujhely
Kassa
Rimaszombat
Nyiregyhaza
Ungvar
Munkacs
Szatmarnemeti
Maramarossziget
Nagyvarad (Oradea)
Des
Kolozsvar (Cluj)
Beszterce
Marosvasarhely
Szekelyudvarhely
Sepsiszentgyorgy
Arad
Maros
Banat

——— Hungary's frontiers after the Treaty of Trianon, 1920

–––– Territories regained, 1938 – 1941

N

0   100 Kms

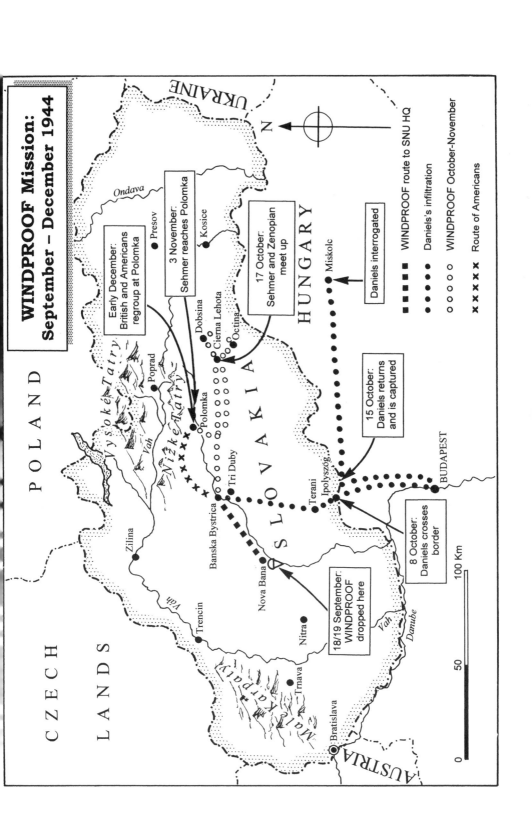

WINDPROOF Mission:
September – December 1944

POLAND

CZECH LANDS

UKRAINE

SLOVAKIA

HUNGARY

AUSTRIA

Ondava

Presov

Kosice

Dobsina
Cierna Lehota
Octina

Poprad

Vysoké Tatry

Nizke Tatry

Vah

Polomka

Tri Duby

Banska Bystrica

Zilina

Trencin

Nova Bana

Nitra

Vah

Trnava

Danube

Malé Karpaty

Bratislava

Terani
Ipolyszóg

Miskolc

BUDAPEST

Early December:
British and Americans
regroup at Polomka

3 November:
Sehmer reaches Polomka

17 October:
Sehmer and Zenopian
meet up

Daniels interrogated

15 October:
Daniels returns
and is captured

8 October:
Daniels crosses
border

18/19 September:
WINDPROOF
dropped here

N

WINDPROOF route to SNU HQ
Daniels's infiltration
WINDPROOF October–November
Route of Americans

0   50   100 Km

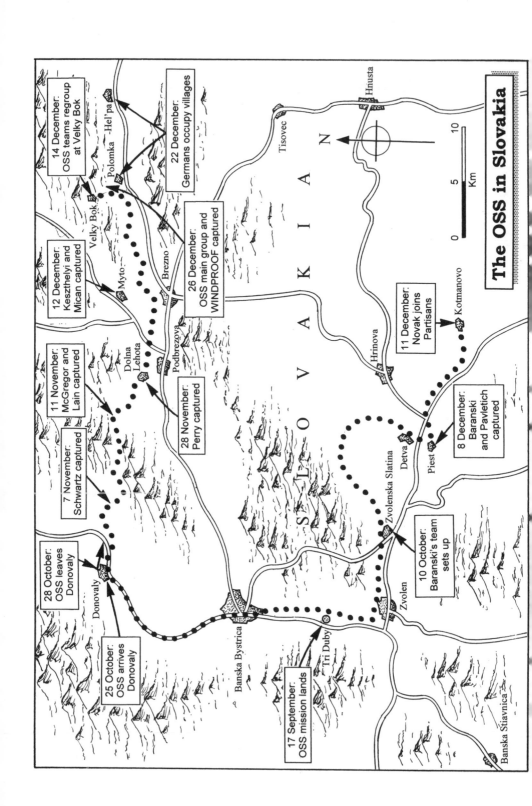

The OSS in Slovakia

28 October:
OSS leaves
Donovaly

25 October:
OSS arrives
Donovaly

7 November:
Schwartz captured

11 November:
McGregor and
Lain captured

28 November:
Perry captured

12 December:
Keszthelyi and
Mican captured

14 December:
OSS teams regroup
at Velky Bok

22 December:
Germans occupy villages

26 December:
OSS main group and
WINDPROOF captured

11 December:
Novak joins
Partisans

8 December:
Baranski
and Pavletich
captured

10 October:
Baranski's team
sets up

17 September:
OSS mission lands

S L O V A K I A

N

0   5   10
Km

Donovaly
Velky Bok
Polomka   Hel'pa
Brezno
Myto
Dolna
Lehota
Podbrezová
Banska Bystrica
Tri Duby
Zvolenska Slatina
Detva
Piest
Zvolen
Banska Stiavnica
Hrinova
Kotmanovo
Hnusta
Tisovec

SOE Personnel in Hungary and Slovakia

SOE Missions in Hungary

✟ **Killed in action/executed/died of wounds**

PILATUS
✟ Lt Lajos Klement aka Lewis/Louis/Tibor Clement aka L. Vadja

DECIMA (later SAVANNAH)
Maj Basil Davidson
Capt Ted Howe
Lt Steve Markos aka István Damo
Lt Wood aka Aurel Weinzierl
W/T Op Cpl (later Staff Sgt) George Armstrong

DANHILL (PILATUS II)
Lt Ivan Agoston aka István Szabo

SANDY (never dropped)
Lt Col Peter Boughey
Capt Coates

SANDY I (FETTES)
Capt Rollo Young
Capt Whittaker
W/T Op Sgt Scott

SANDY II
Lt Gus Bertram aka Betrand aka Gustav Bódó aka Hosszu Zoltan

DARESBURY
Maj Paul Harker (evacuated and replaced by Maj Maydwell)
Capt Hadow

Lt Laban
W/T Op Sgt Peaker (replaced by Cpl Purdhy)

DEERHURST
Lt Col Peter Boughey
✝ Maj Richard Wright
✝ Lt Alex Vincent aka Sándor Vass
✝ W/T Op Cpl Tony Manley
✝ Steve Mate (killed in plane crash en route to join Boughey in
   Brindisi)

DIBBLER
Maj John Coates DSO
(Lt Bertram)
Lt Joe Gordon aka József Gelleny
Lt Mike Thomas aka Miklós Turk
(Lt Tom Byron aka Tamás Révai)

MANGANESE (Czechoslovakia)
✝ O/C Vanura
Sgt Maj Kosina
✝ Sgt Maj Biros

EPIGRAM (Formerly DECIMA)
Capt Ted Howe
Lt Adam Murphy aka Ádám Magyar

DESFORD
Maj Desmond Longe MC
(Maj Kemp)
Capt Houseman

WINDPROOF
✝ Maj John Sehmer MBE
Lt Andy Daniels aka András Durovecz
Lt Stevenson aka BQMS Steve Zenopian
W/T Op Cpl Davies
(Maria Culovics)

DINDER[1]
Capt Dickie Franks[2]
Lt Herbert
W/T Op Sgt Dickinson

MICA
Lt Col Kenneth Greenless
Lt Col Rupert Raw
Capt Scweitzer
W/T Op Sgt Edwards

BAUXITE II (PIGOTITE)
Maj John Foster
Maj George Seymour MC

NATAL (an SOE operation with non-SOE personnel)
Lt Col Charles Howie
Sapper 'Captain' Roy Natusch MM
Sgt Maj Norman McLean
Henry Lowenstein
WO (Warrant Officer) Reginald Barratt

Trained but not deployed:
2 Lt Horovitz
2 Lt Brody
2 Lt Landau
Ádám Herter

SIS (ISLD)/SOE Operatives in Hungary

Col Teague
Sqn Ldr R.H.Lawson, ISLD liaison with MI9 Jewish parachutists
✠ Maj Jack Wilson (Wanndorfer)
'Jack' aka Jacques Dubreuil
W/T Op Keith Hensen
✠ Gabor Haraszty (ALBERT)
Lt Gerit van der Waals RDA
Lt Eddie van Hootegem RDA

Lt F.T.G. Brackel RDA
Karoly Schandl
Lolle Smit

MI9/A Force in Hungary

Lt Col Charles Howie OBE (escaped South African POW) –
   Budapest
Tibor Weinstein aka Tom Sanders
Henry Lowenstein
Evelyn Gore-Symes (MI9 Budapest)
Sapper Roy Natusch MM (escaped POW)
☫ WO Reginald Barratt aka Tim Barker aka G.S.Godden (escaped
   POW)
Rudolph Kasztner
Charles Szladits
Raphael Rupert
Peter Zerkowitz
Revd Alexander Szent-Iványi
☫ Dr Francis Pajor

POLISH UNDERGROUND IN HUNGARY

Countess Janina Tarnapolska ([Mrs Jane Radyszkiewicz)
☫ Prince Andrzej Sapieha
Col Matuszczak
Artur aka Steven Knorr aka Wisniewski aka Woyda

MISSIONS

AMSTERDAM
☫ Rafael Reiss aka Sgt Stephen aka Sgt Stevenson/Stefan Rice
   RAFVR
☫ Sgt Zvi Ben-Yaakov aka Jindrich Grünhut aka 2Lt M. Jamay
   (UNCLE)
Chaim Chermesh aka Martha Martinovic (AUNTIE)
☫ Haviva Reik aka Chaviva Reik aka Ada Robinson

ANTI-CLIMAX
✝ Abba Bardichev/Berdiczew/Berdichev aka Lt Robert Willis
✝ Rafael Reiss – see AMSTERDAM

CHICKEN
✝ Hannah Senesh aka Szenes (MINNIE)
Yoel Palgi aka Sgt Nussbacher (MICKY/HULBERT) DCM
✝ Peretz Goldstein (JONES)
✝ Abba Bardichev – see ANTI-CLIMAX
Sgt Reuven Dafni aka Capt Gary (GARY)
Yonah Rosen aka Rosenfeld (DICKENS)
Sgt Grandville (MAGISTRATE)
Capt 'MacCoy'

CHALLOCK
Zvi Ben-Yaakov (LEADBURN)
'Stickler'
'Morris'

COBWEB
Maj Robert Eden
Maj Macadam

SOE Agents

Mary Miske – FRUIT
Lufti Tozan – PANTS
Not known – PIP
Safet Bey – WOOD
Nandor Stossel – IRON
G. Pothorcky
✝ Erno Nadas
✝ Dezso Marton
Irma Piess
Imre Singer
György Szanto
György Neubauer
Sandor Lengyal

László Békeffi
✝ Bertram Peres aka Walter Bertram
Janos Stark
✝ Anna Visnovitch – MAX
Bobby Pálóczi-Horváth – HOWARD

OSS Hungarian/Slovak Missions

SPARROW
Lt Col Florimund Duke
Maj Alfred Suarez
Capt Guy Nunn

DAWES
✝ Lt James Holt Green DSC
✝ Sgt Joe Horváth
✝ W/Op Cpl Robert Brown
✝ Lt James Gaul DSC
✝ Lt Lane Miller
Sgt Ken Dunlevy

HOUSEBOAT
Lt John Schwartz
✝ Sgt Jerry Mican
✝ W/T Op Charles Heller

DAY
✝ Capt Ed Baranski
✝ W/T Op Daniel Pavletich
W/T Op Anton Novak aka Anton Facuna

BOWERY
✝ F/O Tibor Keszthelyi
Sgt Steve Catlos
Stephan Cora

DARE
✝ Lt Frances Perry

OSS Weapon instructors

Lt Bill McGregor
Lt Kenneth Lain

Others

Emil Tomes (OSS Counter-Intelligence)
✝ Joseph Morton (Associated Press)
✝ Nelson Paris, US Navy photographer
✝ Margita Kockova (interpreter)

SOE in Hungary and Slovakia

A Transylvanian grievance

The modern history of Hungary begins with the coronation of Stefan I on Christmas Day AD 1000. With the blessing of Pope Sylvester II and the Holy Roman Emperor Otto III, this event marked the country's entry into Europe as a Christian state and, with the introduction of Latin as the official language, the beginning of its documented history. For a people who had arrived from the Steppes of Central Asia a mere 150 years before, it represented a remarkable transition.

Three years later, the Hungarians completed their conquest of Transylvania,[3] which was to form the eastern part of the Hungarian lands for the next thousand years. Apart from the obvious attractions of additional land and a defensible border of mountain ridges, three commodities of enormous value came with Transylvania – salt, gold and silver. However, in the sixteenth century, two momentous events occurred which were to shape the next five hundred years of Hungarian history. In 1526, the young Hungarian King Louis was killed fighting the Ottomans at the Battle of Mohács. His death marked the end of the lineage of Hungarian Kings and the crown passed to the Habsburgs in Vienna, where it was to remain until 1918. The second event, dire in the extreme, was the fall of Budapest to the Turks in 1541. From hereon, Hungary was split in two, Royal Hungary to the North and West and Ottoman-occupied Hungary to the South and East; Transylvania was temporarily transformed into an independent principality.

At the end of the seventeenth century the Habsburg Emperors expelled the Turks from Hungary and with their departure, the Transylvanian principality also came to an end, becoming an Austrian province in 1691. Despite the appearance of autonomy with its own parliament and government, Hungary was de facto governed by Austrians from Vienna, so unsurprisingly in the nineteenth century the idea of national self-determination which had originated with the French Revolution took a powerful hold on the Hungarian mind. The independence of Greece, the unification of Italy and the restitution of Poland were all part of the consolidation of peoples into nation states; with their civilization and history, the Hungarians felt it was their turn too and a movement for the restoration of political and cultural independence or *Magyarisation* began

In 1840, when Latin was superseded by Hungarian as the official language of the Hungarian Government and its Parliament, a parallel demand was made for the union of Transylvania with Hungary. Kossuth, the arch proponent of Magyarisation, pushed through sweeping changes in Hungary as soon as the news of the February 1848 revolution in Paris reached Bratislava; the Hungarian parliament symbolically moved back to its ancient seat in Budapest and on 1 April the Union of Transylvania was proclaimed.

By the spring of 1848, the tide of revolution had been stemmed; as soon as the Habsburgs had crushed the uprising in Milan (Savoy), they turned their attention to the far greater problem of how to suppress the Hungarian independence movement. After putting their own house in order by stifling a revolt in Vienna, the Habsburgs gave the task of bringing Hungary back into the Austrian fold to the Imperial General Windischgrätz and his brother-in-law, von Schwarzenberg.

Transylvania became a battleground. Kossuth appointed the Polish General Bem, together with Commissioner Csány, to defend Transylvania against Austria. He then declared himself Governor of Hungary in April 1849, thus provoking the Habsburgs to invite the Russians to assist them. 200,000 of the Tsar's men poured into Hungary from the North. Kossuth's 'hussars' staged a courageous and desperate defence but were defeated at Sighisoara in July. By October, Hungary had been reduced to the status of an Austrian province, with Transylvania placed under the protection of Vienna.

By February 1867, the Emperor finally gave in to Hungarian pressure: the Empire of Austria and the Apostolic Kingdom of Hungary became two equal sovereign states linked by a common monarch. The *Ausgleich* – a compromise between Austria and

Hungary – accepted German hegemony in Austria and Hungarian supremacy in Hungary. A spectacular coronation in Budapest on 8 June 1867 completed the niceties. It was a unique arrangement and if the resulting economic and financial facts are viewed objectively, the Hungarians emerge as beneficiaries, not victims. For the first time since the disaster of Mohacs, they were masters of their own destiny and overlords of Transylvanians, Slovaks, Ruthenes and some of the Serbs.

The assassination of Archduke Franz Ferdinand in Sarajevo in June 1914 met with a muted reaction in Budapest since everyone knew that the policies of the heir apparent had been sympathetic with the minorities. It was clear that the 'Black Hand' had got the wrong man as far as Slavic national aspirations went. Within a month, Germany and Austria-Hungary declared war on Serbia despite the misgivings of the Hungarian Prime Minister, István Tisza, who was the only leading politician to warn the monarchy of its consequences. His words were not heeded and by the time the guns fell silent in 1918, 530,000 men from Hungary and Croatia had been killed, and 1.4 million wounded; over 833,000 were prisoners of war. Greater Hungary as epitomized by the historic Old Kingdom of Royal Hungary had ceased to exist.

The two options for containing a belligerent Austria-Hungary put forward by Lord Northcliffe at the British Department of Enemy Propaganda, were:

> to work for a separate peace with the Emperor, the court and the aristocracy, on the principle of not interfering with the domestic affairs of the Habsburg monarchy, and of leaving its territory almost or quite intact – or to try to break the power of Austria-Hungary, as the weakest link in the chain of enemy states, by supporting and encouraging all anti-German and pro-Ally peoples and tendencies.

The choice was narrowed down to the second by his able anti-Habsburg assistants, Robert Seton-Watson and Wickham Steed. When hostilities ceased, Hungary thus found herself friendless.

1918: Dismay and disbelief

On the night of 30 October 1918, the Hungarian government changed hands in a bloodless coup dubbed 'the Chrysanthemum Revolution'; the pacifist Count Mihály Károlyi,[4] the new Prime Minister, promptly signed an armistice on 3 November in Padua. Eight days later, the Emperor Charles renounced all his interests in affairs of state and the next day the Republic of Austria was declared. Hungary followed on 16 November, but already there were ominous signs at a second round of armistice negotiations in Belgrade that Hungary was going to be in for harsh treatment.

In October 1918, the Romanian National Party had met at Oradea and invoked the right of self-determination for the Romanians of Hungary, appropriately at the same time as President Wilson fully recognized the Yugoslavs and Czechoslovaks. The Habsburg monarchy now finally dissolved into its component parts – Galicia and Ruthenia seceded – causing Greater Hungary to disintegrate. Herbert Hoover described Hungary presenting 'a sort of unending, formless procession of tragedies, with occasional comic relief. Across our reconstruction stage there marched liberalism, revolution, socialism, communism, imperialism, terror, wanton executions, murder, suicide, failing ministries, invading armies, looted hospitals, conspirators, soldiers, kings and queens – all with a constant background of starving women and children.'

The union of Transylvania with Romania was declared on 1 December 1918 and was ratified by King Ferdinand on Christmas Eve. On 20 March 1919, the French Colonel Vyx handed an Allied ultimatum to Hungary, ordering withdrawal to new demarcation lines in the south-east which, if implemented, would sever old Hungarian lands from each other. As Foreign Minister, Oszkár Jászi exclaimed, 'our main trouble was not that we obtained hard armistice conditions, but even these hard conditions were not kept to.' Fearful of the indignation of the Hungarian people, Károlyi called on the Social Democrats to form a government, but he was too late: they had joined the Communists en bloc and after Károlyi's resignation, a new government headed by the Communist Bela Kuhn was formed. Its first act was to proclaim the dictatorship of the proletariat.

Banks, businesses employing more than twenty people and land holdings of more than 100 *jochs*[5] were declared common property and a plethora of commissars appointed. However, in the absence of any experience in government, the new order soon collapsed into a state of chaos, and after a fraught and bloody 133 days including a war against Czechoslovakia and Romania, it was replaced by a reactionary government supported by the newly organized National Army under the command of Admiral Miklós Horthy. Riding into Budapest on a white horse on a rain-swept day in November 1919, Horthy was to be the pivot around which the affairs of Hungary were to turn in the next twenty-five years. After passing through three major convulsions in as many years, the forces of reaction had emerged better ensconced than ever, especially since the first taste of communism had been so bitter.

On 4 June 1920, the Treaty of Trianon was signed – Transylvania had gone to Romania despite Count Apponyi's eloquent plea for it to be constituted as a separate state, and with it a significant slice of Hungary, including Arad, Oradea and Satu Mare. At least the proposal to draw the new Western border on the line of the Tisza River had been rejected. All in all, Hungary lost 66 per cent of her territory (compared to Germany's 13.5 per cent) and 3.4 million of her people were now outside her borders. President Wilson's Tenth Point had been met – 'the peoples of Austria-Hungary, whose place among the nations we wish to see safeguarded and assured, should be accorded the freest opportunity of autonomous development' – but ironically with the exception of the Hungarians.

Not everyone by any means was happy with this outcome: Winston Churchill described the break-up of the Austria-Hungary as 'a cardinal tragedy'. Duff-Cooper commented in 1946 that 'it is surely now generally recognized that the disappearance of the Austro-Hungarian Empire has proved to be one of the major calamities of this disastrous century.' In effect, a free-trade zone of 52 million people covering an area of 267,000 square miles, with a common currency and tariffs, had been dismantled overnight. A cynic might muse that this great internal market, where real income per head between 1904 and 1914 had increased 63 per cent in Austria and 75 per cent in Hungary, way ahead of the UK or Germany, had been too successful for its own good.

Hungary between the wars: the forces of reaction prevail

If old problems were solved, new ones were created. The unilateral advance of the Romanian Army to Budapest in defiance of the Great Powers in Paris was accompanied by a 3 billion gold crown orgy of looting and plundering; nothing was sacrosanct in the name of revenge. Herbert Hoover recounted that 'they looted art galleries, private houses, banks, railway rolling stock, machinery, farm animals – in fact every movable which Bela Kuhn had collected.' The hand of Bucharest was omniscient, overruling the innate liberalism of the Transylvanian Romanians who had, for so many centuries, set out to achieve equality with the Hungarians through passive resistance, not insurrection and brute force.

Just over a year later, the *Agrarian Reform Act concerning Transylvania* was published, after being passed in the Romanian Parliament that March. Whilst there was undoubtedly a case for reform, the effect of this legislation was the destruction of all the great Transylvanian estates owned by Hungarian families. It was, as one Romanian put it, the supreme instrument of the Romanianization of Transylvania. The maximum amount of land permitted to a single owner, even if situated in different districts, was 500 acres, including a limit of 50 acres in the high mountains and a 100 acres in hilly districts; in the plain areas where the demand for land was deemed to be greatest, the limit was a hundred. Expropriation prices were fixed by the government as an average of prices from 1908 to 1913, which amounted to about 5 per cent of current prices including currency depreciation. 11,000,000 acres were thus expropriated and the owners paid in non-transferable Romanian government 5 per cent bonds.[6]

The Hungarian reaction to such events was '*nem, nem soha* – no, no, never' and it was the scion of one of the great Transylvanian families, Pal Teleki, who took on the role of Prime Minister to 'save Hungary from abominable dismemberment'. A descendant of the Transylvanian Chancellor Samuel Teleki, and of József Teleki, first President of the Hungarian Academy of Sciences, Pal had much to live up to. A brilliant scholar as a boy, his studies in geography and political science were published by the time he was twenty. At twenty-six, he was a MP and eight years later elected a corresponding member of the Hungarian Academy of Sciences. Virulently anti-Bolshevik, Pal joined the Károlyi government in 1919 and then became Foreign Minister in the Horthy regency government in 1920. That summer, by dint of his reputation for scholarly objectivity, he was made Prime Minister.

Like many of his contemporaries, Pal had never come to terms with the finality of the Treaty of Trianon. He was sure that 'later on (we) will have the peace revised'. Trianon was acceptable 'only in the *a priori* assumption of a possibility for revision'. The real danger was communism: how could the Great Powers be so blind as to preside over a weak Hungary while Russia grew stronger by the day? But blind they were; just as Hungary had lost the war, so it had lost the peace. In February 1921, Pal resigned and after an abortive attempt by ex-King Charles to reclaim his throne in March 1921, another Transylvanian aristocrat, Count István Bethlen, was appointed Prime Minister. During his tenure of office over the next ten years, Hungary regained much of her pre-war prestige. In 1923, the League of Nations accepted Hungary as a member, granting her a loan of 250 million gold crowns. Fiscal stability was restored and by 1929 industrial production was 12 per cent higher than in 1914.

The Horthy regency, through Bethlen's even-handed and moderate policies, transformed the traumatized society of 1919 into a pluralistic, confident nation with international recognition. The only banned political party was the Communist Party, the press enjoyed almost total freedom and the anti-Semitic legislation of 1920 was watered down. But the global economic crisis of the early 1930s, together with the rise to power of Hitler, paved the way for a right-wing government to take office under Gyula Gömbös.[7] With close relationships to both Hitler and Mussolini, the new Prime Minister, together with his Finance Minister, Béla Imrédy, led his country into the political and economic sphere of the Axis powers.

In early 1935, Gömbös, who had originally given Horthy an undertaking that he would restrain his anti-Semitism, convinced the Admiral to dissolve Parliament and hold new elections. The elections resulted in Hungary's right wing gaining control, which in turn led to a huge increase of Gömbös's power. He expanded and re-equipped the Army, filling it with sympathetic officers, and exerted political control over the Civil Service by allocating key positions to his supporters. In 1936, he boasted to Göring that within two years, Hungary would be completely remodelled along Fascist lines with himself as dictator. Fortunately, Gömbös never lived to see these ambitious plans come to fruition for, after a long illness, he died of kidney failure in Munich on 6 October 1936 and was succeeded by another right-wing pro-German politician, Kálmán Darányi.

However, Gömbös's investment in cultivating the Axis powers appeared to pay off. Half of Hungary's foreign trade was now conducted with Germany, including a high percentage of its exports of bauxite, oil and farm products. It was Béla Imrédy, now Prime Minister, who reaped the territorial rewards and at the First Vienna Arbitral Award of 2 November 1938, under Italian and German arbitration, Hungary recovered nearly 12,000 square kilometres of former territory in southern Slovakia and in sub-Carpathian Ruthenia, with over a million inhabitants.

Like the Iron Guard in neighbouring Romania, in 1935 Hungary begot its own sinister right-wing movement called the Arrow Cross, started by a former professional soldier, Ferenc Szálasi. Its followers originally wore brown shirts, and used the swastika and Hitler salute, but after a ban in 1933, it switched to green shirts emblazoned with the arrow-cross, the emblem of St László, and the party salutation became *kitartás* or 'endurance'. Promising deliverance from Jewish capitalists and an end to the estates of the great landowners, by 1938 it had over 250,000 members. When it contested the May 1939 elections – the only ones in which it stood – the party won more than 25 per cent of the vote and thirty seats in the Hungarian Parliament.

After a gap of twenty years, Pal Teleki became Prime Minister again and once more this brilliant man found himself in an impossible position: how could he placate Germany without antagonizing England? He loved the English with a passion: their way of life and their language; his books and studies had been published in English; his friends included English scientists, academics and aristocrats; he was even head of the Boy Scout movement in Hungary, a position he was inordinately proud of. He was determined to keep Hungary out of the war as a 'non-combatant' state, writing 'we have to stay out of the conflict at any price. The outcome of the war is doubtful . . . the most important thing for Hungary is to remain unscathed when the European conflict ends.'

In March 1939, Czechoslovakia was dissolved and Hungary occupied the rump of Carpathian Ruthenia. Hungary immediately recognized the German puppet state of Slovakia, led by the fascist Jozef Tiso. But on 23 March 1939, disagreements with Slovakia over the new common eastern border led to a localized armed conflict between the two countries. The Slovak-Hungarian War (also known as the 'Little War') ended with Hungary gaining only the easternmost strip of Slovakia.

Yet German troops had already been granted free passage through Hungary to Romania on the pretext of 'training'. In March 1941, Germany demanded the use of Hungarian territory as a jumping-off point for an attack on Yugoslavia; as a quid pro quo, they offered Hungary her pre-1920 lost provinces of Bácska and Muraköz. Horthy and his pro-German Chief of the General Staff, Colonel-General Henrik Werth, were in favour. So the scholar statesman Teleki knew he had failed England, who would be bound to declare war in such circumstances (and she duly did). It was a personal failure above all and in his suicide note written in the small hours of the morning of 3 April 1941, Pal wrote to Admiral Horthy 'we have sided with the scoundrels . . . we are nothing but grave robbers – a most despicable nation. I did not keep you back. I am guilty. Pal Teleki.' A tragic failure or a great hero? Churchill saw him as the latter, for here was a Hungarian who had laid down his life for those very values the Allies held so dear.

Days after Teleki's death, the German Air Force bombed Belgrade without warning and Horthy dispatched the Hungarian Third Army to occupy Vojvodina in northern Serbia. Later, Hungary forcibly annexed sections of Baranja, Bačska, Medimurje and Prekmurje. Hungary did not immediately participate in the invasion of the Soviet Union which began on 22 June that year, but then Hitler had not directly asked for its assistance. Nonetheless, many Hungarian officers argued for participation in the war so as not to encourage Hitler into favouring Romania in the event of revisions to the Trianon Treaty borders of Transylvania. On 26 June 1941, the Soviet Air Force bombed Košice, giving Hungary *casus belli* for joining Operation BARBAROSSA and she duly declared war against the USSR the next day.

On 1 July 1941, under the direction of the Germans, the Hungarian Karpat Group attacked the Soviet Twelfth Army. Attached to the German Seventeenth Army, the Karpat Group advanced far into southern Russia. At the Battle of Uman, fought between 3 August and 8 August, the Karpat Group's mechanized corps acted as one half of a pincer that encircled the Soviet Sixth and Twelfth Armies. Twenty Soviet divisions were captured or destroyed in this action. Now, with Hitler's support, Hungary recovered about two fifths of her Transylvanian losses at Trianon at the Second Vienna Award of 30 August 1941, again under the auspices of Germany and Italy. The new border followed the line south of Oradea, Cluj, Tirgu Mures to Sfantu Gheorghe.[8] The Award was to be short lived but it proved a point: Trianon as an exercise 'to make the world safe for democracy' had been an abject failure.

Early days for SOE: the first networks

From early on, SOE encountered difficulties in setting up a subversive network in Hungary. Before Hungary's entry into the war, and while there was still a British representative in Budapest, the implacable opposition of HM Minister, Sir Owen O'Malley, made the successful establishment of a covert organization almost impossible. Furthermore, it had proved an uphill struggle to find, let alone recruit, active members of a pro-British network as confirmed in a Section D report from Budapest on 24 October 1939: 'Hungary and Romania are in desperate fear of Bolshevism compared to which German domination is the lesser evil.' As a result of this and the German invasion of Yugoslavia, SOE had to start virtually from scratch in 1941.

There was, however, an unexpected turnaround for British Intelligence when military and civilian refugees began to pour across the Hungarian border after the defeat of Poland in early October 1939 and, in consequence, a number of unofficial intelligence initiatives took root. One of the best known was the intelligence-gathering network and POW escape line put together by Countess Kristina Gizycki and her close friend, Andrew Kowerski-Kennedy. The daughter of Count Skarbek, a lately impoverished

Polish nobleman, the 24-year-old Kristina had arrived in Budapest from London in December 1939 as a 'journalist', her cover having been arranged by George Taylor and Freddy Voigt of SIS. Determined to create a role for herself in fighting the German invaders of her homeland, in February 1940 she made an epic journey on skis across the Tatra Mountains into Poland and, after a harrowing five weeks in Warsaw, during which time she gained the measure of the Nazi occupiers, she returned safely to Budapest.

This was the first of four trips she undertook into Nazi-occupied Poland, the last being in November 1940 when she went in to rescue a number of escaped British POWs. On her return, the climate for Polish exiles in Budapest had markedly changed, even for those with diplomatic status like Kristina (her husband, George, was an accredited diplomat). With the Gestapo hot on her heels, she and Andrew took refuge in the British Embassy and it was here that Kate O'Malley, the daughter of the Head of the British Legation, came up with the alias 'Granville', the surname which Kristina was to use for the rest of her life. Issued with all necessary visas, she and Andrew set off on a typically audacious car journey which took them to Cairo via Belgrade, Sofia, Istanbul, Beirut and Haifa. Although warmly welcomed by Colonel Bill Bailey and Colonel Guy Tamplin of SOE, the courageous couple found themselves entwined in vicious internecine politics of the various Polish intelligence outfits now in exile and were unfairly deemed by London as not suited for the British Intelligence services on account of their 'German' connections.[9] Fortunately this decision was eventually reversed and both went on to serve both Poland and Britain with distinction.[10]

During the second half of 1941 and the beginning of 1942, some progress was made by SOE in building up contacts in neutral countries like Turkey, Portugal, Sweden and Spain, and in recruiting agents to send into Hungary from Istanbul. However, owing to the difficulty of infiltrating agents into the country across closely guarded borders, and also due to the mutual enmity between Hungary and Yugoslavia, little headway was made. Towards the end of 1942, SOE experienced a serious setback when their Hungarian network run out of Istanbul was penetrated and all its agents arrested.

In December 1941, Anna Visnovich, a Hungarian with Italian citizenship had been recruited by SOE, together with her lover Eugen Steinwurzl, a German of Russian-Jewish ancestry with a Chilean passport. She had offered her services to go to Romania to establish contact with a Serbian group near Timişoara, who wished to work with the British in sabotaging rail networks. If that turned out to be unpracticable, she proposed that she should go to Hungary and make any contacts SOE might want.

SOE decided to go for both bites of the cherry and she departed after Christmas, with a passport full of visas, for Romania and then Hungary on a four-week mission. Her code name was MAX. Having completed her first task, Anna left Timişoara for Budapest on 16 January 1942 and was next heard from on 12 February when she asked for more money. Shortly afterwards news reached Istanbul that she had been arrested.

In mid-March, a Polish source told London that 'Hungarian authorities recently detained a woman from Istanbul. In her fox furs introductions were found for a group of correspondents and a large amount of dollars.' The lady in question was a flamboyant Hungarian baroness code-named PIP, who had been despatched from Istanbul by Bobby Pálóczi-Horváth to Bucharest and Budapest. Hidden in her blue fox-fur cape was a microfilm containing a 32-page document about sabotage and a 16-page coded letter. The baroness was tried for high treason and sentenced to death. Subsequently her sentence was commuted to twelve years of hard labour.

More disconcerting news was confirmed in a Hungarian newspaper report: 'In the city of Győr enemy agents planned to attempt a large scale sabotage action and had already made all the necessary preparations. This sabotage attempt was foiled by the vigilance of the authorities. The persons concerned have been arrested. Before the completion of the investigation no further communiqués will be published.' When the next communiqué was published it was devastating news. 'The special summary court of the Chief of the General Staff has pronounced the following sentences concerning the Győr sabotage arrests: Erno Nadas, private employee, Dezso Marton, theatrical secretary, Irma Piess (Piecz), servant – to be hanged by the neck.' Marton[11] and Piess were lucky in that their sentences were commuted to imprisonment. Five other members of the network – Imre Singer, György Szanto, György Neubauer, Sandor Lengyal and László Békeffi – were also arrested and sentenced to twelve years imprisonment. Basil Davidson's network,[12] headed by his star agent Nadas, had been totally eradicated. Davidson, a journalist who had originally been recruited by Section D and despatched by train to Hungary in January 1940 without knowing one word of the language, was the first to admit that he and his colleagues were 'very young, very inexperienced and very amateurish' in these early days.

Another incident that occurred that May revolved around Mary Miske,[13] code name FRUIT, the English wife (née Walters) of Baron Miske Gerstenberger, the Hungarian Consul General in Istanbul. She had been approached by Davidson to take letters to the Social Democrat, Arpad Szakasiks, and the Peasant Party politician, Imre Kovacs.[14] The letters denied that the Anglo-Saxons had ceded Hungary to the Russians and urged both men to form a Popular Front to force Horthy to disengage from the Axis. Not wishing to implicate herself, Mary had wisely pushed the letters through the two men's letterboxes. The unfortunate Kovacs was caught by the Hungarian counter-intelligence authorities with the letter in his possession and imprisoned.

At around the same time, a Polish organization in Hungary with which SOE worked was also compromised and entirely liquidated by the Gestapo. SOE's Hungarian cupboard was now bare. An internal reorganization in spring 1942 resulted in operational control being passed to London from Cairo and Istanbul; little changed as a result of this bureaucratic pass-the-parcel and, in May 1943, control reverted to Cairo.

Early in 1943, Horthy had visited Hitler. It had not gone well. The Führer, well informed by the Abwehr, demanded the dismissal of Kállay and Szent-Györgyi on the grounds that they were Anglo-Saxonphiles. He had a point for Albert Szent-Györgyi had gone to Istanbul on 7 February and managed to brief a German agent masquerading as a British Army officer, well and truly spilling the beans. He then berated the Admiral for his 'betrayal' over the Jewish question and demanded a quota of 100,000 Jews per month to be delivered to Germany. He finally finished his tirade by accusing Horthy of failing to support Germany economically. This meeting ended on a distinctly fractious note, with Horthy asking Hitler to put the German demands in writing. This was duly done and Hungary refused to answer.

On 13/14 March 1943, SOE launched their first external Hungarian operation, PILATUS. A 23-year-old former Foreign Legionnaire, Lieutenant Klement (code-named VADJA), was dropped into Poland with a W/T set and codes with orders to make his way to Budapest. Klement had had a chequered past, fighting in Norway with the French Marines, then transferring to the Paratroops, where after a frustrating few months, he deserted and tried to join the British Army. The French authorities tried him for desertion and after several spells in prison he was handed over to the British authorities in the Isle of Man. After his release in August 1942, he was 'highly recommended' for SOE work.

A further set was smuggled into Hungary by Count Peter Pejačević,[15] the Hungarian Ambassador to Madrid. On 26 May, SOE bemoaned the fact that 'neither SIS nor ourselves have any active agents inside the country nor any reliable information about what is happening there.' What they did not know was that Klement was still en route from Poland and only reached Budapest on 11 June. Two days later he tried to contact Count Peter only to find that he had left for Portugal and the abandoned Countess implored him to go away. Catherine Schandl in *The London-Budapest Game* tells a different version of this story. Count Peter had in fact deposited the set with his sister, Countess Marie, in her apartment in the Royal Palace. Before he unexpectedly left for Portugal, he told her about the contents of 'the yellow case' and that she should expect a British agent to come and collect it. Klement duly arrived in August but the Countess was away and her brother Count Geza had no knowledge of any such arrangements. On her return, he told her about her mysterious visitor and, after a family council of war, Count Geza and another brother, Count Marcus, took the suitcase and buried it some distance from Budapest. The Countess burned the cipher papers. When Klement showed up again in September, the Countess was this time at home and duly received him. She told him where the set was buried and that was the last she saw of him.

According to his statement later given to the Russians, Klement was instructed by SOE to wait until a new contact could be activated and when that failed, was then told to sit it out until February 1944. This prompted him to 'do some work on my own account' and after being liberated by the Russians on 26 January 1945, he reported to General Chernikov, the military governor of Budapest, and was last heard of in Tura on 1 March. He never reappeared in the West and is presumed to have died in captivity.

In London, SOE had been trying to instil a sense of unity into the three Hungarian organizations active there: Revai's Association of Hungarians in Great Britain, Count Károlyi's New Democratic Hungary and The Hungarian Club. Revai was reluctant to adopt the programme of the Hungarian Front for National Independence which had been enthusiastically embraced by the other two, probably because Károlyi refused to treat him as an equal. To circumvent this, SOE proposed to the FO and the PWE that Kalasy should come to London and take control of the Association of Hungarians in Great Britain.

The Surrender Group

The initial Hungarian intention was to sit out the war on the side-lines enjoying its recouped lands, but by mid-1942, under pressure from the Germans, Horthy had had to despatch a whole army to the Russian Front. It was the destruction of this 207,000-strong army at Voronezh in January 1943 and the German disaster at Stalingrad that heralded the turning point in Hungary's participation in the war. Worried about Hungary's increasing reliance on Germany, Horthy forced Prime Minister Bárdossy to resign and replaced him with Miklós Kállay, a veteran conservative politician of Bethlen's government. Kállay continued Bárdossy's policy of supporting Germany against the Red Army while he also put out feelers to the Allies through emissaries in various neutral capitals.[16] Attempts to establish covert contacts with British diplomats were coordinated by the executive director of the Revisional League, starting with Ambassador Aladár Szegedy-Maszák in Sweden in 1942, then Istanbul, Portugal and Switzerland. Yet the vast majority of the Hungarian upper class and officer corps still gambled on a German victory. Such wishful thinking came from the desire to hold on to the territories recovered post-Trianon and from a dread of Soviet retribution, combined with the ruling elite's pathological fear of communism. The spectre of Bela Kuhn and his debilitating brand of incompetence and chaos was never far away.

To formalize his peace initiative, Kállay created the Surrender Group which comprised a distinguished group of statesmen, diplomats, civil servants, lawyers, financiers and landowners; the line-up included Interior Minister Keresztes Fischer, Under-Secretary of State Jëno Ghiczy (later Foreign Minister), Deputy Foreign Minister Szentmiklóssy and his assistant and Head of the Political Department, Aladár Szegedy-Maszák, Head of the Press Department Ullein-Reviczky,[17] and elder statesmen like Count Bethlen and Count Móric Esterházy. Importantly, the group was inclusive of the left as well and radical social reformers like J. Kovács and Peter Veress were part of it. However, there was a glaring weakness in the group's make-up for no senior soldiers had been recruited. Without the whole-hearted participation of top Army officers, the levers of a *coup d'état* remained out of reach.

From the outset, there was little expectation that Horthy would ever embark on a proactive anti-German policy since his power base inside Hungary depended too much on the pro-German elements in the Army and Civil Service which he himself had so assiduously cultivated since 1932. Unless a realistic alternative to remaining on Germany's side was constructed, there was little point in risking alienating Hitler before Stalin arrived on the doorstep. It was to this end that a Foreign Ministry official, László Veress, travelled to Lisbon in January 1943 to make contact with the Allies through the offices of the Hungarian Legation. Described as having 'a keen mind, a willingness to risk his life, an ardent love for his country and a love of Great Britain',[18] Veress returned to Budapest with a stark message from the Allies. It was only a matter of time before the Axis collapsed and in the light of the Russian advance it would be apt for Hungary to accept the 'unconditional surrender' formula recently promulgated by the Allies at Casablanca as a basis for securing their future goodwill.

Kállay's group was aghast at this proposal since it would invite German retribution. A mollifying message was therefore sent to the Allies in Istanbul that Hungary would under no circumstances resist the British or American armies inside or outside Hungary, and furthermore was prepared to facilitate their access to her territory and infrastructure provided that no Russian, Yugoslavian, Czechoslovak or Romanian troops were involved. The problem was that without the participation of the Hungarian military, there was no chance for the group to enter into detailed military negotiations.

When Veress arrived in Istanbul in March, SOE officers, who had been forbidden by the FO to talk to him in Lisbon, were allowed access.[19] One of them, George (Bobby) Pálóczi-Horváth,[20] code-named HOWARD, caused some unease since he was known to have written before the war for *Gondolat*, the monthly paper of the Hungarian Communist Party. The result was an agreement in principle to establish a W/T link between Kállay and HMG, with the possibility that a mission, codenamed SANDY, would follow. When Veress suggested this to Kállay on his return, the Prime Minister was horrified and refused to discuss it until his son had driven him and Veress to the hills outside Budapest,[21] where they could not be overheard. Although he did not veto the idea outright, neither did he endorse it and it was only after the fall of Mussolini that he agreed to have a staff officer appointed for conversations with Istanbul. Due to a Machiavellian mix-up, the pro-German Hungarian Military Attaché in Sofia managed to get himself appointed as the new Military Attaché in Istanbul, with the result that no bilateral conversations ever took place at a military level.

On 15 August 1943, DECIMA, consisting of Major Basil Davidson, Lieutenant Markos,[22] Lieutenant Wood and Corporal Armstrong was infiltrated into the Frushka Gora area of Northern Yugoslavia with the objective of contacting left-wing elements in Hungary. In between times, Davidson frequented Novi Sad, the capital of Hungarian-occupied Yugoslavia, and spent his days in civilian clothes, insouciantly sitting in cafes and counting passing German military traffic. Ten months later, an internal SOE report noted that 'little has been accomplished owing to constant German pressure.'

Wood, real name Aurel Weinzierl, had a colourful past. As a band leader at the Pars Hotel in Teheran, he had been arrested by the British as an enemy alien and deported to India; when he arrived there in 1942, he was interned in Sultanabad. Here, he volunteered for SOE despite his relatively advanced age of forty-eight and parachuted in with DECIMA. He returned to Cairo in June 1944 after being on the run almost non-stop for nine months.

In the late summer of 1943, Veress arrived back in Istanbul, this time by train to avoid suspicion, after the Allies had made it clear that unless Hungary brought its interests fully in line with their political and military objectives, there was nothing further to discuss. However, for Hungary, the viability of 'unconditional surrender' was predicated on a rapid Allied advance through Italy, with troops reaching Hungary in the foreseeable future; in fact, the opposite happened. As the Allied advance became bogged down and drastic German reprisals took place, any attempt to cooperate with the Allies looked doomed to failure and likely to provoke a vicious German reaction.

So on 17 August, having committed the Hungarian outline terms to memory before he left Budapest, Veress passed them to John Sterndale-Bennett, the Councillor of the British Legation, who in turn relayed them to London. The Western Allies were pre-occupied with the invasion of mainland Italy at the time and it was not until 9 September that Veress, with an SOE escort, stepped aboard the British Ambassador's yacht, *Macao II*, late at night to receive the FO's response. Anthony Eden wanted Hungary first to confirm her offer of unconditional surrender through regular diplomatic channels. While no one questioned Veress's bona fides, he was not the head of an official delegation or legation. Secondly, any agreement was to be kept secret while Hungary progressively withdrew her troops from Russia and wound up her economic participation in the German war effort. Finally, 'at a given moment', Hungary was to place all her resources at the disposal of the Allies. Ladened down with two SOE W/T sets in large wooden boxes, Veress gingerly made his way back to Budapest on German troop trains, where he successfully established contact with Cairo on 29 September. The Surrender Group meanwhile pondered the Allied terms and wondered what exactly an SOE Mission would actually do once it had arrived. SOE's specialities of armed insurrection and sabotage were not on their political menu.

The lack of progress experienced by SOE in their dealings with the Surrender Group to date had caused a rethink in London. It was all very well for the Hungarians to come into the open when

Allied success in Sicily had become apparent and to seek some form of re-insurance, but in the cold light of day Hungary's contribution to the war so far had been to commit two divisions in support of the German offensive on the Russian Front. She was therefore an enemy country as far as the Allies were concerned and would continue to be regarded as such unless she proved, by her actions, her right to different treatment. Wishy-washy negotiations involving the Surrender Group 'angling' for better terms did not constitute such action and on 15 November a recommendation was made to the Chiefs of Staff that the bombing of Budapest should be undertaken without delay. Aside from sending a strong political message to the Hungarians, the bombing of Budapest could be justified on purely military grounds, since it was the most important railway junction for German traffic to and from Romania, Serbia and Turkey.

At around this time, SOE underwent another bureaucratic spring clean. General Gubbins, in a memo of 9 December, split the role of SOE in Hungary into two: London was charged with developing high-level contacts in 'the hope that a dividend will eventually come', and SOE Cairo was to 'press on the direct attack by physical contact with subversive action parties in Hungary who are prepared to take direct action'. This directive was duly implemented and London took charge of SANDY while Cairo relaunched FETTES as SAVANNAH, a mission based in Yugoslavia with the purpose of carrying out non-political sabotage and subversive activities. At the beginning of January 1944, the heads of the Hungarian Sections of SOE in London, Cairo and Istanbul met in Cairo to coordinate their activities, although the background was somewhat bleak, with 'abundant evidence that Russian military successes, slow Anglo-American progress in Italy and the example of Count Ciano,[23] have caused the Hungarian Government to increase its collaboration with Germany.'

In December, in a sarcastically worded message to force the hand of Kállay's 'powerful Group' within the Hungarian government, SOE proposed to drop a two-man team 'blind'; their cover story was to be that they were escaped POWs. Bad weather prevented this operation but at the end of that month the Hungarians finally came up with a pinpoint and preparations went ahead for a January drop on the estate of Count Mihály Andrássy near the Yugoslav frontier where the Chief of the Metropolitan Police and Veress were tasked to take care of reception arrangements. This time it was the FO who prevaricated and put a halt to it on the grounds that it might upset the Russians and lead to unpleasantries in forthcoming negotiations. As Denis Allen, a FO official, had noted the previous autumn, 'it is clear that any attempt on our part to impose a solution [on Eastern Europe] in the face of Soviet opposition would be fruitless.' Frank Roberts of the FO reinforced this view when he wrote to Christopher Steel, SOE's political adviser in Cairo, that 'the Secretary of State had been to Moscow and had gained the definite impression that the Russians were very touchy about Hungarian affairs . . . and withheld authorisation for the Mission to go in.' Kállay's activities in Hungary at the time also sent mixed messages to London. His reconciliation with the Imrédy Party, with its strong pro-German leanings and the proposed trial of three prominent Social Democrats for treason, seemed to indicate that he was swaying towards the Germans.

February came and went and in March, under pressure from SOE's chief, Lord Selborne, the Foreign Secretary finally withdrew his objections to the Mission with the proviso that the matter went before the Prime Minister. Churchill approved the operation, subject to the consent of the Chiefs of Staff who met on 16 March and gave it their blessing. It was now on for the April moon, but it was too late. The Hungarian Army Security Section Radio Branch had located the W/T set used by the Surrender Group in Budapest and arrested its operators. All notes were passed to the Gestapo and soon it was evident that the Germans, in the words of von Ribbentrop, were fully apprised of the extent of Hungarian 'treason and ingratitude': indeed, the German Minister in Budapest pointedly refused to meet with the Prime Minister.

By 15 March, reports reached Kállay of German troop concentrations on the Hungarian border; Vienna, the historical centre of East European intelligence, was full of rumours of an imminent German invasion of Hungary. On 17 March, Hitler invited Horthy to visit him at Ober-Salzburg. At a meeting of the Crown Council, for Hungary was still a regency, both the Chief of Staff and the Minister of War urged him to decline. After all, it had been Horthy himself who had declared in April 1943 that he would never again go and see that 'horrible house-painter'. Nevertheless Horthy decided to go and left on the Friday night with his Foreign Minister, War Minister and Chief of Staff. As soon as they arrived at Schloss Klessheim, they were virtual hostages and it was only through the quick wit of the Foreign Minister that a message was sent to Budapest that an invasion was imminent. The meeting was far from cordial. According to the Hungarian Foreign Minister, Hitler told Horthy 'in his rudest manner' that he had proof of the Hungarian government's treacherous activities. He therefore asked Horthy to sign a declaration inviting German troops into Hungary to defend the country against a common enemy. The Admiral flatly refused on constitutional grounds and managed to negotiate his return to Budapest.

By the time, he arrived back on Sunday morning, Hitler's Plan *Margarethe* had been implemented and all key points in the country were in the hands of the Germans, including the airfields. Nazi paratroopers and SS men seized the Budapest police HQ and the Gestapo began a wave of arrests on the Saturday night. Initially, the Regent refused to form a government, but when he was informed three days later that Croatian, Romanian and Slovak troops would be joining the occupying forces, and that Hitler was unable to guarantee the safety of the Admiral's own family, he acquiesced to the appointment of Döme Sztójay, the Hungarian Minister to Berlin, as Prime Minister.

Within hours a witch-hunt began and within days the Surrender Group leadership had been rounded up: Szentmiklóssy and Szegedy-Maszák were arrested and handed over to the Gestapo, the former later dying in Dachau; Keresztes-Fisher, dragged from his bed on the night of 19 March, was sent with his brother[24] to Flossburg Concentration camp; and Kállay himself only escaped arrest by taking refuge in the Turkish legation in Budapest.[25] Other high-profile arrests included Baron Bánffy, Minister of Agriculture, Sombor-Schweinitzer, Chief of Police, and his deputy, Gyula Kádár. There was no civil or military resistance, as correctly predicted by some members of SOE, to the arrest of over 3,000 patriotic and pro-Western citizens who were packed off to concentration camps, nor was there any protest at the wave of Jewish deportations which were unleashed.[26]

The death of a SPARROW

In the summer of 1943, the USA began to hatch its own plans for making contact with Hungary. The brainchild of Royall Tyler in Geneva, and nurtured by Allen Dulles, the OSS representative in Berne, and Szentmiklóssy in Hungary, the plan was code-named SPARROW. Tyler, an American scholar and long-time expatriate in Europe, had been in Hungary with the League of Nations in connection with a reconstruction loan and, after effortlessly mastering the language, had become a financial adviser to the Hungarian government, in the process accumulating a large number of highly placed contacts. Always supportive of Tyler, Dulles remained equivocal about the Hungarian situation. In a telegram of 17 December 1943, he expressed:

> serious doubts regarding separating Hungary from the Axis . . . There is greater fear of the Russians than of the Germans among the Hungarian governmental strata at the present time. It is the belief of these people that Hungary will suffer through Russia's intent to compensate Romania for the probable loss of Bessarabia and perhaps Dobrodgea. Hungarians believe that Russia's hostility towards their country is even greater that the Soviet enmity towards Romania . . . In the opinion of the Hungarians . . . the only thing that could hit them which would be worse than the Trianon Treaty would be a Russian occupation and they are not certain that the Anglo-Saxons will protect them from the latter eventuality or allow them anything better than the aforementioned treaty.

Nevertheless, the three-man SPARROW Mission, headed by 49-year-old Lieutenant Colonel Florimond Duke, was dropped into Hungary on the night of 15 March 1944, the last night of the moon period, and landed uneventfully near the village of Podturen, where the next morning they were extended a warm welcome orchestrated by a Hungarian waiter recently returned from Paris. Expected by General Ujszászy, the head of Military Intelligence, they were soon collected by Major Király, his top aide, and housed at a barracks at Nagykanisza. Unknown to SPARROW, all was not well for on the evening of their arrival, Admiral Horthy had been handed a note by von Jagow, the German Minister in Budapest, during the interval of the premier of the new opera *Petöfi*. He demanded a meeting that night to hand over a letter from Hitler and it resulted in the departure of the Admiral and key ministers to Klessheim the next day.

On Saturday 18 April, Duke and his team-mates, Major Suarez and Captain Nunn, were taken by army ambulance to Hungarian Intelligence HQ in Budapest, near the Parliament building and ushered into the office of General Ujszászy. Duke began by requesting a meeting with Horthy in order to deliver to him a personal message from President Roosevelt, but the General stalled and announced that the Admiral was out of town for the weekend. When he followed with a request to send a signal to OSS Balkan HQ in Algiers, it was again declined. In a matter of hours, the Americans found themselves at the epicentre of the German invasion, with their status quickly changing from peace emissaries to that of POWs. Determined to keep them out of the clutches of the Gestapo, the Hungarians transported them to Belgrade and on to Pancevo, the HQ of Luftwaffe Balkan Intelligence, where they were handed over to Major Krüger, an impeccably well-behaved young officer.[27] It was only when they were being transferred to the main Luftwaffe POW camp in Frankfurt that they were intercepted by the Gestapo and taken back to Belgrade for interrogation. From there, they subsequently found themselves incarcerated in Gestapo HQ in Berlin, then Budapest City Jail on Fö Utca until finally, in June 1944, they ended up under Gestapo supervision in the Landesgericht prison in Vienna, where they were stripped of their POW rights and told that they would be summarily shot.

Fortuitously, hard on the heels of the successful Allied landings in Normandy, the precarious fortunes of SPARROW now took a turn for the better and they were taken to the large Allied POW camp at Kaisersteinbruck 20 kilometres outside the city. From there, on 23 August, they eventually arrived at Oflag 4C, better known today as Colditz, where they spent the remainder of the war. By any yardstick, Duke, Suarez and Nunn had been through an extraordinary, harrowing ordeal which they faced with great courage, deploying subterfuge and stubbornness in equal measures to frustrate their captors and protect their friends.

A follow-up two-man mission consisting of an Austrian businessman, Franz Joseph Messner (CASSIA), and his secretary was sent to Budapest by the Americans to pick up a radio and then return to Vienna and make contact with the Allies.[28] The Gestapo were waiting for them. After being tortured, Messner revealed the names of the Austrian resistance cell; twenty were shot, two survived. The café-society era of US intelligence-gathering operations in Istanbul, presided over by Roosevelt's convivial friend, the 'US Assistant Naval Attaché' George Howard Earle III, had reached its end. At the strategic level, the former US Minister in Vienna and Governor of Pennsylvania had served as a magnet to attract visits from Admiral Canaris,[29] the chief of the Abwehr, and from Count von Moltke,[30] head of the Kreisau Circle, but the relaxed and indiscrete lifestyle of the millionaire, bon viveur, naval officer in the bars of Istanbul compromised security.

It is still unclear as to the extent that the OSS had shared details of SPARROW with their British and Russian allies. While the OSS Generals Donovan and Magruder defended their unilateral action on the grounds that the role of SPARROW was solely to collect military intelligence, the involvement of Baron Bakach-Bessenyey, the Hungarian Minister in Bern, suggests otherwise. After the war, former Prime Minister Nikolai Kállay asserted that, having broken the US codes, the Germans were aware of SPARROW and it was a contributing factor to their decision to invade Hungary.[31]

Another contributory factor to the demise of SPARROW was the parlous state of OSS's intelligence-gathering operations in Istanbul, overseen by Lanning MacFarland. These had started in early 1943 with Project Net-1, a program of subversion and infiltration in south-eastern Europe, and initially produced a plentiful crop of reports under the aegis of its director, Alfred Schwarz (code name DOGWOOD). Within a year, to the consternation of the British, he had sixty-seven sub-agents working for him in the Cereus Circle, all with floral code names. The problem was that many were unreliable and shoddily vetted; one, Lieutenant Colonel Otto Hatz (JASMINE), was undoubtedly a double-agent and there are indications that he too betrayed SPARROW. Another, Andre György (TRILLIUM), had proved unreliable on several occasions and is thought to have been the bearer of a secret message from Himmler to Churchill.

The fate of Ujszászy has never been established. Dulles received information on 2 May that he had been shot by the Nazis and that a Hungarian actress, Katalin Kárady, had been arrested in connection with meetings between Ujszászy and 'British parachutists' in her home. Later reports suggested that he had been taken by the Russians after a period in German captivity, and although an unwilling prisoner, had provided pro-Soviet evidence at the Nuremberg trials, and also made broadcasts from Moscow. For certain, he was never seen again in the West.

Yet, even if Hungary had failed to disengage itself from the German camp, the efforts of the Surrender Group, SOE and OSS had not been in vain. Despite the strength of the pro-German lobby and the assumption by the German government that Hungary was in safe hands, Hitler had been forced to mount a punitive expedition to retain political control, including the deployment of nearly thirty divisions and an accompanying number of Gestapo.[32] It was a result of sorts, even if it left SOE almost back in the same position as it had started in 1941. The only difference was that it now had a number of trained Hungarians on its books, ready to infiltrate into Hungary, and had acquired by good fortune some valuable Hungarian intelligence assets in Velios and Bogdan, two Hungarian diplomats in Athens who had been evacuated to Cairo by caique on 26 April, and in the tenacious László Veress, who by way of a dangerous journey through Romania and Bulgaria, had managed to reach Zagreb from where he was exfiltrated to Bari on 10 June.[33]

After the German invasion, SOE reorganized its Hungarian operations. The main Hungarian section and the operational base moved to Monopoli in southern Italy and came under the command of Major General Stawell. HQ Force 133 in Cairo became the rear link to C-in-C Middle East, while SOE London continued its role of maintaining contact with the FO, which retained political control of UK military policy in Hungary.

MI9: Escape and evasion

In 1943, tasked with rescuing escaped POWs and Allied airmen in Hungary, MI9 began to train up agents with the intention of dropping them into Yugoslavia from where they could make their way North into Hungary to set up escape lines. Two operations were subsequently carried out in 1944: Operation CHICKEN on 13 April and Operation CHALLOCK on 20 August.

It should be borne in mind that, since its expansion in 1941, MI9 had signed an unofficial pact with SIS – its head, Brigadier Norman Crockatt, had agreed with Sir Claude Dansey, the SIS No. 2, to pass all signals traffic through his service and, in line with SIS's de facto control of all of MI9's operations in Holland, Belgium, France, Spain and Portugal, there was a high degree of supervision by the 'professional spies' of its role in south-east Europe.

The teams had been selected from Jewish volunteers from Palestine[34] by R.H. Lawson of the SIS and trained by Lieutenant Colonel Tony Simonds, a former SOE man, now the commander of N Force in Cairo. As well as assisting POWs, their brief was to rescue Jews. The first stick to drop into Yugoslavia in early April included Hannah Senesh (code name MINNIE), Reuven Dafni, Abba Bardichev and Yonah Rosen. They were shortly followed on 13 April by Captain MacCoy, Sergeant Grandville, Yoel Palgi and Peretz Goldstein, who parachuted into the Partisan HQ at Metlika where they met up with Major Robert Eden of the COBWEB mission and made their way south of Zagreb to the Sava River, and then north-east to the Hungarian border villages of Cazma and Donji Miklous. Here they met up with the first stick and were briefed by Hannah, who had recently conducted a reconnaissance of the border. She expressed doubts that neither the Partisans nor the gangs of smugglers who operated there could be trusted, so the decision was taken to split the party into two.

On 13 May, Palgi and Bardichev left to cross the border in the Papuk mountains where they were welcomed by the BLO, Captain Owen. Goldstein and Rosen then joined them and after Bardichev had split off en route to Romania, the three of them crossed the Drava River on 13 July in a rowing boat. Intercepted by Axis security patrols, they had to retreat and it was only on 19 July, during which time Rosen had lost patience and sought another crossing point, that Palgi and Goldstein successfully crossed into Hungary and caught a train to Pécs, then on to Budapest. Meanwhile, Senesh and Dafni had also managed to cross the Drava River with three new agents she had met there, two Budapest Jews,

Fleischmann and Kallós, and a French POW called Tony. They were almost immediately captured, together with their W/T transmitter; Kallós committed suicide by shooting himself in the temple. Dafni, who had been told by Senesh to wait for her to return, remained in Yugoslavia for the next six weeks and facilitated the escape of hundreds of Jews.

The situation for Budapest's large Jewish population had catastrophically deteriorated since the German coup of March – thousands had been arrested and sent to extermination camps. So understandably, Palgi made the rescue of the remaining Jews a priority and became immersed in negotiations between Adolf Eichmann and the Jewish Agency over the question of 'buying Hungarian Jews'. The head of the Jewish delegation, a small manufacturer called Yoel Brand, along with a disreputable carpet smuggler, Andre György (aka Bandi Gross), had arrived in Istanbul on 19 May on a German courier plane from Vienna. They had been instructed by the Germans to present the following proposals to the Americans and British:

- The Germans are willing to consider the release of the Jewish population in Hungary as fast as the Jews can be admitted to Spain, Portugal and Turkey.
- In exchange, the Germans expect to receive the following from the Allies: 2 million bars of soap; 800 tons of coffee; 200 tons of cocoa; 800 tons of tea; 10,000 trucks. (Of special interest is the fact that Brand made clear that the Germans were willing to give a guarantee that the 10,000 trucks would be used only against the Russians, and would not under any circumstances, be sent to the Italian or 'Second Front'.)

The proposition received a frigid response as it stood to split the Allies – the trucks would have been used on the Eastern Front – and to highlight Britain's paltry Jewish immigration policy into Palestine. Unaware of the controversy generated by the Brand Plan, after introducing himself to Rezsö Kastner,[35] the leader of the Budapest Jewish community, Palgi stepped into Joel's shoes and presented himself to the Gestapo as an intermediary.[36] Not surprisingly, he was arrested, savagely interrogated and despatched to Pécs prison. After a spell there, he was transferred back to

Budapest, first to a Hungarian prison and then to the Gestapo prison on Fö Utca, where he met up with Senesh and Goldstein. Here, he heard for the first time the story of Senesh and how the Gestapo had brought her mother into her interrogation and threatened to harm her unless Hannah gave them the radio codes.

On 7 November 1944, as the Russian Army was completing its encirclement of Budapest, Hannah Senesh, after being incarcerated, interrogated and tortured for five months before being subjected to a mock trial, was executed at the age of twenty-three.[37] This courageous, intelligent, heroic girl, described by a close friend as 'a poet-tomboy', left a last poem for posterity:

> One-two-three . . .
> Eight feet long,
> Two strides across, the rest is dark . . .
> Life hangs over me like a question mark.

> One-two-three . . .
> Maybe another week,
> Or next month may still find me here,
> But death, I feel, is very near.

> I could have been
> Twenty-three next July;
> I gambled on what mattered most,
> The dice were cast. I lost.

Later, Palgi and Tony escaped from a train taking them to Komarom in western Hungary and, after a futile attempt to find shelter in the French legation, linked up with the MI9 Budapest cell run by WO (Warrant Officer) R. Barratt and Dr Raphael Rupert. Meanwhile Goldstein and Fleischmann reached Oranienburg to the north of Berlin on 8 December, where Goldstein was killed in an Allied bombing raid.

Operation CHALLOCK experienced the same difficulties as the SOE missions did in trying to cross into Hungary from Yugoslavia, and it was withdrawn to Bari; its two agents were rerouted to Hungary via Slovakia where they dropped on 14/15 September near Banská Bystrica. Their set was captured but a new one was taken in and they started off on their journey to infiltrate Hungary from the North. However, increasing German activity against the Partisans forced them to link up with MI9's Slovak project, Operation AMSTERDAM, and retire, together with an OSS mission, deep into the hills above Banská. So, of the six agents earmarked for infiltration into Hungary, three reached Budapest, where they were promptly captured, and the other three failed to cross over the border. Hungary was proving a tough nut to crack. However, the MI9 mission on the border, Operation COBWEB, first under the command of Major Eden, then Major Macadam, managed to round up and successfully evacuate over 120 Allied airmen before it was withdrawn in October 1944.

Carry on subverting

On the night of 8/9 April, as a follow-up to PILATUS, another lone operator, Hungarian-born Lieutenant Steve Agoston,[38] was dropped blind to the east of Szeged near Mako (DANHILL Mission) with the objective of contacting friends of his who were in the area with a view to establishing communications and making reception arrangements for future parties. No contact was made, or as SOE put it, 'nothing heard from him after he left the aircraft', and two further attempts to drop another set were stymied due to bad weather. Another Hungarian, Lieutenant Steve Markos, who had been a member of Basil Davidson's DECIMA Mission, was reinstated into the Bačska area on 11 May where he remained at large until arrested by the Russians in late October. And as a follow-up to DECIMA, SANDY 1 (FETTES) consisting of Captain Young, Captain Whittaker and Sergeant Scott dropped in to VI Partizan Corps HQ in northern Yugoslavia to set up a forward base in the Papuk area for operations into Hungary. They were joined on the night of 3/4 June by SANDY II (Lieutenant Bertram),[39] whose orders were to proceed to the Pécs area where he was known and arrange a safe house for the reception of further personnel. An additional mission, DARESBURY, consisting of Captain Hadow and Sergeant Peaker, parachuted into Yugoslavia on 20/21 June with the same brief as SANDY I. Here they met up with Major Harker,[40] who had been collecting information about conditions in Hungary.

Lieutenant Bertram left for Pécs in mid-June, intending to find a safe house and to reconnoitre suitable areas for missions to be dropped into. Travelling in civilian clothes, he boarded the train at the Yugoslav frontier and alighted at Pécs, where he spent the following week before moving to the small village of Orfű to the North. Here he opened a courier line back to Captain Young and on the basis of this success it was decided to send Major Coates to join him.

DEERHURST: ill conceived and ill fated

The aim of DEERHURST was to make contact with a group of '300 people' led by former Hungarian Army officers, who had made the wild and inaccessible area to the NW of Lake Báláton the HQ of a potential resistance group. This was in flat contradiction to SOE's assessment that same month that:

> none of the pre-requisites of resistance existed [in Hungary]. Hungary had never been actively engaged in the war. She had suffered no severe casualties, she was not a defeated nation and, above all, there was no suffering among the civil population. Far from her alliance with Germany leading to a deterioration of conditions of life, Hungary in the last four years has derived nothing but benefit from her association with Germany and the standard of living has, if anything, continued to rise.

Major Basil Davidson, one of the most experienced SOE operatives in Central Europe, was even more specific about the difficulties faced in infiltrating agents into Hungary:

- Vigorous German and Hungarian counter-espionage services.
- Efficient and strong police forces.
- The apathy and even the hostility of the Hungarian population.
- The lack of any established resistance group or movement in Hungary.
- The enmity which the brutality of the Hungarian occupiers has roused against themselves in all areas of Serbian population.

- The activities of Yugoslav traitors in the Voj Vodina area.
- The impossibility of obtaining forged Hungarian papers outside Hungary itself.

He concluded that 'the present mood and morale of the Hungarian population is apathetic, indifferent and terrorized. The prospects of active resistance to the enemy are very poor indeed; considered prior to the opening signs of German collapse, the prospects are indeed so small as not to be worth considering.'

DEERHURST had been planned by Major Dickie Wright, who was earmarked to lead it. The idea was to drop into the Bakony region about 45 miles NW of Vezsprem. However, when another mission led by a former cotton merchant, Lieutenant Colonel Peter Boughey,[41] was cancelled due to the presence of a German SS Division in Pécs, the personnel of the two missions were combined and a four-man advance party formed, consisting of Boughey, Wright, Lieutenant Vincent[42] and Corporal Manley (W/T Op). If, on arrival, the position proved suitable, the remainder of the party would be dropped, with Wright staying in place and Boughey going south to Pécs or the area south of Lake Báláton.

The OC of SOE Security Section was far from happy:

I understand that the plan has been sent to London in writing and that no active disapproval to an operation of this kind taking place has been expressed. I understand, however, that Lt Col Perkins of London HQ has expressed, in a signal, his disapproval of Lt Col Boughey going on this particular operation.

I understand that Lt Col Boughey has been provided with a false identity as Sgt John Connor, Black Watch [BW]. From the information available to me, this would seem to be a most incomplete, not to say inaccurate cover, likely to lead to the most severe consequences for Lt Col Boughey if he were made prisoner. My reasons for this are:

a. The cover story says that Lt Col Boughey joined the BW as John Connor in August 1940. He spent 6 weeks or so at the BW depot, and then, owing to his linguistic abilities, was transferred to Field Security [FS] (I understand that in fact Lt Col Boughey speaks some French and German). This appears to be a hopeless cover if Lt Col Boughey goes in as a BW NCO because while officers of other units may be transferred to FS or Intelligence duties, and remain members of their original unit, NCOs and ORs, on transfer, become FS NCOs and members of the Intelligence Corps.

b. Lt Col Boughey as an officer with long and varied experience of SOE work is in possession of a great deal of valuable information, which is likely, it seems, to fall into enemy hands if this operation is allowed to take place. In this connection, it should be borne in mind that Lt Col Boughey is undertaking a blind drop into enemy occupied territory – the first in this country – in the most hazardous circumstances, and in so doing, is running far greater risks that those incurred on normal operations.

Lt Col Boughey's cover story, as I have said, seems inadequate. Further reason for its inadequacy is that he volunteered for operations in Hungary as he knew the country in peacetime. I understand that in fact this is not so, and that Lt Col Boughey knows the area into which he is to be dropped only through studying aerial recce photographs and from general briefing. If he is broken down on this point in interrogation, then this will only serve to increase suspicion and will certainly lead to severe action against him when linked to his obviously false BW/FS cover.

I understand that Lt Col Boughey will say, if necessary, that he has been sent to establish himself in advance and make preparations for the arrival of other members of the Mission. This will, of course, be a fairly obvious admission, except that it is probably unlikely that two sergeants (Connor and Dickinson) would have been sent without an officer to perform such a task.

Further points making likely Lt Col Boughey's capture, and therefore disclosure of information, are:

a. The addresses in his possession date back, I understand, to before the occupation. It is not known whether these persons are still at the addresses, or how they will act if contacted.

   b. Lt Vincent, Lt Col Boughey's Canadian/Hungarian companion, does not know the district and has no contacts there.

   c. The drop is to take place in a clearing in the woods, on a moonlight night, two miles from a village. It will be surprising if attention is not attracted, or if some of the stores are not dropped wide.

I understand that a land route already exists, and that a Canadian/Hungarian has already gone in by land through Partisan routes from Papuk and that he is now awaiting documentation by the Partisans. The object of the operation is, I understand, to start courier lines between Lt Col Boughey at Pécs and VI Partizan Corps at Papuk. This could seemingly be achieved, and later the Mission might expand its activities among the resistance groups said to be in the neighbourhood, if the initial point were made by the overland route. Thus when the base had been established, Lt Col Boughey might well go in with much less chance of capture.

If this is not practicable, then perhaps the operation might be carried out by a BLO less acquainted with SOE.

In view of the precautions taken with SOE agents, to ensure they have the minimum knowledge of installations, staff work and future plans, it seems illogical to send into the field an officer of Lt Col Boughey's standing and experience, to take risks which, in spite of his uniform and cover, are as great as those normally incurred by any agent.

I should be grateful if this matter might be reviewed, and also if London might be consulted if thought fit, in order to decide if the advantages which might accrue to the organisation from the successful completion of this mission by Lt Col Boughey, warrant the danger to the security of the organisation, inherent in the operation.

Captain Maydwell, who had been due to jump with de Chastelain and Porter into Romania in January, also expressed his unease:

I am frankly not optimistic about our work in Hungary. Things have been left so late out here, and in SOE work . . . one must have a certain amount of time to start with. I hate the thought of dropping blind, particularly in a country like Hungary, but there it is . . . the whole business is most unsatisfactory and goes against all SOE teaching but if quick results are wanted there is no alternative.

On 3 July 1944, after one abortive attempt, the DEERHURST plane was reported missing[43] and it transpired later that the whole team had dropped next to a Jewish labour camp and had been captured by its guards.

What actually happened is recalled by Lieutenant Colonel Boughey in a letter to Roy Maclaren:[44]

Our parachutes were draped over tree tops and I for one was left hanging about 30 feet up a tree . . . There was no hope of concealing our whereabouts. At dawn, the Army assisted by the Home Guard were soon out in force. Despite this, both Vincent and I (the other two had landed on the other side of the hill) managed to conceal ourselves for about twenty-four hours, escaping detection by only feet from the lines of troops who were combing the area. On a subsequent drag, a soldier came right upon our hideout. We were lucky he did not shoot us in his fright! . . . after a thorough search when we were stripped naked and a brief interrogation, we were taken by truck to Vesperem where we were told we were going to be shot the next day!

News reached SOE at the end of July that they had been taken to Gestapo HQ at Fö Utca in Budapest, and later to Stalag VIII in Silesia. The loss of DEERHURST came as 'a very great blow' to the Hungarian Section and as it was the second party which had been dropped blind and lost, future parties who hoped to drop blind could not get permission.

Lieutenant Colonel Threlfall, a former head of the Hungarian section with considerable experience of living in pre-war Hungary, reflected after the war that DEERHURST 'was very badly organised and rather nonsensical'. He had always been very much against these sorts of missions for the simple reason that they would only have worked if there had been a widespread Hungarian resistance movement. Having presided over the negotiations with the Surrender Party, Threlfall knew only too well the difficulties that lay in wait for madcap SOE Hungarian adventures. Major Coates also recalled that Boughey had gone in 'against all the rules' but fondly described him as an 'exceptionally original, brave and courageous character'.

In a memo dated 12 July 1944 entitled 'Hungary: Liaison and Planning of Operations', the mood of SOE planners was expressed in no uncertain terms:

> Irrespective of the desires of either London HQ or Italy, the actual facts of the background to almost every operation in Hungary are as follows:
>
> • In the majority of cases we are unable to put an operation into effect without the FO being involved – frequently, contrary to our wishes – because political ramifications usually arise and the FO's apprehension of offending Russia raise susceptibilities and means the passage of numerous letters between SOE and the FO, causing regrettable procrastination . . .
>
> • In addition to the frustration caused by the above, operations frequently originate from information gained in Istanbul, Lisbon, Stockholm etc. and in view of the FO's decision not to utilize the knowledge of the dissident Hungarian diplomats as a consulting – and possibly advisory – group in London, [we are unable to proceed].

The show goes on

In July 1944, a Mr Shertock of the Jewish Agency approached SOE with a view to sending two missions into northern Hungary,[45] comprised of Jewish operational personnel under the command of Zazlani to form Hungarian-Jewish resistance groups. With 300 Palestinian Jews at his disposal, many who served with the British

Army in North Africa, Zazlani was confident he could deliver whatever was required of him. The offer was turned down by SACMED on the grounds that Russian advances rendered the plan unworkable, but SOE remained active, beefing up DARESBURY with Major Maydwell and his Hungarian interpreter Lieutenant Leban after Major Harker was withdrawn in early August due to malaria, DIBBLER with Lieutenants Gordon[46] and Thomas,[47] and DECIMA with Captain Ted Howe, a former *Times* correspondent in Budapest.

However, little went according to plan. Veress, who by now was an advisor to SOE, wrote on 22 July: 'It would be a mistake to underestimate the stiffness and toughness of the thoroughly Nazified political, administrative and military set-up established after 19 March 1944. This is a suicide set-up which is resolved to carry on to the bitter end.'

He concluded that:

There seems to be only one effective weapon to make German use of Hungarian territory as a military base unsafe, at the same time cracking the government system serving Germany: both militarily and politically effective bombing . . . and bring home the certainty to the Hungarian people that cooperation with Germany is not only suicide in the long run but is a deadly danger now and must be ended without delay.

By early September, Lieutenants Gordon and Thomas had been evacuated from FETTES/DIBBLER after making several unsuccessful attempts to cross the frontier to link up with Lieutenant Bertram in the Pécs area; Bertram himself had managed to send only three messages,[48] one of which was indecipherable. Captain Young and Sergeant Scott were also evacuated from FETTES on 10 September, having 'had it' mentally and physically. But the Hungarian Section was determined to persevere in the Pécs area and on 13 September dropped DIBBLER, consisting of Major John Coates and Lieutenants Thomas and Gordon, both Hungarians, to the north of Pécs to try and make contact with Bertram.

DIBBLER: an endangered species from Day One

Although Lieutenant Bertram had established himself just outside Pécs, all was not well. Captain Young had received an undated message on 28 June, saying that Bertram had safely arrived, and another one on 2 July which was undecipherable. On 23 July, a final message was received with the correct security checks, advising that 'place is safe. Inform when bodies coming. If possible should be soon. Greetings.'

The decision to send in DIBBLER was both at the time and in hindsight controversial. Threlfall for one was against it. The tasks given to the mission were ambitious, yet vague:

a. To make contact with actual and potential resistance groups, particularly in the Pécs area, particularly amongst the industrial workers; to encourage and help organise them.
b. To draw up a plan for mass military and industrial sabotage; not however to put any part of it into effect until receipt of orders.
c. To organise passive resistance, propaganda etc.
d. To encourage Hungarians to join Tito and to provide evacuation routes.
e. To reconnoitre lines further into the country and prepare ground for further missions.

There was scant evidence of resistance in the area but nevertheless the mission pressed ahead. Coates later speculated that the notion that Pécs was a suitable centre for fermenting resistance may well have been part of a German deception plan.

John Coates was an unusual young officer in that he had started the war as a 21-year-old conscientious objector after reading Modern and Medieval Languages at Downing College, Cambridge. Educated at Abbotsholme, a progressive school in Staffordshire, Coates had spent two terms in Germany as an exchange student – in Buchenau (1931) and Bieberstein (1936) – and had also been on a study tour in Austria (1936), as well as mounting his own expedition by bicycle to Italy, returning through Austria and Germany in 1938.

In his attitude to the war, which was far from straightforward, Coates was strongly influenced by his time at Abbotsholme, where a number of the staff had pacifist leanings, and where the boys had been encouraged to take a critical interest in politics and international affairs. Coates later recalled that at this stage of his life 'war [seemed] basically morally wrong'.[49] When he appeared before a tribunal in July 1940, since part of his sixth form studies had included preparation for a First MB (Medical), he opted to join the RAMC and was posted to 132 Field Ambulance.

Once in uniform, Coates decided in due course that he might as well become a fully-fledged combatant; after transferring to the Somerset Light Infantry, he applied for officer training and was sent on the 162 Infantry OCTU at Bulford, where, with his flair for French and excellent knowledge of German in particular, he was selected for the Intelligence Corps, and subsequently commissioned in August 1941. After a stint with the 61st Division in Northern Ireland, he was posted, partly on account of his linguistic ability, and having volunteered for and passed commando training, to No. 10 (Inter-Allied) Commando in north Wales. There, as Intelligence Officer, he enthusiastically set about training and liaison with the French, Belgian, Dutch, Norwegian, Polish and other troops, often in their own languages. The Commando also included a highly secret troop of German, Austrian and one or two Hungarians, mainly Jewish volunteers, who had all taken on British identities for their cover and protection.

In September 1943, Coates transferred to the elite, top secret 34 Section of 30 Commando Assault Unit in Italy,[50] whom he later recalled as 'a curious, mixed bunch of people, very interesting folk'. His joining instructions were far from simple, involving first a flight in plain clothes to Lisbon, then a transfer to Fez, this time in uniform, and finally reporting to his new commanding officer, Lieutenant Commander Quentin Riley, under fire on the beaches of Salerno. Riley promptly despatched him to Ischia, which had just been occupied by Captain Pat Martin-Smith and a small troop of commandos and intelligence specialists in the wake of the retreating Germans. It was to prove an idyllic interlude in the midst of a bloody campaign and gave Coates the perfect opportunity to brush up his Italian which he had started to learn before the war.

Before long, the troop was relocated to Corsica where it energetically acted in support of a SOE unit under the command of Colonel Andrew Croft. Withdrawn to Naples to wait for the fall of Rome, Coates concluded that 30 Commando was 'a somewhat chaotic sort of unit' in the unpredictable manner in which it was deployed and as such he was 'getting no action', so when Peter Boughey tracked him down in Naples, he eagerly accepted his offer to join the Hungarian section (ME 76) of SOE as a member of SANDY, the planned semi-diplomatic mission to the Surrenderist Party. But by the time SANDY was ready to go, the Germans had invaded Hungary and so a new strategy was devised which was predicated on the idea of sending fluent Hungarian speakers into the country to set up preliminary contacts and safe houses, and then to send small missions in to reinforce them.

DIBBLER was one such mission and after flying in to VI Partizan Corps HQ at Vocin in the Papuk area of Yugoslavia, where he linked up with the BLO Captain Sutcliffe and the ME 76 representative, Captain Young, Coates spent from 13 July to 6 August examining the feasibility of an overland infiltration route to Pécs. He concluded that any crossing of the Drava was likely to be fraught with danger since the whole area was infested by gangs of smugglers, who were in the pay of both sides and hence totally unreliable, as well as heavily patrolled by Hungarian gendarmerie and police on the northern bank. Therefore it was impractical for him as an 'imperfect' Hungarian speaker to cross into Hungary to link up with Bertram and on his return to Italy on 15 August, he despatched the two new members of DIBBLER, Lieutenants Thomas and Gordon, both fluent Hungarian speakers, to VI Partizan Corps HQ with instructions to proceed into Hungary and reconnoitre DZs in the Pécs area, with a view to receiving Coates himself. After failing to cross the Drava on three occasions, they returned to Bari in the second week of September; now it was clear to all that DIBBLER would need to drop blind, close to the village where Bertram had established a safe house.

SOE meanwhile was alert to the possibility either that Bertram might have been turned by the Germans or that his messages might be being read by them or the Hungarians, and therefore had decided not to communicate any reception committee requests to him or give details of the in-bound party. He was merely told to expect a W/T operator at his safe house in due course. In his post-operation report, Coates explained the rationale for the high-risk profile of the Mission:

It must be emphasised that the successful penetration (or rather – repenetration) of Hungary had not, even at this late stage, been accomplished; the Russians were already fighting in Temesvár [Timişoara]; it was therefore considered necessary to take exceptional risks. It was realized not only that a blind drop on a moonless night might lead to disaster but also that our contact was insecurely placed, perhaps even in the hands of the SD.

Before leaving Bari, Coates liaised with Force 399, ISLD, PWE, PICME and A Force.

After an aborted drop on 11 September,[51] the DIBBLER Mission jumped on the moonless night of 13 September and almost immediately got into difficulties. Firstly, they had been dropped on opposite sides of a mountain and had become separated from each other; secondly, Coates and Thomas, who had managed to find one another, realized they were in the wrong place (near Abaliget) about 10 kilometres from their true target, but thanks to the excellent air photographs that they had with them, were quickly able to get their bearings; thirdly, their 'package' or container that held most of the mission's kit, rations and signals equipment, was nowhere to be found. After staying put for the first twenty-four hours during which time they conducted a fruitless search in the vicinity of their drop point, the pair walked for two days through the thickly wooded hills until they came to the village of Orfű, where their contact awaited them. They had yet to link up with Gordon who, they assumed, was making his own way to the RV.

On the evening of 16 September, Coates sent Thomas, wearing civilian clothes, into the village to make contact with Bertram and to return with a party of helpers to go in search of the missing container. If he was not back by 1800 hours the next day, they had both agreed that Coates should move on and probably head for the Yugoslavian border. When 1800 hours came and went and there was no sign of Thomas, Coates decided to stay put in 'his little lair', a fateful decision which led to his capture the next morning as a line of police, gendarmes and peasants swept the fields and woods surrounding the village. Later, Coates's Hungarian interrogator told him that they had been expecting DIBBLER for at least a month as they had captured Lieutenant Bertram near Kaposvar in July and made him send out messages under duress.[52]

In what turned out to be a difficult and dangerous three months' captivity in four different prisons, Coates and his team were at first brutally interrogated by both the Hungarian and German security services, particularly Thomas who had been caught in civilian clothes and identified as a fluent Hungarian speaker, and on occasions all were tortured by the Germans. Later on, they were treated in a generally friendly way by the Hungarians, who in some ways tried to protect them from the Germans. Indeed Coates succeeded in building a relationship of sorts with their Hungarian captors, who after Horthy's speech in October and the subsequent Fascist coup by Szálasi, effectively became co-conspirators. This greatly strengthened the position of the team and the Hungarians managed to move them to the Zugliget internment camp on the edge of Budapest, where they were held in a guarded compound and treated as POWs. They also supplied them with civilian clothes and addresses to which they could go in the event that they managed to escape.

The first to escape was Andy Daniels of the WINDPROOF Mission, who Coates had assessed as a priority since he, like Thomas, had been captured in civilian clothes and was in serious danger of being shot as a spy. When it came to Thomas's, Gordon's and his own escape, Coates, as the senior British officer, first insisted that Thomas be sent to hospital because of a pain in his ear, and ordered him to escape from there. Then he and Gordon managed to escape together on 15 December and made their way to Budapest where they wisely separated at the first address they stayed at. Coates was hidden by a Hungarian family until he handed himself over to the Russians just after Christmas. This turned out to be far from easy and, mustering all the Russian he could remember from his Cambridge days, he eventually convinced the battle-hardened and suspicious Red Army soldiers that he was a British officer under the protection of anti-Fascist Hungarians by getting hold of some wine and toasting Churchill, Stalin and Roosevelt.

Coates was later awarded a well-deserved DSO. His citation read:

During this period (of capture and interrogation) Major Coates showed unfailing bodily courage and strength of mind. He not only kept the real purpose of his mission secret, but succeeded in leading his captors off the scent, thus undoubtedly saving his party from being shot out of hand. By his sterling example, Major Coates encouraged other members of his party to stand up to their interrogators . . . his leadership and sense of responsibility were worthy of the greatest praise.

Major Maydwell's mission, having made no progress in penetrating the frontier, was withdrawn on 13 October.

The strange case of Lieutenant Colonel Howie

The only live mission now left was EPIGRAM with Captain Ted Howe and Corporal Armstrong on their way from Frushka Gora to the Banat in Romania, to join up with Lieutenant Markos and Lieutenant Wood; after that, they planned to go to Budapest and establish a mission with direct communications to Bari. They got as far as Petrograd where they met up with the Russians, but their request to accompany their new Soviet friends to Budapest was denied and they were withdrawn to Belgrade on 1 November. The FO had made it plain on 20 October: 'There is no useful purpose by which he [Howe] could serve by going to Budapest in advance of the Mission [BMM] since arrangements for their arrival will in any case have to be cleared through Moscow.' A blind drop led by Major Kemp was planned for the Matra mountains area and a study was being conducted about the suitability of Count Wenckheim's estate at Sekes, 220 kilometres south-east of Budapest as a courier line to be run by his English wife or her sister. Neither was actioned.

An extraordinary entry in a report dated 13 December 1944 written by Captain Page for the commander of Force 399 says: 'On 22 September Lieutenant Colonel Howe [Howie], a British POW with who we had been in intermittent contact during the past, crash-landed near Termoli in Italy from Budapest in a Heinkel 111 with General István Náday, [53] Hungarian Deputy Chief of Staff.

The General had come to offer peace terms.' The background to the unusual storyof this officer,[54] aptly described by his SOE debriefer, Major Morton, as 'intelligent, resourceful and a natural leader', could come straight from a John Buchan novel. As a captain in the South African Active Citizen Force, the 34-year-old Howie had promptly joined the Cape Garrison Artillery after the South African House of Assembly had passed General Smuts's motion to declare war on Germany in September 1939 and, furthermore, he volunteered to serve outside his homeland. After active service in East Africa and Abyssinia, Howie, by now a lieutenant colonel, was sent with his regiment to Tobruk, which fell to the Afrika Korps on 21 June 1942. Taken prisoner, Howie was initially sent to Italy but was then moved to Stalag VIIIB in Eastern Silesia from where, together with fellow inmateTibor Weinstein,[55] a Hungarian Jew who spoke fluent German, he escaped in broad daylight on 26 September 1943, crawling 75 yards down a 2 foot by 2 foot tunnel. His fake papers, forged by POW Henry Lowenstein, were sufficient to fool the Gestapo at Vienna station, though shortly after their departure to Hungary, Howie and Weinstein had to hurl themselves from the train to avoid detection, and by the first week in October they had reached Budapest, en route at that stage for Yugoslavia. Uncertain of how the land lay, the two escapees approached the Swiss consulate, where a friendly secretary put them in touch with a Hungarian Unitarian pastor, the Harvard-educated Reverend Alexander Szent-Iványi, who offered to put them up in his church complex in the city centre. This marked the beginning of Howie's extraordinary and unexpected Hungarian adventure.

After Weinstein, who had lived in Budapest for a long time before the war, moved on to touch base with his own contacts, on the advice of Szent-Iványi, Howie reported to the Hungarian authorities and was sympathetically received by Colonel Baló, head of XXI Department of the Hungarian War Ministry, which dealt with all internees and POWs. The outcome of this meeting saw Howie move to the Polish internment camp at Zugliget on the outskirts of the city, from where he had more or less a free rein to move about, even though he did not speak any Hungarian and was chronically short of funds. However, in late November, on the orders of Colonel Utassy, the new head of XXI Department,

Howie was sent to Szigetvár camp on the estate of Count Andrássy, in the southernmost region of Hungary.

By now, Howie had already established contacts with the Polish underground and, through Prince Andrzej Sapieha's signalling group, was in touch with London; through another contact, Lolle Smit, the Managing Director of Philips in the Balkans, he was also able to get messages through to the Allies in Istanbul. It was not long before SOE had identified him as a possible asset and on 10 December Lieutenant Colonel Threlfall contacted Colonel Protasewicz of the exiled Polish General Staff in London to send a message to Howie – could he identify an address to which a SOE group could come after dropping by themselves? By Threlfall's normal cautious standards, this was an unusually bold move, for although SOE had managed to conduct satisfactory background checks on Howie, they had no way of assessing his ability to conduct clandestine operations. This was the beginning of Operation NATAL, which was run in parallel with the SANDY Mission about which Howie was never informed, for all communications about SANDY were conducted through the Veress-London channel, not through the Poles. Wisely, Threlfall was hedging his bets since the success of SANDY depended on the cooperation of the Surrender Group, which at that stage showed signs of flagging due to Hungarian dithering and FO prevarication. Although not an accredited member of SOE, Howie immediately went to work, put together a small untrained team of Allied POWs to prepare for a drop and organized a reception committee on Count Andrássy's estate, the same proposed dropping point as for the SANDY Mission. As it turned out, neither NATAL nor SANDY took place, but that did not prevent Howie from continuing his anti-German activities, despite the dramatic and dangerous new restrictions imposed on his movements in Budapest as a result of the March 1944 German occupation.

Through his Hungarian and Polish acquaintances, word about a senior escaped POW 'British' officer had long ago reached Buda Castle, the heart of Horthy's regency. Yet it came as somewhat of a surprise to Howie in late July when he was approached by an intermediary seeking a meeting between him and Admiral Horthy's younger son, Miklós Horthy. On the night of their first meeting, Howie was spirited into Buda Castle and found himself face to face with the Regent himself. This was the first of several meetings which Howie had with Horthy,[56] and soon Howie and Prince Sapieha had been moved into the apartment of General Károly Lázár, commander of the bodyguards, for added security while they set up a radio link to London.

During his meetings with Horthy, Howie urged him to arrange an immediate armistice with the Allies, but Horthy could not make up his mind, partly because his honour would not permit him to stab his country in the back, and partly because, since the British attitude to Hungary appeared ambivalent, he still felt that he had time on his side. However, when the Regent learnt of Romania's capitulation and defection from the Axis camp on 23 August, he sent for Howie and Sapieha, and installed them in a disused wing of the royal palace where they could safely make contact with London, and ask the British and American governments for terms.

Unfortunately the Germans picked up their first signal and Veesenmayer, the Reich Plenipotentiary in Budapest, threatened the Hungarian government that he would order the shelling of the city unless all transmissions ceased forthwith. This was sufficient to close the operation down and Howie's little group was whisked away that same night to a small cottage on Lake Báláton. Here they resumed their transmissions but once again the Gestapo picked up their signal trail and they had to make their way hurriedly, via Esztergom, to a safe house on the Romaszhan's estate in Czechoslovakia. Shortly thereafter, Horthy's aide-de-camp, Colonel Tóst, arrived and persuaded Howie to return with him to Budapest for another meeting with the Regent. This time Howie insisted that the only course of action at this late stage was to fly envoys out of Hungary to make direct contact with the Allies. Horthy agreed and noted in his memoirs: 'On September 22 I dispatched General Náday and the British [sic] Colonel Howie by plane for the Allied Headquarters at Caserta, near Naples. Colonel Howie . . . had been taken by Polish intermediaries to my son who had him smuggled into the palace. He had hidden in the apartments of my aide-de-camp, Tóst, until the time came for him to fly to Caserta.'

Their flight in a Heinkel 111 was far from straightforward. First, having failed to file a flight plan, it had to evade German anti-aircraft defences and then fly into Allied airspace with German markings. Relying on a code Howie had brought with him proved a non-starter, for the aircraft's radio failed. While the pilot, Captain János Marjoros, proposed flying to Benghazi, Howie insisted on reaching Allied Headquarters at Naples by the most direct route. This proved unrealizable as there turned out to be no facilities for night landings at Naples, so finally Marjoros brought the aircraft down at Madna Airbase just south of Termoli, executing a perfect belly landing. Minutes later, an American anti-aircraft battery commenced firing.

After an overnight stay in Bari, they were flown to Caserta, where General Náday and Howie presented the Hungarian request for Anglo-American support: in essence a proposal for a joint occupation of Hungary by Allied troops so that the country would not be entirely left to the Communist vicissitudes of the Russians. General Wilson, Supreme Allied Commander Mediterranean Theatre, and Air Marshal Sir John Slessor, Air Force chief of the Eighth Army, listened attentively, although Náday was at a disadvantage in that he had no written credentials from Horthy. The meeting ended with a promise to forward the Hungarian overtures to the British and American governments, but within a few days, word from Washington and London was passed down the line that there was no question of deploying Anglo-American forces to Hungary. The US State Department considered that the request 'failed to reflect the realities of the situation', an accurate assessment given that Soviet troops had crossed the Hungarian frontier on the night of 22/23 September. Wilson's aside to Náday that Hungary must find her own way of communicating with the Russians was not lost on Horthy; a mission, this time with written credentials, was despatched to Moscow, leaving Náday redundant as an intermediary. Howie was repatriated to South Africa, bitterly disappointed that he had failed to secure armistice terms for the Hungarians, and deeply concerned about the fate of all those who had so selflessly and courageously harboured him during his time in Budapest.

From all perspectives, Howie's story is most remarkable. At every turn in it, there is an unexpected twist, a chance encounter and a lucky escape, but throughout his service as a soldier, POW, escapee and finally 'accidental agent', Howie's personal traits of devotion to duty, level-headedness, approachability, loyalty, courage, consideration for others and unwavering determination to succeed, like beacons in the fog of war, all shine through the intricate and fragile web of his knife-edge existence in Budapest. Hungarians from all walks of life and members of the Polish underground in Budapest quickly came to trust him, both with their lives and with the future of their country. Although he was never able to disguise his military bearing, his two crucial assets were that he was very quiet man and had a knack of being able to slip away. Never officially accredited to HMG, it was through an unshakeable belief in his self-appointed mission, together with sheer persistence coupled with an ever-ebullient optimism, that he eventually made his way into the inner sanctum of the Horthy family, a goal much desired but never achieved by SOE. The fact that he failed to attain the desired outcome of Hungarian withdrawal from the Axis camp in no way reflects on his own almost superhuman efforts.

Charles Howie was not the only Allied soldier acting as a freelance agent in Budapest. Warrant Officer Barratt of the RAF aka G.S. Godden, a name he had adopted from another POW in order to effect his escape from Stalag VIIIB, had arrived in the city in September 1943 after evading capture and soon met up with a pro-British lawyer, Dr Károly Szladits aka Rupert Raphael (code name RUPERT), and Miss Evelyn Gore-Symes,[57] an Englishwoman living in Budapest.[58] Together with other escaped POWs and evaders, he was given shelter in the crypt of the Revd Szent-Iványi's Unitarian Church. Barratt was later recaptured attempting to cross the River Drava into Yugoslavia and sent back to Stalag VIIIB. Once more he escaped and, arriving back in Budapest in July 1944, made contact with Howie. On 8 December, he was captured by the Russians and held as a prisoner in Bratislava. It was later learnt by his widow that he had been 'shot while trying to escape', although this was never officially admitted by Moscow. Raphael Rupert and a Dutch officer, Lieutenant van der Waals, were also taken prisoner by the Russians; both disappeared without trace.

Another extraordinary figure who showed up in Budapest around that time was an escaped New Zealand POW, Sapper Roy Natusch of 6th Field Company, New Zealand Engineers. In April 1941, he was among the members of the Anglo-Anzac force left behind on the beaches of Kalamata in Greece. He teamed up with an Australian sergeant, Johnny Sachs,[59] and for the next eight months they roamed the Peloponnese, living off the generosity of patriotic Greeks, before their group was captured by Italian troops.

After several escape attempts, including jumping off a boat at Poros on his way to Turkey and tunnelling his way out of Camp PG 57 at Grupignano, the Italians sent Natusch to a German POW camp in Austria. While on a work farm near Gaas, he and two others, Dai Davies and Joe Walker, escaped into Hungary. When they were subsequently captured at Szombathely, Natusch decided to pass himself off as an officer and apparently succeeded, for after an interview with Colonel Utassy of XXI Department, he was introduced to Szent-Iványi and through him met with up Howie.

As early as 1941, some Allied POWs had managed to get away from their work camps in eastern Austria into Hungary. At first they were held in a prison at Siklos but later they were treated as military internees and housed in the old fortress of Komarom, where there were refugees from all the countries of German-occupied Europe. Later still, they were given the rights of 'free internees', corresponding to the status laid down in the Hague Convention for escapers who reached a neutral country,[60] and were accommodated on Count Mihaly Andrássy's estate where an internment camp for POWs had been established in August 1943. They were allowed the freedom of the town of Szigetvár and its neighbourhood to a radius of 6 miles.

By December 1943, there were some twenty British ORs living there and being well looked after, doing nominal work on the estate in return for their board and lodging. *The Official History of New Zealand in WWII* notes that 'there was some dissatisfaction . . . among the local Hungarians, who worked long hours but noticed that although the British escapees did not, they always had plenty of money to spend in the local taverns.'

Lieutenant Colonel Howie decided that 'Captain' Natusch should take command of this group and on New Year's Eve 1943, briefed him about the impending arrival of the NATAL Mission and ordered him to make the necessary preparations for a reception committee. Natusch also claimed after the war that he had been approached on behalf of the Hungarian government by Baron

Biedermann to organize POW camps on the border of Yugoslavia, the idea being that in the event of a German occupation of Hungary, the Hungarians would arm and then release the POWs, who would head south and link up with the Yugoslav Partisans.

This leisurely life style at Szigetvár came to an abrupt end when the Germans occupied Hungary in March 1944 and the Allied escapees, no longer protected by the Hague Convention, were swiftly rounded up and taken back to Austria by the Germans. Natusch, however, had managed to escape and through the offices of the Bierdermanns, reached the house of Evelyn Gore-Symes in Budapest. Here he was introduced to a network of Dutch officers who had escaped from a POW camp in Poland and, after expert tuition, he adopted a new persona, that of Lieutenant Eddie van Houtegem.[61] Arrested by the Gestapo at a dinner hosted by the lawyer Károly Szladits, he had been so meticulously schooled that his captors even told him they were looking for a notorious New Zealander, 'Captain Roy Natusch', before despatching him to a Dutch POW camp.

In transit, Natusch jumped from a train, was injured, again recaptured and put in hospital in Bratislava. His next stopover was a camp for British POWs from which he duly escaped and, walking south through Hungary, he finally reached Semic in Yugoslavia on 9 October 1944 where he was flown by one of Tito's supply aircraft to Bari. His SOE debrief by Major James Klugman was controversial – Klugman found his story so incredible and inconsistent that he recommended his immediate discharge and return to New Zealand. The New Zealand government reacted somewhat differently and awarded 'The Double Dutchman' a MM for his hair-raising escapades.

WINDPROOF but not bulletproof: the Slovak national uprising

Six months before the beginning of the Second World War, Czechoslovakia, a nation state only created in 1918, had ceased to exist. Prague and the Czech lands of Moravia and Bohemia had been annexed by Germany, while Slovakia had allied itself to Berlin,[62] under the auspices of Father Josef Tiso, a staunchly pro-

Slovak independence Roman Catholic priest. Hungary had helped herself to the little Ruthenian rump on the Eastern extremity.

It was Edward Beneš, the leader of the Czechoslovak government in exile in London, who, in 1943, instigated the idea of a Slovak national uprising when he formed the Slovak National Council, composed of the government in exile, various Czechoslovak democrats and communists and the Slovak Army, and signed the so-called 'Christmas Treaty', a joint declaration recognizing his authority with the goal of reconstituting Czechoslovakia after the war.[63] Supported by Colonel Frantisek Moravec, the former head of Czech Military Intelligence, he informed SOE of his intentions on 10 July 1943, only to meet with a lukewarm response from Lieutenant Colonel Perkins. Not only was Slovakia well inside the Soviet sphere of influence as laid down by Churchill and the FO, but the sheer scale of the logistical effort needed to support such an uprising was beyond Britain's capabilities – over 40 per cent of long-range bombers and transport aircraft would have to be redirected.[64]

In March 1944, a Slovak army officer, Colonel Ján Golián, took charge of the planning of the insurrection, stockpiling money, ammunition and other supplies in military bases in central and eastern Slovakia. A Slovak Army Corps comprising of two divisions – 1st Infantry *Giraltovce* Division and 2nd Infantry *Radvaň* Division – with a total strength of nearly 32,000 and fifty tanks – together with the entire Eastern Slovak Air Force Group of two air squadrons, were deliberately relocated to Prešov in north-east Slovakia that summer in readiness. At a meeting of the Slovak National Council on 29 July, two alternative plans were drawn up and agreed. Under Plan A, the divisions were to secure the Dukla and Lupkov passes (which linked Poland and Slovakia through the Carpathian Mountains) in conjunction with the advancing Soviet 1st Ukrainian Front under Marshal Ivan Konev; or in the event of an unexpected German occupation of Slovakia, under Plan B they were to deploy to the area around Banská Bystrica-Zvolen-Brezno nad Hronom and hold it until the Soviet Army reached it. Either way, if successful, the effect would be to shift the Allied front line in the east 250-300 kilometres to the west.

After the ill-considered killing by a group of communist Partisans of thirty members, including a full colonel, of a German military mission en route to Berlin from Romania, on 29 August, German troops entered Slovakia from the north, south and west with the objective of suppressing further Partisan activity. Tiso's Defence Minister, General Ferdinand Čatloš, duly announced on state radio at 1900 hours the same day that Germany had occupied Slovakia and ordered all Slovak forces to remain in barracks. This precipitated events and at 2000 hours Colonel Golián sent a coded message to all units to begin the uprising in an hour's time. It was at this point that things began to go badly wrong. The Corps Commander, General Augustín Malár, left his post and flew to Bratislava where he pleaded on national radio on the evening of 30 August for the Slovak Army to stand down to the Germans. Not surprisingly, this caused considerable confusion in the East Slovak Army and Air Forces group, even more so when, instead of adhering to the agreed plan, Malár's Deputy and Chief of Staff, Colonel Viliam Talský, ordered the Eastern Slovak Air Force to fly his staff to a prearranged landing zone in Poland to join the Soviet Army. The two divisions, left leaderless, were quickly surrounded by the German 24th Panzer Division and disarmed on the afternoon of 31 August without a single shot being fired. Many of the 20,000 soldiers were sent to camps in Germany while others escaped and joined the Soviet-controlled Partisans or made their way home. Consequently, the uprising got off to a catastrophic start, losing its only two heavily armed divisions capable of resisting any German advance.

Nevertheless, the rebels commenced operations on 29 August at 2100 hours, entering Banská Bystrica the next morning. With his forces in central Slovakia now amounting to 47,000 men, Golián predicted that he could resist German attacks for about two weeks. By 10 September, his insurgents had gained control of large areas of central and eastern Slovakia, which included two airfields, allowing the Soviet Air Force to fly in equipment.[65] However, at a political level, the revolt was destined to failure. The pro-German government of Tiso remained in power in Bratislava, allowing Germany to deploy 40,000 SS troops under SS-Obergruppenführer Gottlob Berger to suppress the uprising. And despite the assurances given to Beneš by Stalin and Molotov in Moscow in December 1943, STAVKA failed to deliver the promised support to the insurgent army and even blocked Western offers of military aid, just as they had done a few weeks earlier in the Warsaw uprising. Simultaneously, Marshal Konev and the Soviet Partisan headquarters in Kiev ordered Partisan groups operating in forward positions in Slovakia not to coordinate resupply drops with the Slovak insurgent army. The result was that the vast majority of Soviet air drops of weapons over insurgent-held territory in eastern and northern Slovakia were quickly confiscated by Soviet Partisans, with little ending up in the hands of the Slovak rebel army.

On 8 September, the Red Army began its offensive towards Dukla Pass on the Slovak-Polish border and tried to fight its way through the Carpathian Mountains into Slovakia. This poorly planned and hasty action resulted in tremendous casualties[66] on both sides and became bogged down for nearly two months. Beneš, the Soviet Partisans and various Slovak factions began to argue among themselves for operational control. Although he tried on repeated occasions, the newly promoted Brigadier General Golián could not bring the sides together to coordinate their efforts, and on 7 October he was replaced by General Rudolf Viest, flown in from London via Moscow.

The WINDPROOF Mission, which finally dropped into Slovakia, had originally started off as DESFORD. Designed by Major Longe to overcome the restrictions of movement imposed by Tito, which had made penetration into Hungary from Yugoslavia so difficult, two areas were proposed as suitable for operations – north-east Hungary around Gyöngyös and the Bükk hills, close to the Slovak border, and south-west Hungary in the Zala countryside between Szentgotthárd and Nagykanizsa, on the Austrian border.

Longe's plan was to use the densely forested Bükk hills and a story of a crashed bomber after raiding Miskolc rail centre as 'cover' for the party, so that they appeared to be evading capture rather than running a clandestine operation. Major Longe would lead the party with Captain Houseman as his second in command, together with a Hungarian W/T operator and a Hungarian contact man.

The prime objectives of DESFORD were: to establish communication lines between the infiltrated team and Force 399, and also London; find a suitable location to receive stores and personnel;

investigate and report on German movements within the area; establish contacts with any dissidents within the area who might be willing to go into action against the Germans; organize and co-ordinate the activities of the Partisans against German targets, and delay and demoralize withdrawing enemy forces; and obtain political and military intelligence on the area.

It was agreed to use the northern area around Gyöngyös as it was deemed more suitable, and the team were despatched to Bari for insertion on 20 May 1944, but the operation became delayed until August 1944 through shortage of W/T operators and no Hungarian being available for the drop. Major Kemp, who was recovering from a hand injury, had been proposed as a replacement for Major Longe, who was now actively involved with Special Forces Unit 22 in northern France. Major Kemp was later sent to Poland on the ill-fated FRESTON Mission. Even the mode of infiltration was altered constantly as SOE became stretched over logistics. At the last moment, DESFORD had its name changed to WINDPROOF ('D' was the designator prefix letter for Hungarian missions and the new prefix letter indicated a Slovakian destination).

Churchill still harboured hopes of reaching Hungary before the Russians. On 5 September, he sailed to Quebec for the Octagon Conference with President Roosevelt and the Joint Chiefs of Staff. In the ensuing discussions, he expressed his desire that British forces should forestall the Russians in certain areas of central Europe – for instance, the Hungarians had expressed the intention of resisting the Russian advance and would surrender to a British force if it could arrive in time. It was therefore, in his view, imperative that British forces, having secured the ports of Trieste and Fiume by way of an amphibious landinglaunched from Ancona or Venice, should enter Yugoslavia and advance north and north-east into Central Europe. However, the Eighth Army had not even reached Rimini and looked destined to face yet another winter of bitter fighting in the Apennines. Budapest lay 850 kilometres away by road and all US and British airborne troops had been earmarked for Operation MARKET GARDEN in Holland.

However, while Churchill mused in Quebec, Horthy had already contacted the Russians. His emissary was a relative, Count Ladomér Zichy, who, from his estates in northern Hungary, was able to contact Slovak Partisans and through them a Russian officer, Colonel Makarov, who claimed to be the representative of Foreign Minister Molotov. Zichy returned with a set of written promises which gave Horthy grounds for optimism: Russia would stop bombing as soon as a Hungarian peace delegation arrived in Moscow; the emissaries would be treated as diplomats and given free use of cypher and radio; the Romanian Army (now joined with the Allies) would stop where they were at the time; only the Russian Army would advance; there would be a census in Transylvania; the Soviet High Command would arrange for an immediate cessation of hostilities and send partisan groups to Hungary to help the Hungarians with the changeover; and the Hungarian police gendarmerie and administration would continue. The most important clauses of the communiqué concerned Hungary's integrity and independence, which would be assured. Her present frontiers would be guaranteed and the Soviet Union would not interfere with her internal affairs. The letter, dated 14 September 1944, and bearing the signature of Lieutenant Colonel Makarov, ended with a declaration that the Soviet Union had no intention of expanding in Europe. A similar message was brought back by Baron Ede Aczél, the governor of Cluj Province in northern Transylvania, who had gone through the lines and contacted Colonel General Fedor Kuznyetsov. With Lieutenant Colonel Howie on the run at this time and unable to make radio contact, the likelihood of London having detailed knowledge of these negotiations is hard to determine.

WINDPROOF made its first attempt on the night of 2/3 September but the aircraft failed to take off due to mechanical trouble. After that, all available aircraft were retasked to supply the Polish Resistance in the Warsaw Uprising, which had started on 1 August. It was not until 18 September that SOE were given another aircraft, which managed to drop the Mission, consisting of Major John Sehmer, Lieutenant Andy Daniels[67] and Sergeant Steve Zenopian,[68] Corporal Bill Davies, the Mission's W/T operator, and twenty containers, at Nova Bana, some 30 miles from its pinpoint. By this time, the situation on the ground had changed dramatically.

John Sehmer's background was unusual to say the least. His German grandfather, Theodor Sehmer, had been a partner in the Ehrhart & Sehmer engineering firm in Saarbrucken, and had sent

John's father, Ernst, to study at Bonn University, then Buffalo in the US, where he obtained a law degree. In 1907, aged twenty-eight, Ernst married into the Bayley family of Cheshire and settled down to life as a country squire, first in Staffordshire and then in Sussex, where he farmed throughout the First World War. Life as a German national was far from easy and at one point *The Times* published a letter suggesting that Sehmer was signalling to the German Army from the top of a folly. After the war, his wife had their five children rebaptized as Catholics since she said that the only person who had shown them any understanding was the local RC priest.

Shortly after the war, Ernst fell on hard times and, after letting their Sussex property, moved to Oberammergau in Germany, where John, who had been born in 1913, attended school at Kloster Ettal. After a time, Ernst sent his family back to England and in 1927, while staying at the Dom Hotel in Cologne, he committed suicide; the dire state of his financial affairs had proved too much to bear. John, now fourteen, attended Collyers School in Horsham, and then The Oratory School at Caversham, ending up working as an engineer with the International Combustion Company in Derby. He then moved to Leeds to work for another company and in January 1938 was commissioned in the Territorial Army.

On the outbreak of war, Sehmer joined the 45th Battalion of the Royal Tank Regiment and in May 1942 embarked for the Middle East. His military service records show an attachment to the Intelligence Training Centre from 2 August 1941 to 9 May 1942, but the nature of his duties there are not clear. He was recruited by SOE on 26 January 1943 and after training, which he completed on 8 April, 'this determined and reliable' officer joined the Yugoslavian desk.

Almost immediately, and at very short notice, he was earmarked for HACKTHORPE III,[69] one of three Missions planned to support General Mihailović and his *chetniks*.[70] The previous commander, Major G.C. Morgan, had been redeployed at his own request to launch Operation FLESHPOTS, a blind drop into Macedonia with the objective of disabling the Allatini chrome mines of which Morgan had been the Managing Director before the war.[71] Sadly this daring endeavour failed, with Morgan, his W/T Operator, Bombardier Buchan, and liaison officer, Flight

Lieutenant Tasic, all captured. Together with Corporal Leslie Blackmore and Lieutenant Jovan Gaitski, Sehmer parachuted into Yugoslavia on the night of 19 April 1943. Following Colonel Bailey's decision to reinforce the *chetnik* Missions with trained military engineers, so that they could more effectively sabotage German lines of communication and economic targets, HACK-THORPE was joined by KIDMORE on 21/22 May, consisting of Captain Hawksworth RE, two New Zealand sappers, Sergeants Harvey and Lindstrom, and Sergeant Dusan Leban. The expanded force then linked up with the HENBURY Mission, commanded by Captain Michael Lees, which also had two sappers, Lieutenants Smith and Tomlinson. Soon after, all three Missions were caught up in a ferocious battle with Bulgarian troops, during which Sehmer lost one of his New Zealand sergeants and his W/T operator.[72] After over a year in Macedonia and Serbia, he was flown out on 29 May 1944 to Bari in a Dakota with the other *chetnik* BLOs; by coincidence, Lees was sitting on the same plane.[73] Together with Kenneth Greenless and Jasper Rootham, Sehmer had gone to say goodbye to Mihailović. After a farewell glass of *rakia*, they shook hands, saluted and left.

The first WINDPROOF message received by Bari was positive: 'All arrived safe. Deposited thirty miles west of pinpoint on wooded mountain at Velikople. Fires arranged to burn all night to give visibility to A/T guns covering approach Huns who were only eight kilometres away. Excellent reception from Army and peasants. Motoring today to see General Golian at Banská Bistrica. American mission beat us to it, down there, arrived 17th.' Sehmer was referring to the OSS Mission that had flown into Tri Duby[74] the day before. (The fact that WINDPROOF was not on that plane strongly indicates that the Mission was not destined for any role in Slovakia with the SNU.) The British were aware that the OSS was using the cover of exfiltrating Allied aircrew as a pretext for flying in arms and equipment to the Slovak Uprising. This strategy had been personally sanctioned by its commander, General Donovan, irrespective of the broader political picture and inevitable friction with the Soviets.

When Sehmer arrived in Banská Bystrica, he was surprised to be introduced to members of the MANGANESE Mission. Dropped some 75 kilometres off target at Velky Uherec on 9 June 1944, this all-Czechoslovak Mission consisting of Cadet Officer Vanura, Sergeant Major Kosina and Sergeant Major Biros had made its way to Bratislava to contact members of the Resistance there. Finding little support, they were then ordered to proceed to Banská Bystrica at the end of July, where they arrived in August and installed themselves in the town, putting their W/T set at the disposal of Colonel Golián.

Sehmer was equally bemused on 26 September when he signalled Bari: 'A Force AMSTERDAM turned up . . . Were dropped in Hun lines forty miles from pinpoint . . . All kit bar cash lost . . . all Jews.' Run by Lieutenant Colonel Tony Simonds out of Cairo, their official brief was to arrange the evacuation of Allied airmen, but unofficially they were charged to organize Jewish resistance groups. Before the war, Simonds had worked alongside Orde Wingate and the Zionist 'special night squads' and had kept in touch with their leaders. This had resulted in a deal. The Zionists would provide Simonds with contacts, safe houses and field operatives across the Balkans, and in Czechoslovakia and Hungary, on the understanding that they could extricate a Jew for every Allied POW they rescued. Between June 1943 and August 1944, Simonds sent in twenty-five Jewish agents. As Foot and Langley put it,[75] 'the idea was splendid but the results did not live up to it.'

Three members of the Jewish Agency, Rafael Reiss aka Reisz, Zvi Ben-Yaakov (team commander) and Chaim Chermesh, all trained by and accredited to SOE, arrived in mid-September;[76] their female colleague, Haviva Reik,[77] who had been banned by SOE from dropping on the grounds that it was too dangerous, hitched a lift with an American aircraft and joined them a few days later on 21 September. At the end of the month, Abba Berdiczew, a W/T operator, completed their number. Caught up in the fierce fighting that followed, four of them, including Reik and Reiss, were captured by the SS and shot by the Gestapo on 20 November in Kremnica.

The first five members of an OSS intelligence and liaison team had arrived by a B-17G aircraft on 17 September. Headed by Navy Lieutenant James Holt Green, the other members of the group were Sergeant Jerry G. Mican (originally from Prague and a friend of Beneš's brother), interpreter Sergeant Joseph Horváth (originally from Polomka), W/T operator Robert Brown, W/T operator

Charles Heller, and a former Foreign Legionnaire, Lieutenant John Schwartz, cover name Križan, (originally from Slovakia).

With the OSS since March 1943, Green, a softly spoken North Carolina cotton baron, had worked with SOE in Yugoslavia on the Albanian border from January to June 1944, and had established an excellent rapport with his British opposite number, Major Anthony Hunter. When he was recalled to Bari in June, he was given the OSS Yugoslav desk, which included planning missions in Slovakia. He gave the task of supporting the Slovak uprising to Captain Don Rider but when he was deployed to Yugoslavia with the ASH team, Holt took it on and was confirmed as head of DAWES.

Their mission was to establish cooperation with Colonel Golián and to organize American military supplies of weapons, ammunition and explosives for the Czechoslovak First Army. They were also tasked to evacuate American airmen from Tri Duby airfield and to inform SACMED about the situation in Slovakia. To accomplish these aims, the team planned to split into two: the DAWES Mission (Green, Horváth, Brown) and HOUSEBOAT (Schwartz, Mican, Heller), the latter's assignment being to penetrate Czech and Moravian territory and accomplish certain tasks there. However, the situation in Slovakia forced both groups to stay together in Banská Bystrica.

The German counter-attack began on 19 September and by 25 September, the tone and content of Sehmer's messages had changed dramatically: 'Situation grave. Slovaks begging us for arms and ammunition.' In addition to his precarious military situation, Sehmer was also concerned by the arrival of 'vast numbers of refugees . . . of all nationalities'. As they were all seeking protection and then evacuation, he needed some form of directive to work to.

Having sent Daniels and Zenopian ahead to Terany on the Slovak/Hungarian border, Sehmer and Corporal Davies, neither of whom spoke Hungarian, wisely remained at the Slovak Army HQ, where WINDPROOF had mutated into the official British Mission to the Czechoslovak First Army (CFI). Bombarded with a string of intelligence reports about the situation in Slovakia, SOE London chided Sehmer on 4 October that he had forgotten about his original mission which was to infiltrate into Hungary.[78] Sehmer replied two days later, stressing that since he was on excellent terms with General Golián, who thought that the British had accredited the WINDPROOF Mission to him, it made sense for him to stay put. 'Please do not think I am being disloyal in any way, but I do feel I can be of more use here.'

On 7 October, a flight of six Flying Fortresses landed without problems at Tri Duby and unloaded sixteen tons of bazookas, sub-machine guns, Bren guns, ammunition, explosives and general stores. Two infantry officers, Lieutenant Bill McGregor and Lieutenant Kenneth Lain, arrived at the same time and joined the OSS group because of their expertise with various weapons. On the flight were two OSS staff officers, Major Ross and Lieutenant Deranian, who held a meeting with Lieutenant Green during the unloading.

Besides Ross and Deranian, Lieutenant Colonel Henry Threlfall, commanding officer of SOE's Bari base, also arrived at Tri Duby (Operation QUARTZ) together with an SOE Jewish operative, Lieutenant Robert Willis (real name Abba Bardichev),[79] Jindrich Souhadra,[80] a Slovak colonel from London and a large quantity of field dressings and other medical supplies. As the commander of Force 139 in Bari, Threlfall had taken it on himself to find out what was going on and held a thirty-minute conference with General Golián in order to glean from him personally the military situation in Slovakia.[81] Threlfall later recalled that 'the situation was very obscure . . . we didn't know what was happening.' The fact that such a senior officer, and one who was in charge of the Czechoslovak desk, was sent in on a spur-of-the-moment fact-finding mission suggests that SOE were taken unawares and had little forewarning of the SNU. This certainly explains the shock experienced by Sehmer and his mission on finding themselves in the middle of a major military conflict.

In a Most Immediate signal, Threlfall notified London that he had:

> spoken Windproof leader. Explained briefly SOE and FO position. Confirmed his functions both to him and Golián. Is definitely no misunderstanding. He says one of his men already in Hungary; another on frontier. Controls very tight and doubts if possible for British officer to cross. Moreover says he has several other lines into Hungary working or in

preparation which necessitated his staying Slovak HQ as they lead thither. Instructed him leave HQ for point nearer Hungary if possible but left him discretion since he is on spot and must decide according local circumstances.

As a result of this meeting, Sehmer understood that politics prevented him from playing the role of British Military Mission to the SNU and that any such arrangement would need the blessing of Moscow.

Threlfall, a senior manager with Lever Brothers before the war, had been with SOE since 1940. His first appointment as 'clerk to the British Naval Attaché' in Stockholm had ended in somewhat farcical conditions, when Swedish police arrested a man who claimed that Threlfall had supplied him with timers and dynamite to blow up ships in the Kiel Canal and place time bombs on German trains in transit to Norway. Forced to leave the country in August 1942 for engaging in 'illegal purposes', after his stint as head of the Hungarian section in 1943–4, Threlfall took over command of SOE's Polish and Czechoslovak desks, arriving at a critical moment at the start of the Warsaw Uprising.

The Allies had agreed to supply the Poles from the air, using a north and a south corridor. The former soon proved impractical in terms of the unacceptable risks involved in overflying Germany, so for the first half of August, Threlfall, as the senior SOE officer involved, found himself coordinating the airlift out of Bari. He recalled:

The flights covered Italy, Yugoslavia where the planes were battered by anti-aircraft, then across Hungary with more anti-aircraft potting at them; and then Poland, and dropping down over Warsaw . . . The loss of aircraft was colossal and tragic. Many Allied pilots, having dropped supplies on Warsaw and finding that their planes had been severely damaged, were not allowed by their allies, the Russians, to land in their territory, although it was only on the other side of the Vistula.

As losses began to mount, RAF chiefs, dismayed by the costly havoc in the skies above Warsaw, finally and reluctantly halted all flights.[82] For Threlfall, this was a salient lesson in the politics of ill-considered promises when it came to dealing with the Russians. In his discussions with Golián, he was appalled but not surprised to hear that there were 15,000 men without small arms and that Russian arms deliveries to date amounted to a paltry 600 SMGs, 50 LMGs, 12 HMGs and 300 rifles. The twenty-four Soviet fighters that Czech pilots had flown into Tri Duby were not of much use since they did not have 'proper' petrol or oil. He observed that 'the Slovaks were tactful but clearly most dissatisfied with Russian deliveries which not up to promises. [They] made several remarks about paper deliveries. Also complained that many of weapons sent unusable.' Despite his recent experience in the politics and practicalities of long-range aerial supply in the Russian sphere of influence, Threlfall's 'inclination would be to send him [Golián] everything one can without respecting too closely the agreement which may have been made that the Russians alone should supply the rising'. This may have been prompted by Golián's profuse thanks to Threlfall for the anti-tank bazookas unloaded from the B-17s!

On the return flight to Bari, Threlfall took with him three senior Slovaks, Lieutenant Colonel Mirko Vesel (Slovak Army), Jan Ursiny (Social Democrats) and Alco Novomesky (Slovak Communist Party) who were to report to Beneš in London.

Two other SIS/SOE operatives were also in the area – Major Jack Wilson and his W/T operator, Keith Hensen.[83] Jack Wilson, a Viennese Jewish SIS agent, whose real name was Wanndorfer, had been parachuted 40 miles to the east of his pinpoint near Vienna, and was subsequently captured by a group of Partisans and escaped US airmen on or about 1 September. On him was a set of forged German identity papers and, thinking that his captors were pro-Allied Slovaks who would cheerfully set about dismembering him, he had swallowed his cyanide capsule. Fortunately it only made him sick.

Although Green had counselled caution in reinforcing the DAWES Mission due to the deteriorating military situation, an additional fourteen OSS intelligence and liaison officers were flown in on 7 October. Lieutenant James Harvey Gaul, Lieutenant William McGregor, Lieutenant Kenneth Lain, Lieutenant Lane H. Miller and Sergeant Ken Dunlevy joined the DAWES group, and Lieutenant Green divided the remaining eight men into two groups. Captain Edward Baranski, W/T Daniel Pavletich and Anton Novak, alias Anton Facuna (born in Slovakia) were assigned to group DAY. The DAY team's mission was to obtain tactical information from the western parts of insurgent territory, to penetrate combat lines and to be active in the enemy's rear. Lieutenant Green assigned Flying Officer Tibor Keszthelyi (commander), Sergeant Steve Catlos, Stephan Cora and Francis Moly to the BOWERY team. The mission of the last two individuals was to cross the Hungarian border and verify information obtained about Horthy.[84] Cora and Moly reached Hungary on 11 October but by then the BOWERY team had ceased to exist. Keszthelyi and Catlos became a part of the DAWES team. The mission of the sole DARE team member – Lieutenant Francis Perry – was to make connections between Vienna and Bratislava. Finally, Emil Tomeš from the OSS counter-intelligence department, AP correspondent Joseph Morton and photo-journalist Nelson Paris, a member of the US Navy, attached themselves to Green's HQ party.

Sehmer, meanwhile, was busy infiltrating his team into Hungary. After establishing contacts at Ipolyszög about 7 kilometres west of Balassa-Gyarmat, Daniels had crossed the border on 8 October; wearing civilian clothes, he had boarded the train and managed to reach Budapest in the early hours of 9 October, where he booked into the Brtania Hotel. After activating a number of contacts, he was told that there was no point him being there since there was already another British mission in town – presumably a reference to the activities of Lieutenant Colonel Howie – so he took the night train back to Ipolyszög on 15 October. The next day, travelling with a deserter's pass, his luck ran out, he was captured by the Gendarmerie and taken to Miskolc where he was repeatedly tortured before eventually being sent to a Polish prison camp at Zugliget.[85]

Zenopian, who had been waiting at the border for Daniels to return, arrived back in Banská Bystrica on 16/17 October and almost immediately left for Dobšiná, 100 kilometres to the east of Banská, where Sehmer had arranged for him to meet a captain in the Hungarian Army who would take him on to Budapest. After a 'no show', he went to Ochtiná with a view to crossing the border between Jelšava and Rožňava, but returned to Dobšiná where he met up with Sehmer, Willis and Davies who were reconnoitring 'lines', and moved with them to the remote village of Čierna Lehota in the hills west of Dobšiná. Here they received the order not to proceed to Hungary but to return to Slovak HQ at Banská Bystrica.[86] However, this time their path was blocked by the Germans.

By 19 October, SOE, presumably with FO clearance, had altered its stance with Golián: it was therefore suggested at one stage, after proposing to withdraw Daniels and Zenopian from Hungary and evacuating them back to Bari, to send a Czech-speaking officer to join Sehmer and to convert the mission into an official Slovak one,[87] on a par with the Russians and Americans. Confusion followed since from the very beginning the FO and British Chiefs of Staff had made it clear that the uprising was to be a Russian affair and that any support of the SNU by air should likewise be a Russian commitment. Moreover, there was a move afoot in London to send in a high-level British Military Mission, code-named MICA. Composed of Lieutenant Colonel Kenneth Greenless, Lieutenant Colonel Rupert Raw, Captain Schweitzer and a W/T operator, Sergeant Edwards, the Mission left London on 21 October and arrived in Bari three days later. Scheduled as the official Mission to General Viest, the team prepared to drop into the Donovaly area on 29 October. However, the situation on the ground remained extremely fluid and when Radio Bratislava announced the capture of Viest on 4 November, MICA proposed that it should join the Czech Airborne Brigade under Prikryl. This idea immediately ran into problems since Marshal Konev had ordered the Brigade to place itself under the command of the senior Partisan leader, and any British mission would need Russian approval at the highest level. The hapless MICA remained grounded, eventually returning to the UK on 21 January 1945.

On 19 September, OKW had replaced SS-Obergruppenführer Berger with SS-General Höffle and a major German counter-offensive began on 17–18 October when 35,000 German troops entered the country from Hungary, bringing the western advance of Soviet forces to a halt in late October. The encircled insurgents had to evacuate Banská Bystrica on 27 October, along with the SOE and OSS missions, and retreated to the mountains where they switched to guerrilla warfare tactics. On 28 October, Viest sent London a message that said the organized resistance had ended and on 30

October, President Tiso celebrated a thanksgiving mass in Banská Bystrica and awarded medals to General Höffle's SS and Wehrmacht troops. On 3 November, the Germans captured Golián and Viest in Pohronský Bukovec, later interrogating them before executing them.

Not surprisingly, the situation for WINDPROOF had deteriorated and the Mission, now consisting of Sehmer, Zenopian, Davies and Willis from A Force (ANTICLIMAX), was completely cut off.[88] On 23 October,[89] in a signal requesting an arms drop, Sehmer added: 'We are completely cut off . . . unless help comes we can't hold out . . . fully realize difficulties (re air drops) but situation here desperate.' Holt Green's message to OSS in Bari was almost identical: 'Believe situation getting worse. Possibly we may discard radios . . . Have arranged to split [the forty-three Americans] into 4 groups . . . Organised resistance rapidly deteriorating.' On 30 October, now joined by the OSS interpreter Margita Kocková, Sehmer signalled that the Germans had taken the Slavosovce Valley and, after being deserted by his Slovak army and Partisan guard force, he had, only by luck, run into a 200-strong group of Partisans commanded by Lieutenant Dymko. WINDPROOF was complete with the exception of Daniels, who was out of contact, but they had lost all their personal kit, including that all-important luxury, tobacco. As the weather continued to deteriorate, in a signal to HQ, Willis advised of 'very bad conditions . . . living in improvised huts in woods with weather worst possible'.

Unknown to Sehmer, all members of MANGANESE had by now been captured. Sergeant Major Kosina was taken prisoner and interrogated by the Gestapo, whom he managed to bluff; Vanura and Biros, separately captured on 31 October, were taken into the woods near Bahnicky and shot.

The Germans had entrusted the hunt for the Allied missions to Major Erwin Graf Thun und Hohenstein, commander of Frontaufklärungstrupp 218 based in Banská Bystrica.[90] Born in 1896 into a distinguished Bohemian military family (his grandfather and father[91] were both highly decorated officers in the Austro-Hungarian imperial army), he attended the Cavalry Cadet School and reported on the outbreak of the First World War to the aristocratic Ulanenregiment II Furst zu Schwarzenberg. After the war, the highly decorated young Graf was involved in the

March 1920 Kapp Putsch in Berlin, when the Freikorps failed to oust the Weimar Republic, and subsequently he emigrated to Argentina where he became a farmer.

1940, Graf Erwin volunteered for military service, more as a patriot and adventurer than a committed member of the Nazi Party, and due to his linguistic skills, especially Russian, he was posted to a special forces unit, No. 1 Lehrregiment Brandenburg zbV 800. After the German invasion of. the Soviet Union, he instructed volunteers from Russian POWs (mostly Ukrainian nationalists) in counter-Partisan operations. Dressed casually in a loden jacket and breeches, the Graf soon became a legend for sangfroid. Sometimes, wearing the uniform of a Russian major, he joined bands of anti-German Partisans and, after winning their confidence, eliminated their leaders. On one such occasion his group was unmasked, resulting in a bloody *handgemengen*, when the guerrilla leaders were killed with daggers.[92]

By 11 November, heavy snow had begun to fall and soon Thun und Hohenstein's troops met with success, rounding up a group of American fliers including the British agent Keith Hensen.[93] In the meantime, Sehmer and his group had found refuge on the ski slopes of Velky Bok above Polomka village and managed to make contact with Bari. The cold had by now become intense and still there was no sign of resupply. Over a month later, on 18 December, Bari informed Sehmer that there were three planes stood by as soon as the 'met' conditions improved. By now, 3,000 retreating German and Hungarian troops had arrived in the valley below the SOE hideout, making foraging for food even harder.

Lieutenant Zenopian takes up the story in his debrief by the Americans in Bucharest on 1 March 1945:

> I was with Major Sehmer when he got into trouble and had to bury his radio, but through a Partisan band we were able to effect recovery of the wireless and then intended to go back to Banská Bystrica but on the way learned that the Americans had been forced to move. It was reported that the American Mission was somewhere in the Domber area[94] . . . Lt Willis and Lt Gaul then went to get the rest of the Americans and brought them to our location in the mountains of Domber (6 December).

The American flyers who had been with Green and Gaul, had previously 'packed in'. Meaning that they could not take it and had gone to the nearest village to give themselves up.

. . . the situation at the beginning of December was that the Americans lived in one house (an hour's walk from the village of Polomka) with the British living further up the mountain in another (another hour's walk). Conditions were not too good, food was scarce and five of the Americans were seriously ill because of frostbite in their feet. Major Sehmer and I were making an attempt to supply everyone with food and we had to put the pressure on the Partisan stores in order to get enough to keep us going . . .

One of the members of the American Mission acted as a sort of doctor and seemed to know something of first aid, but I do not remember his name. There was also an Englishman named Wilson with the Americans, but I do not know what his story was and so do not know why he was with the Americans rather than us. He was, however, captured with the rest of the Americans on 26 December 1944 . . .

Some of us used to go down to the village of Mojanu and also to other villages in order to send messages (having lost all battery power, it was essential to find mains electricity to power the sets) . . . in our messages, we told our people that it was very dangerous and difficult to operate the wireless and we hoped constantly that a plane would come to drop us equipment . . . we could not understand why planes did not come, as I know definitely from 16 December to the day of capture on 26 December, the weather was perfect both day and night.

By now, the Chiefs of Staff had figuratively washed their hands of the Slovak National Uprising. In a minute dated 15 November 1944, they noted: 'As the FO have now accepted military arguments against our assisting the rising as decisive and have so informed Czechoslovak Government, and as rising has now collapsed and Czechs are inclined to attribute its failure to lack of Russian support, FO consider it undesirable to press matter any further.'

SOE were very much aware of the precarious situation of

Sehmer and his team, and of their OSS colleagues. On 5/6 December, Sehmer had signalled: 'For God's sake send a charger – risking lives working from occupied villages is not amusing.' On 16 December, Green, using Sehmer's set, had sent an equally succinct report: 'All equipment lost. Majority in bad condition because of exposure and frozen feet. Exhausted by long mountain marches and starvation diet.' On 18 December, it was decided to send in the BAUXITE II team of Major John Foster and Major George Seymour with a W/T operator, but the plan was scuppered on the basis of 'why reinforce failure'. Renamed PIGOTITE on 3 April 1945, the Mission was disbanded on 17 May, having never dropped.

The problem of resupply remained and the RAF offered three options: the drop of a generator in a jettison tank by a lone fighter, a normal night sortie if 'met' permitted or a daylight sortie of three aircraft escorted by fighters. On 21 December, a sortie did take off but had to return due to excessive icing. A week later, the RAF signalled SOE: 'WINDPROOF successful'. It was tragically too late and the stores had most likely been dropped to Russian or Partisan camps marked by fires.

Zenopian continues the story:

The Christmas eve party was very touching and everybody had a wonderful time together. We had done some decorating and had a Union Jack as well as the Stars and Stripes on the walls. I will never forget the scene, and I have with me the pencilled text of a prayer given by Lieutenant Gaul during the party:

'*O God, we who are gathered here in Thy name and by Thy name and by Thy blessing, on this day of Thanksgiving do offer with deep gratitude our most heartfelt thanks for our deliverance from the blizzards and high winds of the wintry mountains and from the cruel snows fallen upon us, and from the perils of the black night and dark valleys. Gratefully we thank Thee for preserving our group together and for maintaining our physical health and strength and for buttressing our wavering courage and for providing food, even in our darkest days, and we ask Thy blessing on us and our allies, particularly the Slovak nation, and Thy mercy on our*

*comrades who are missing by enemy action and wintry storms.
Amen.'*

. . . on 24 December, after the party, I went from the
Americans' house back to our place, taking with me Sergeant
Davies, a wireless operator, two Americans and a Slovak girl,[95]
who had been with the American Mission since the time of
Banská Bystrica . . . Major Sehmer, as well as Lieutenant
Willis, both of our house, stayed with the Americans,
intending to come back on 26 December.

On the morning of 26 at eight o'clock we were given a
warning from below that the Germans were coming from the
direction of Polomka . . . about ten o'clock, from a vantage
point we could see the Germans as they came up the mountain. There were about 250 . . . a Slovak Lieutenant of the
Partisan group, who was taking care of the British house,
decided to go with his commissar and meet them . . . in a short
time the commissar disappeared from the scene and the
Germans started shooting . . . and firing artillery shells at the
house. When this started the Partisans decided to move off
and so did we [Lieutenant Zenopian, Sergeant Davies, the two
Americans[96] and the Slovak girl][97] . . . Later we contacted a
Partisan group about fifteen miles distance from the house
and heard the story of one Slovak soldier of the American
guard who had escaped.

On the morning of 26 December, when everyone was
dressing and breakfast was being prepared, a helluva of
machine gun fire burst on the house from all directions (the
soldier,[98] though wounded, had managed to escape) and
watched as the whole group surrendered. After which all of
them were marched out by Hlinka Guards . . . all fully dressed
in complete uniforms . . . to Polomka town . . . from where
they were taken to Bratislava from which point they were
taken to Bruck a/d Donau. That is all I know of what
happened to them. Ironically we heard that planes had come
that night, 26 December.

From 26 December until the last of January our party
stayed in the area, still hoping that we might be eventually
able to get clear. However, we had no equipment, no food,
and we knew that the Germans had decided to clear the

mountains of all Partisan bands because of the retreat. Therefore, on 1 February 1945, I tried to get through to the Russian lines. We started at six o'clock in the morning and after four days reached the place called Radova in Slovakia ... eventually we arrived at a place called Bystro where we made contact with the Romanian army fighting with the Russians.

On 23 January, Culovics, Catlos, Dunlevy and Davies met up near the Hungarian border with Romanian troops who by now were fighting for the Russians. Two days later they were handed over to the Soviet Army at Rimavská Sobota, where they were put in a KGB holding camp. En route to Odessa, from where they were due to be repatriated, the group found themselves in Bucharest, waiting for an overnight train connection. Catlos had become very concerned about Culovics who had been told by the KGB that she would have to stay on and join the Soviet Security Services. He managed to make contact with the US Military Mission and soon all four had been 'kidnapped' by four jeeploads of British and American soldiers who stormed the Red Army billets where they were staying.

As a postscript to his debrief, the debriefing officer, Lieutenant Colonel Walter M. Ross, the OSS officer who had conferred with Holt Green at Tri Duby on 7 October, records that Zenopian said: 'The cold in the area was really terrific and that they escaped death by freezing is a miracle ... in one night eighty-two men of a Slovak Brigade were frozen to death.'

The Dachau detachment of the War Crimes Commission confirmed much of Zenopian's story in their report of 11 October 1946. Willis and Wilson are identified as members of Sehmer's Slovak Mission. On capture they were taken to the Gestapo jail at Banská Bystrica and then to Mauthausen Concentration Camp on 6 January 1945, where they were incarcerated in individual cells in the 'bunker'. On 7 January, Sehmer was interrogated by five members of the RSHA.[99] During his interrogation he was beaten by the Camp Commandant before being tortured, first by having his fingers pressurized by wooden stakes after which he was suspended from the ceiling by his arms. He was then re-interrogated. On 26 January, after the camp received a telegram from Kaltenbrugger in Berlin, the 31-year-old Sehmer was executed, shot at close range in the back of the head by Franz Ziereis,[100] the Camp Commandant, in person. He left a wife and young son.

Two other British servicemen were shot in similar circumstance: Willis and Wilson.

According to a telegram sent by RSHA Chief Ernst Kaltenbrunner, the following members of the American OSS were executed at Mauthausen on 24 January 1945: Lieutenant Holt Green,[101] Sergeant Mican, Sergeant Horváth, Corporal Brown, W/T operator Heller, Lieutenant Gaul, photographer Nelson Paris, Lieutenant Miller, Captain Baranski, Lieutenant Keszthelyi, Lieutenant Perry, W/T operator Pavletich, AP correspondent Joseph Morton and the team's Slovak interpreter, Margita Kocková. Eight members of the OSS – S. Catlos, K. Dunlevy, McGregor, K. Lain, J. Schwartz, F. Moly, S. Cora and A. Novak-Facuna – escaped captivity and survived until the end of the War.

On 24 January 1945, the following statement was published by the German Overseas News Agency:

> Eighteen members of a group of Anglo-US agents led by an American named Green and by an Englishman called Sehmer who pretended to be a major, were rounded up on Slovak territory in the rear of the German sector, so competent German quarters announce. The interrogation revealed that it was their task to commit acts of sabotage in Slovakia and to carry out economic and political espionage for the Anglo-Americans. The agents were wearing civilian clothes when arrested, were sentenced to death by Court Martial and were shot.

Maria Culovich's recollection was altogether different. For example, when asked by her debriefers what people were wearing, she recalled of Sehmer that he 'wore a black wool "tam" with "Fear Not" and a picture of a tank on the front, a British wool OD shirt, British battle dress and trousers and heavy brown shoes. He wore a major's crown on the shoulders of his battle dress and parachute wings over the left pocket. He also wore three ribbons.'

This ill-starred uprising, which started on 29 August 1944, achieved little. The Russians finally entered Banská Bystrica on 25 March 1945, seven months later. By his shenanagins, Stalin had outwitted his Western Allies once again. Wearing his priest's robes, Monseigneur Tiso was hanged as a traitor in 1947.

Lieutenant Daniels, the one member of WINDPROOF who had crossed into Hungary in civilian clothes on 23 September, was captured on 16 October 1944 and held in various jails until he escaped with the help of Gordon and Coates from Zugliget near Budapest. He managed to contact the Russians on 11 February 1945 after being on the run for sixty days.

A botched coup d'état and the end of a free nation

Six months after the German invasion and the eradication of the Surrender Group, on 11 October 1944, Admiral Horthy finally decided to 'defect' from the Axis camp and sent a delegation[102] to Moscow to follow up Aczél's and Zichy's overtures. They took with them a handwritten letter by the Regent in which he pleaded for his country, asking the Russians to spare her further sufferings. He pointed out that Hungary entered the war only under enormous pressure by the Germans and asked Stalin to use his influence with the Allies to ensure fair armistice terms for his country. No date was fixed. He believed that by announcing this volte-face over the radio, he could take his country out of the war. The Germans were well informed and well prepared – they kidnapped the Regent's son, Miklós, in broad daylight on 15 October, the day of the proposed proclamation as Horthy recalls in his memoirs:

> I was fully aware that a dramatic race was in progress. I knew that the Germans would do all they could to prevent Hungary from concluding an armistice which I saw as the only way out. Like our Finnish cousins, we had fought the Communist menace as long as there seemed to remain a chance of success. If I wished to spare Hungary the horror of warfare on her own soil and to assure Hungary's existence as a state being recognized by the victors, now was my very last chance. Hitler, on the other hand, had every incentive to keep the war away from Germany's frontiers as long as possible. I could not know the details of his plan, so that I do not know whether the events of that Sunday morning were part of his general plan or not.

The German Security Service had informed my son Nicholas through intermediaries that envoys of Tito wished to talk with him. Nicholas had not kept a first appointment on observing suspicious-looking persons lurking in the vicinity of the proposed meeting-place. Another meeting was fixed for 15 October early in the morning at the offices of Felix Bornemisza, the Director of the Hungarian Danube harbours, on Eskü Square on the Pest side. Thinking it possible that there were envoys from Tito who might have important information to give, I had, on the assumption that the meeting would take place in the Palace, empowered Nicholas to negotiate. My son did not realize that I had made that assumption and went into town accompanied by three Guardsmen. He told them to come to his assistance should they observe anything untoward, or should he be away longer than ten minutes. His suspicions proved only too well founded. He had hardly set foot in the building before he was attacked by fifteen armed Gestapo men who beat him mercilessly until he fell to the ground and feigned unconsciousness. He was then rolled in a carpet and carried to a van that was waiting outside, but before he was thrust into the van he succeeded in giving a cry for help. In the fight shots were fired and one Hungarian and one German were killed. This abduction had obviously been planned well beforehand. Nicholas was to be a hostage to force my hand.[103]

The news of his abduction reached me just before a meeting of the Crown Council that was scheduled for 10.00 am. The meeting did not begin until 10.45 am. Facing me across the rectangular table sat Vörös, the Chief of the General Staff; on either side of me sat the members of the government and the Chiefs of the Cabinet and Military Chancelleries. I can here refer to the minutes which give my address as follows:

'I have called together the members of the Cabinet in this darkest hour of Hungary's history. Our situation is gravely critical. That Germany is on the verge of collapse is no longer in doubt; should that collapse occur now, the Allies would find that Hungary is Germany's only remaining ally. In that case, Hungary might cease to exist as a State. Hence I must sue for an armistice. I have made sure that we shall receive acceptable conditions from the enemy, but it is certain that we shall be

*subjected to German atrocities when that armistice is
concluded. We shall have much to suffer; our troops may be
dispersed. But against that suffering must be set the fact that if
we continue this hopeless fight, our race and our fatherland
will be in jeopardy and will surely be destroyed. We have no
alternative. We must decide to sue for an armistice.'*

The Chief of the General Staff gave a survey of the military
situation. The troops of Marshal Tolbuchin were on the
southern outskirts of Belgrade. There was fighting between
Szeged and Csongrád to force a passage across the Tisza.
South of Debrecen armoured units were engaged in a violent
battle. Vörös went on to say that the Russians might be
battering at the gates of Budapest itself in two days time. He
told us that at 10.10 am he had received an imperative order
from Guderian:

*'The entire area of Hungary has been declared a German
operational area. Only the German Supreme Command may
issue orders. The orders for withdrawal issued to the First and
Second Hungarian Armies are hereby countermanded and this
counter-order must be implemented within twelve hours.'*

The Arrow Cross group took my radio proclamation as a
signal to go forward with their plans for seizing power. One
of the first buildings they occupied with German aid was the
radio station. An Arrow Cross Party member drew up a
counter-proclamation, allegedly in the name of Vörös, the
Chief of the General Staff, which was broadcast. It served its
purpose. My military orders had not yet reached the troops
and everything was thrown into the utmost confusion. The
two units of the Army that were still in Budapest went over
to the Arrow Cross after their commander, Bakay, had been
arrested and his second in command, Aggteleky, had disappeared. It is not known to this day how Vörös's signature
came to be appended to the false proclamation. Vörös assured
me personally that he had had no knowledge whatsoever of
the communiqué sent out in his name.

Indescribable excitement reigned in Budapest. To many, my
radio proclamation had come as a relief after almost unbear-
able suspense. A number of political prisoners were released.
The underground movement began to carry out its plans. At

the same time, there was fear of German reprisals and coun-
tervailing measures; the Germans had quickly sent some Tiger
tanks to patrol the streets. Those who had hoped for an
armistice were now thrown into despair by the spurious
Vörös orders. These conflicting emotions made it easier for
the Arrow Cross supporters to achieve their ends. In the
afternoon, the radio sent out the first speech of Szálasi,
accompanied by blaring Hungarian and German marches.

The Palace was in a state of siege. The approaches had been
mined, incidentally isolating the German Embassy on the
Palace Hill. As we learned during the night, the German
attack on the Palace had been timed for the early hours of the
morning of 16 October.

We had just lain down, fully dressed, when Lieutenant Field
Marshal Vattay, Chief of the Military Chancellery, and
Ambrózy, head of the Cabinet Chancellery, were announced.
They had come to deliver the message that the Fuehrer
'offered' me asylum, provided I abdicated, relinquished all
powers, and surrendered the Palace. I refused this 'offer' and
emphatically told the messengers that I was not to be
approached again concerning this matter.

In expectation of the attack, I sent my wife, daughter-in-law
and grandson at four o'clock in the morning under guard to
the residence of the (Papal) Nuncio, who had in the past
offered us sanctuary.

Yet, what was the sense of allowing the situation to develop
into a fight? In view of the enemy's superior strength in men
and artillery, we had nothing to oppose to their armoured
vehicles, a fight could lead only to the decimation of our
faithful Guards. Though I had been unable to achieve my aim
of bringing peace to Hungary, my radio proclamation had
nevertheless proved to the world that Hungary was not will-
ingly submitting to occupation. But I intended to ask no one
to lay down his life for me. I therefore ordered that no resistance should be made. This order failed to reach only one unit
in the Palace park, a unit that was commanded by the son
of the former Premier, Kállay. Shots were fired, and four
German soldiers were killed. Andreas Kállay was taken
prisoner and sent to Dachau.

The Admiral was placed in 'protective custody' by the Nazi leadership and never returned to Hungary.[104]

Almost immediately, the Arrow Cross instigated a reign of terror that resulted in the deaths of tens of thousands during the final months of the war. They rounded up thousands of Jews, shooting them on the banks of the Danube, while at the same time, Adolf Eichmann organized the notorious death marches to Austria. But non-Jewish Hungarians were to pay a high price for their continued alliance with Germany; Hitler's order of 23 November to defend Budapest 'house by house' resulted in one of the longest and bloodiest sieges of the Second World War. It certainly gave the lie to any notion that Hungary was still in control of her own affairs, and completely undermined Szálasi's statement that 'I would regard it as necessary to hold Budapest only if any offensive operations were to be undertaken from there. However, if this is not intended, Budapest must definitely be evacuated and we must make a strategic retreat to the Transdanubian hills.' The battle for Budapest, which raged for 102 days, engulfed the lives of over 800,000 non-combatants – more than 30,000 houses were destroyed – and every other victim on the defending side was a civilian, 38,000 in all. The grand total of civilian and military dead was a staggering 160,000.[105]

The Soviets had set up an alternative government in Debrecen on 21 December 1944, but as soon as they had completed the capture of Budapest on 18 January 1945, Zoltán Tildy became the provisional Prime Minister and on 20 January, along with representatives of the Hungarian provisional government, signed an armistice in Moscow. Officially, Soviet operations in Hungary ended on 4 April when the last German troops were expelled. Meanwhile, Szálasi and his entourage had left Hungary on 29 March, taking the crown of St Stephen with them. Horthy, still in 'protective custody' in Germany, was released by the Americans and interned in a series of camps.

In elections held that November, Tildy's Smallholders' party won 57 per cent of the vote. The Hungarian Communist Party, now under the leadership of Mátyás Rákosi[106] and Ernő Gerő, received support from only 17 per cent of the population. The Soviet commander in Hungary, Marshal Voroshilov, refused to allow the Smallholders to form a government, instead establishing a coalition government with the communists holding some of the key posts. On 1 February 1946, the Republic of Hungary was declared, with Tildy as President and Ferenc Nagy Prime Minister.

When Hungary signed the Treaty of Paris on 10 February 1947, she lost all the territories gained between 1938 and 1941 for neither the Western Allies nor the Soviet Union supported any change to her pre-1938 borders. The decisions of the Vienna Award of 2 November 1938, so dear to Horthy, were declared null and void. Half of the ethnic German minority (240,000 people) were deported to Germany in 1946–8, and there was a forced exchange of population between Hungary and Czechoslovakia. Hungary's pre-war national strategy lay in smithereens.

Despite its failure to influence the political outcome in Hungary, SOE continued to apply itself to the problem and proposed that HMG should revive the Károlyi Council with a view to it forming a post-war government.

The Hungarian Workers Party (formed by a merger of the Communist Party and the Social Democratic Party) became the largest single party in the elections of 1947 and served in the coalition People's Independence Front government. Within a year, the Communist Party headed by Mátyás Rákosi was in total control. Now came the reckoning. The Smallholders' Party, which had won 57 per cent of the 1945 vote, was liquidated after a series of trumped-up conspiracy trials. Likewise, the Social Democratic Party ceased to exist as an independent organization and its leader, Béla Kovács, was arrested and sent to Siberia. By March 1948, the People's Courts had sentenced 16,273 persons, of whom 146 were executed, including Szálasi, Bárdossy, Imrédy and Sztójay. Yet this was in hindsight the calm before the storm of purges perpetrated by Stalin in 1949.

On 18 August 1949, Parliament passed a new constitution modelled on the 1936 constitution of the Soviet Union. The name of the country changed to the People's Republic of Hungary and socialism was declared as the main goal of the nation. A new coat of arms, complete with Communist symbols like the red star, hammer and scythe, replaced the thousand-year-old badge of the Hungarian kings. Democracy on any scale in Hungary had disappeared.

Horthy's words ring true:

It is easily said that we should have preferred to engage in a hopeless struggle rather than to submit to Hitler's demands, and such a view reads well on paper. In fact, it is total nonsense. An individual can commit suicide, a whole nation cannot. For Hungary's tragedy was that, for the first time in her history, she saw herself simultaneously threatened on all sides. And the fate that overtook the Hungarians, who, as has been confirmed by subsequent events, made a correct estimate of the Communist peril, was the same as that which overtook those who allowed themselves to be misled into sharing Roosevelt's illusion that the Soviet Union was developing into a 'peace-loving democracy' and would, after the war, collaborate loyally and peacefully with the Western powers.

1945: looking for lost property

When the European war ended in April 1945, a worrisome missing list was posted by SOE's Hungarian Section. Operations against Hungary had proved costly, both for agents, politicians and civil servants and SOE personnel, with the DEERHURST and WIND-PROOF failures top of the list. As it turned out, the cost in terms of loss of life was not as bad as anticipated. The DEERHURST team had been transferred in October 1944 from Gestapo HQ in Budapest to Vienna where they found themselves in the notorious Elizabetstrasse Prison with its daily ritual of executions. A few days later, they were despatched by train to the Luftwaffe interrogation centre at Ober Ursel near Frankfurt-am-Main and from there sent first to the Luftwaffe POW distribution centre at Wetzlar, and thence to the Wehrmacht centre at Limburg. It was here that two of its officers, Major Wright and Lieutenant Vincent, were killed in an Allied air raid. Boughey recalled that 'as a sergeant, I was already in a train in the sidings and although some damage was done and some killed, I survived!' 'Sergeant' Boughey ended his journey at Sagan Stalag VIIIC, but his troubles were far from over. 'With the approach of the Russians through Poland in early 1945, the Germans decided to march all the POWs out of the camp westwards on foot. As it was mid-winter with much snow on the ground, I felt that this held no future for me already suffering from acute bronchitis so I hid up in the camp and after the evacuation slipped out the other way east to reach the Russian front lines. This was successful and after an eventful trip travelling partly on foot, by truck and by train through Poland I arrived at Odessa on the Black Sea. From thence by boat to Istanbul and Naples and then to London by air.'[107]

Major Coates, after capture in September 1944, had been moved to three separate prisons before ending up at the Polish Internment Camp at Zugliget outside Budapest. Here, he and Gordon helped Thomas and Daniels of WINDPROOF to escape[108] before escaping themselves on 12 December. Hidden by a Hungarian family in Kamaraerdő,[109] Coates contacted a Russian patrol on 26 December and, after repatriation, was sent to the BMM in Budapest in June 1945 to locate and pay off SOE's remaining twenty agents and thirty-six functionaries, together with any other deserving individuals.[110] Gordon, Thomas and Daniels individually managed to survive the terrible siege of Budapest before handing themselves over to the Russians, who then transferred them to the BMM in Debrecen in March 1945.

Lieutenant Colonel Howie, the South African officer who had led such a Scarlet Pimpernel existence in Budapest, put in a personal plea for the Polish Tarnopolska family who had provided him with shelter:

> It is impossible to describe in words just how one in my position in Hungary feels towards people like this; they took the risk of torture and death as a matter of duty when no Hungarian, after the German occupation, would look at me until I had completely covered my tracks, and it was comparatively safe. The Tarnopolskas are too proud to accept financial assistance as agents ... if the possibility exists of my sending as a personal gift some funds [to the family] ... I should be deeply grateful. I know that my connection with the Poles and their underground army must be very embarrassing, but I feel under an overwhelming personal as well as national obligation towards them as a whole and in particular those with whom I worked.

While with the BMM, Coates[111] signalled the WO for information about a group of six agents under the command of a Mr

Kovács, aka Stephen Cora, who had been dropped into Hungary early in November 1944 to organize resistance. Apparently all had been arrested on 6 December and subsequently executed. There was no reply to this request. It may well have been a mix-up with the activities of the OSS BOWERY team of Cora and Moly, who had reached Hungary on 11 October.

The other Canadian Hungarians who had formed the backbone to SOE's activities in Hungary were also recovered safely – Bertram, Agoston and Mark. Klement, the first to be dropped, was reported as being captured by the Russians in early 1945, although his name mysteriously appeared on a British military memorial at Brookwood Cemetery with his date of death shown as 1943.

It was not until June 1945 that Mrs Sehmer received a telegram and then a letter stating that her husband had been posted 'missing believed killed'. There then followed an amazing coincidence and a long delay. A younger sister of Sehmer had been with the Army in Cairo and seen something of her brother while he was there. She wrote to her sister-in-law on 5 September 1945 stating that the OC of her regiment had been in Vienna on business and, while unpacking her suitcase at an officers' hotel, had found a bit of paper in one of the drawers. It read: 'Lt O'Neill, US Navy, has identified John Sehmer, he thinks, but must have a photograph and/or relation to confirm they were executed (dated August 1945).' There then followed a prolonged correspondence with the WO while they tried to locate Lieutenant O'Neill. Although on 14 January 1946, a letter was received saying it had been officially recorded that John Sehmer was 'presumed killed in action', it was not until November 1946 that the family were finally notified by the WO that they had heard from the American authorities and confirmed what was by then already known, for Zenopian had already written in May 1946 to George Usher, a relation of the Sehmers, with the true account of the fate of WINDPROOF.

Together with her son, Jamie, Mrs Sehmer managed to visit Zenopian in Vienna in the winter of 1954/55 to thank him for his kindness. Zenopian told her that 'as a soldier, leader, companion, John was one of the best. If I ever have to undertake another such mission again, I will never have such a commanding officer.'

On 20 August 1996, Jamie Sehmer, with his son Alexander, arranged for a simple plaque to be placed on the wall of the hut at Polomka, which has been preserved by the Slovak government as one of the memorials to the Slovak National Uprising.

> *In Memory of Major John Sehmer,*
> *The Royal Tank Regiment,*
> *Head of the British Mission to Free Slovaks,*
> *and of other members of the SOE who gave their lives for freedom.*
> *Captured December 26th 1944 with members of the American Mission*

On 4 January, three weeks before his death, the award of Major Sehmer's MBE was published in the *London Gazette*. The citation, addressed 'Dear Sehmer', followed on 18 February 1945 with a comment that, for security reasons, it could not be published:

Major Sehmer was dropped into Yugoslavia by parachute on 10 April 1943 and has spent over twelve months in east and south Serbia under difficult and trying conditions, when relationships between the Yugoslavs and Allied officers might have developed into an open breach. He at all times did his best to promote goodwill between the Mission and General Mihailović's forces. It was not for lack of endeavour or organising ability that he was unable to bring off any effective sabotage actions, but entirely due to the evasive actions employed by the Jugoslavs to prevent such action being carried out. By his behaviour and restraint he has maintained cordial relations as far as was possible between the Allied Mission and the Chetniks.

John Sehmer was never decorated for his heroic efforts in Slovakia.

Notes for Part One
1. The original team of Lt Col Boughey, Capt Coates, Lt Vincent and a W/T Op never dropped.
2. Later Head of SIS.
3. Ardeal to the Romanians, Erdely to the Hungarians and Siebenburgen to the Saxons.

4. He had made covert contacts with the British and French in Switzerland during the war.
5. One *joch* was the equivalent of approximately 2.8 acres.
6. In contrast, prices of land owned by Romanians were based on average prices between 1917 and 1922.
7. It was Gömbös as the leader of MOVE who gave shelter to the assassins of the Centre Left German politician and pacifist Matthias Erzberger in 1921.
8. Another result of the Second Vienna Award was, of course, that Hungary gained all of northern Transylvania's population: 1.3 million Hungarians, 1 million Romanians and some 170,000 other nationalities.
9. This was supposedly through their work with 'The Musketeers', a resistance group run by an eccentric engineer called Stanislav Wirkowski.
10. Christine Granville GM OBE and Croix de Guerre.
11. Marton died of typhus in Dachau Concentration Camp; Békeffi was also in Dachau where he contracted terminal TB.
12. Basil Davidson was a journalist who had been recruited by Section D in 1939 and despatched to Hungary in January 1940 to establish a British news distribution agency. His other tasks were to develop anti-Nazi propaganda and identify potential members of the Resistance.
13. Arrested by the Russians in Vienna after the war when she was looking for her husband (unknown to her he was dead), she spent ten years in a gulag before being repatriated to the UK where she was subsequently employed by the FO.
14. According to an unnamed SOE source, she also had letters for two newspaper editors, Robert Kertesz and Mr Barankovics.
15. The Pejačevićs were a Croatian family and Count Petar had been ambassador in Spain since 31 October 1941.
16. Kállay had no time for Károlyi in London whom he dubbed 'the red count'.
17. Later Ambassador to Sweden.
18. He had practised as a lawyer in London before the war.
19. Lt Col Threlfall, who conducted the negotiations between October 1943 and March 1944, described him as 'very quiet and modest'.
20. He was a friend of Basil Davidson, the author of the 1942 letters, and had worked with him in Budapest.
21. Another account has Veress talking to Christopher Horthy in almost identical circumstances. Afterwards, Horthy reported to his father, the Regent.
22. Marcos was a 40-year-old Transylvanian who had Canadian/British nationality. SOE recruited him from the Canadian Army in England and considered that 'although he does not admit it, he is probably a communist.'
23. On 24 July 1943, Count Ciano, the Italian Foreign Minister, organized a vote against Mussolini to take Italy out of the war. He was later arrested and shot in January 1944.
24. General Lajos Keresztes-Fisher (1884–1948). Both he and his brother Ferenc survived their imprisonment in Buchenwald Concentration Camp.
25. He finally left it under immense German pressure on 18 November 1944 and was sent to Mauthausen Concentration Camp.

26. Over 437,000 Jews were deported to Auschwitz out of a Jewish population of 700,000.
27. Kruger later served as Air Attaché at the German Embassy in Washington and went on to become a Luftwaffe Brigadier General in 1968.
28. This instruction came from Alfred Schwarz (DOGWOOD).
29. In January 1943, Canaris walked into Earle's room in the Park Hotel and berated him for the unconditional surrender clause which he stated merely served to impede the efforts of Germany's generals to extract their country from the war.
30. 5–10 July 1943 and 11–18 December 1943.
31. Lt Col Wilhelm Höttl, SD head of intelligence and counter espionage in central and south-east Europe, had intercepted the message warning of SPARROW's arrival and alerted Himmler and Walter Hewel, von Ribbentrop's representative at Klessheim.
32. From the south came three task forces composed of two army regiments, an SS police regiment, one armoured battalion, one SS brigade; two thirds of the 42nd Light Mountain Division; strong elements of 8th SS Cavalry Division. From the south-west came two task forces of infantry supported by tanks. From the north-west came two armoured divisions, plus an armoured battalion with new tanks. From the north came three reinforced motorized infantry regiments and a heavy artillery regiment from Denmark. All four thrusts were reinforced with specialist river-crossing engineer battalions and with militia battalions to keep order. In addition, there were nine squadrons of fighters, seven anti-aircraft battalions and sixty transport planes filled with paratroopers.
33. Veress survived the war and died in London in September 1980.
34. Of the 240 men and women who volunteered for operations behind enemy lines, 110 underwent the Cairo-based training program. Nine were subsequently sent to Romania, three to Hungary, five to Slovakia, ten to Yugoslavia, three to Italy and two to Bulgaria. Twelve were captured; seven of them were later executed. The first group was dropped into Yugoslavia in May 1943; the last was dropped in southern Austria on the final day of the war.
35. Palgi later felt that Kastner had betrayed him. He was assassinated in Israel in 1957 by Jewish zealots.
36. Brand was arrested by SIME and interrogated in Cairo from 15 June until released to Palestine on 5 August. On Russian objections, the Allies denied his return to Budapest where his wife and family were held hostage by the Germans.
37. She was later immortalized in the 1988 film *Hanna's War*.
38. Ivan Szabo.
39. Gustav Bodo.
40. The 24-year-old Harker had already completed a nine-month mission in Thessaly and the Pindus Mountains in Greece (ARCHIPELAGO).
41. Boughey had returned to Europe in 1937 and after a spell of ill-health, had gone to Maribor in Slovenia as the British Consul in 1939, presumably as an officer of SIS. The following year he joined the British Legation in Belgrade

with the annotation in his file 'cypher experience'. Deeply involved from then on in all aspects of SOE's work in the Balkans, he played a key role in trying to save Mihailović.

42. Alexander Vass.
43. It crashed on the return journey, killing all crew.
44. Source: *Canadians behind enemy lines*.
45. Mukacevo and Satu Mare were the selected areas.
46. Jozsef Gelleny
47. Mike Turk.
48. 2 July, 23 July, 15 November 1944.
49. All quotes by Coates are from his IWM tapes.
50. The majority of 30 Commando Assault Unit had been redeployed in support of D-Day landings.
51. Two ISLD agents were successfully dropped from the aircraft near Szeged. DIBBLER's equipment, including its wireless set and food, was inadvertently dropped to DECIMA that same night and it was the combination of ground mist over the drop zone and no moon that convinced the pilot to return home without dropping DIBBLER.
52. Coates later minuted that Bertram had been captured at the end of July and his cover and codes completely broken.
53. General István Náday (1888–1954) was an openly pro-British officer, convinced from the beginning of the final victory of the Allies. He had the habit of writing his personal notes in English.
54. The *Independent* 22 December 2000.
55. Howie's South African colleague, who had been scheduled to escape with him, announced at the last minute that he did not feel linguistically confident enough to make the journey to Hungary.
56. Count Bethlen was also in attendance.
57. Awarded the King's Commendation for Brave Conduct in 1946.
58. After the war, Gore-Symes listed Károly Szladits, Rupert Raffel, Anthony Reinprecht, Dr and Mrs Tibor Szalay, Mr Weissenmeyer, Jozsef Schmaltz and Baci Rozsi as being deserving of recognition by the British authorities.
59. Sachs did escape, was awarded the MM and was later killed on operations in the Far East.
60. Hungary had not formally responded to Britain's Declaration of War, hence this loophole.
61. Curiously, John Coates in his debrief report for DIBBLER recounted meeting a British captain called 'Reynolds', who had been a POW for three and a half years after being captured in North Africa. His actual rank was flight lieutenant but he had crossed the Austrian border into Hungary with a corporal's paybook. Once he had ascertained that the Hungarians were more or less 'on side', he told them he was a British Army captain, the RAF being extremely unpopular at the time on account of the bombing of Budapest. Reynolds told Coates that he was in touch with Van Houtegem and could help him escape. He also told him that Howie had been flown out of the country.

62. Under pressure from Hitler, who threatened to hand over the Slovak lands to Hungary and Poland, Slovakia seceded from Czechoslovakia on 14 March 1939 and declared its independence 'under German protection', thus becoming Germany's first ally.

63. The Slovak Military Revolutionary Council (VRV) had a somewhat different agenda, including the establishment of an independent Slovak state.

64. This stance was supported by the Chiefs of Staff who minuted on 6 September 1944: 'We consider that all air operations in support of Slovak uprising should properly be carried out by Russians.'"

65. This proved far from easy. Inclement weather and pilots' inexperience resulted in the crash landing of eleven out of thirty aircraft on 5 September alone.

66. Between 8 September and 28 October, they suffered 85,000 casualties (21,000 dead).

67. Andrew Durovecz.

68. Steve Zenopian was of Armenian extraction but had grown up in Lancashire and spoke English with a broad Lancastrian accent. His Hungarian was fluent (he had lived for some years in Budapest) as was his French.

69. Later changed to NECRONIAN.

70. HACKTHORPE covered the Pristina area, SMOULDER Homolje and HUGGATE Kopaonik.

71. Allatini Ltd was UK-owned and accounted for 26,094 tons out of a total chrome production of 30,547 tons in 1939.

72. HACKTHORPE was consequently reinforced by ORCHARD (ROUGHSHOD): Capt R.Purvis, Scots Guards, 2/Lt Newlyn RE, Sgts Sheraton and Faithfull, and W/T Op Cpl Thompson.

73. *Special Operations Executive.*

74. 'Three oaks'.

75. *MI9: Escape and Evasion 1939–1945.*

76. Chermesh aka M. Kaszas aka 2/Lt Harry Morris states 15 September (letter J.Sehmer 25 November 1994).

77. Code name Ada Robinson.

78. Threlfall is adamant that Sehmer was not dropped to support the SNU.

79. Also Berdiczew.

80. He was a right-hand man of General Miroslav who was in charge of the SNU in London.

81. The fighter escort of Mustangs never even landed, such was the speed of the turnaround of the B-17s.

82. *SOE Recollections and Reflections 1940–45*, pp. 195–9.

83. A US photograph identifies these two men in a group of US flyers.

84. Cora and Moly reached Hungary on 11 October 1944.

85. There is another unsourced version in circulation of this infiltration into Hungary. In its initial stages, around 15 October, two members of the WINDPROOF Mission, Lt Daniels and Lt Zenopian, had managed to cross the border into Hungary in civilian clothes and set up a base camp in the Matra Mountains, close to the waterfalls at Vizesés and a few kilometers

from Gyöngyös. Most of the area had been a shooting estate once owned by Count Mihali Karolyi. Here they set up a courier route back to Sehmer in Slovakia. However it took a week to get a message through to Sehmer and with increasing German activity in the area and the application of stringent conscription and labour laws, there was little point in keeping it going, so they withdrew and in the course of doing so, Daniels was captured.

86. 17 October 1944 Force 399 to WINDPROOF: 'Orders received no rpt no further missions will be sent Hungary and all attempts infiltration will cease forthwith. You will therefore return SLOVAK HQ and await further orders. You will recall Daniels and Zenopian.' Chermesh recalls Sehmer driving to the Hungarian border on 16 October, the day after the coup against Horthy, to check for infiltration routes.

87. One report states that Lt Gibbs, an interpreter, was dropped at an emergency airfield at Brezno on 21 October. However, SOE signal traffic denied any knowledge of a flight to Brezno on that night.

88. There is a suggestion that SOE's Czech Mission, MICA, consisting of Col Greenless, Lt Col Raw and a W/T operator, joined WINDPROOF on 17 October before being evacuated to Italy.

89. One account states that Sehmer left Banská Bystrica on 13 October with three men and Margita Kochova, his interpreter.

90. Also known as Abwehrgruppe 218.

91. Feldzeugmeister Franz Graf Thun und Hohenstein and Feldmarschal-Leutnant Felix Graf Thun und Hohenstein.

92. After being captured by Russian troops, he was tried on 18 January 1946 by a Soviet military tribunal, sentenced to death and shot a few days later.

93. Probably Frank Hensque.

94. Dumbier.

95. Maria Culovics.

96. Dunlevy and Catlos.

97. Maria Culovics aka Gulovičová was later awarded the US Bronze Star for her heroism.

98. Pavol Kamensky aka Kemenevsky Rovel.

99. Werner Mueller, one of Berlin's best linguists, and Dr Hans Wilhelm Thost, an interpreter for the RSHA, were present. Thost later testified about the torture he witnessed.

100. According to the Federal Council of Anti-Fascist Fighters, Prague, 30 June 1971, they were shot by a gun hidden in a camera.

101. Green's US Navy insignia were discovered in the drawer of Ziereis's desk when the camp was liberated in May 1945.

102. The Chief of the Hungarian gendarmerie, Lieutenant General Gábor Faraghó, Professor Count Géza Teleki, the son of the former Prime Minister, and Domokos Szentiványi of the Ministry of Foreign Affairs.

103. He was flown to Vienna and from there taken to Mauthausen Concentration Camp.

104. He died in Portugal in 1957.

105. Red Army official statistics show 80,026 killed and 240,056 wounded. Russian soldiers described it as 'worse than Stalingrad'.
106. Born Rosenfeld in 1892 in the village of Ada, near Subotica.
107. Boughey note to FCO dated September 1979.
108. Daniels reached the Scandl villa on 13 November 1944 and remained in hiding until Budapest was liberated by the Russians.
109. Count Markovics and his daughter Kati(ka) Boné.
110. SOELIQ mission.
111. John Coates joined the FO after the war and, after retiring in 1960s, became Dean of Students and Lecturer in Finno-Ugrian Studies at the University of East Anglia.

Part Two

Bulgaria

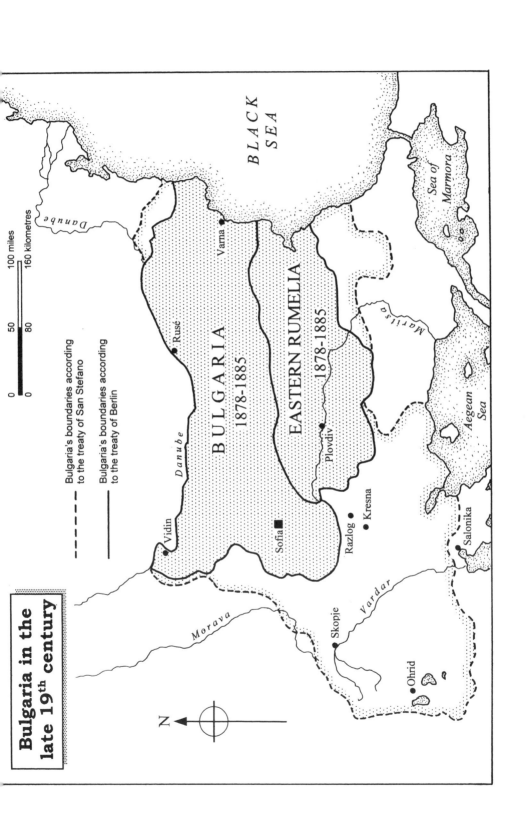

Bulgaria in the late 19th century

Bulgaria's boundaries according to the treaty of San Stefano

Bulgaria's boundaries according to the treaty of Berlin

BLACK SEA

Sea of Marmora

Aegean Sea

BULGARIA 1878–1885

EASTERN RUMELIA 1878–1885

Danube

Morava

Vardar

Maritsa

Vidin

Sofia

Ruse

Varna

Plovdiv

Razlog

Kresna

Skopje

Ohrid

Salonika

N

0   50   100 miles
0   80   160 kilometres

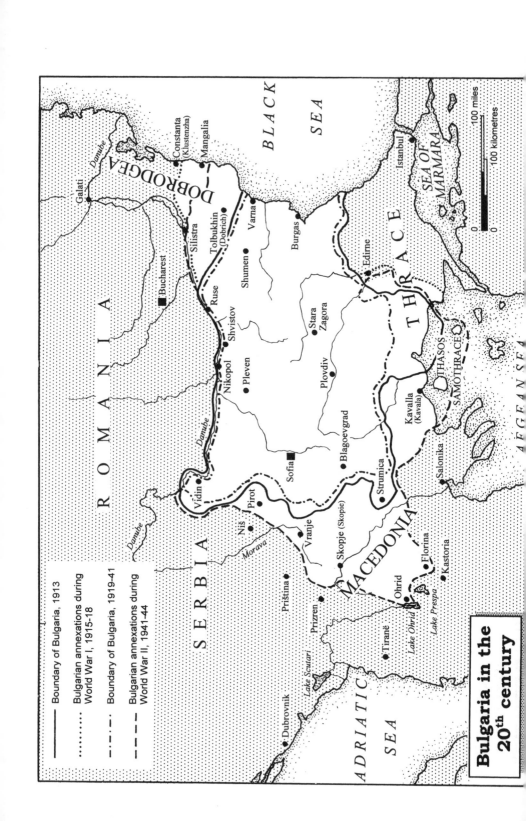

Bulgaria in the 20th century

Boundary of Bulgaria, 1913

Bulgarian annexations during World War I, 1915-18

Boundary of Bulgaria, 1919-41

Bulgarian annexations during World War II, 1941-44

BLACK SEA

DOBRODGEA

ROMANIA

SERBIA

THRACE

MACEDONIA

SEA OF MARMARA

AEGEAN SEA

ADRIATIC SEA

Danube
Danube
Danube
Morava

100 miles
100 kilometres

Galati
Bucharest
Constanta (Klustenzha)
Mangalia
Silistra
Tolbukhin (Dobrich)
Varna
Shumen
Burgas
Ruse
Shvistov
Nikopol
Pleven
Stara Zagora
Plovdiv
Edirne
Istanbul
THASOS
SAMOTHRACE
Kavalla (Kavala)
Vidin
Sofia
Blagoevgrad
Strumica
Salonika
Pirot
Niš
Vranje
Skopje (Skopie)
Florina
Kastoria
Priština
Prizren
Ohrid
Lake Ohrid
Lake Scutari
Lake Prespa
Tiranë
Dubrovnik

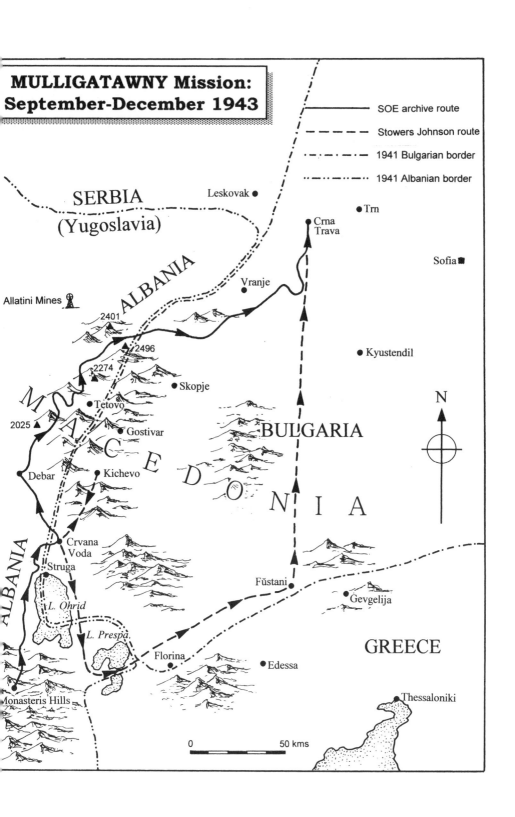

MULLIGATAWNY Mission:
September-December 1943

SOE archive route
Stowers Johnson route
1941 Bulgarian border
1941 Albanian border

SERBIA
(Yugoslavia)

Leskovak

Trn

Crna
Trava

Sofia

ALBANIA

Allatini Mines

2401

Vranje

2496

2274

Skopje

Tetovo

BULGARIA

Kyustendil

2025

Gostivar

MACEDONIA

Debar

Kichevo

N

Crvana
Voda

Struga

L. Ohrid

Fŭstani

Gevgelija

ALBANIA

L. Prespa

Florina

GREECE

Edessa

Monasteris Hills

Thessaloniki

0   50 kms

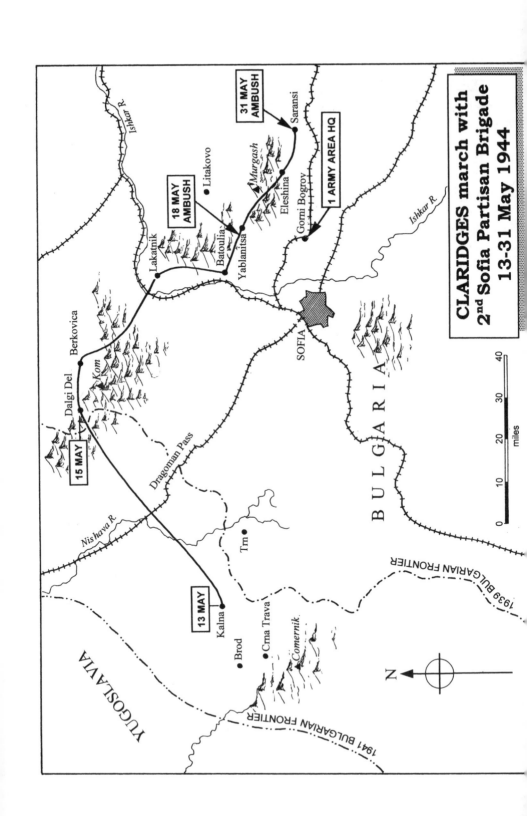

CLARIDGES march with
2nd Sofia Partisan Brigade
13-31 May 1944

SOE Personnel in Bulgaria

Bulgaria

☦ *Killed in action/executed/died of wounds*

MULLIGATAWNY
☦ Maj Mostyn L. Davies DSO
☦ Sgt J. McC. Walker
☦ Sgt N. Munro
☦ Cpl J.R. Shannon
☦ W/T Op Sig R.G. Watts

CLARIDGES
☦ Maj W.F. Thompson MC
(☦ Sgt J. McC. Walker)
W/Op Sgt Scott DCM
(☦ Sgt N. Munro)

Trained but not deployed:
Toncho Naidenoff

Other Missions which interfaced/liaised with operations in
Bulgaria:
Albania
CONSENSUS

DONKEYWRENCH
Capt MacDonald

INFLATION
Sqn Ldr Hands DSO

Yugoslavia
SNAFFLE
Maj The Hon T. Strachey
Lt Dawson
2/Lt Kombel
Cpl Stamper
Partisan liaison: V. Dimitrov

ENTANGLEMENT
Maj Dugmore
Sgt Rogers

BUMBOAT
Capt Dowd

CONSERVE
(Mission to *chetniks* on Mt Kagalica)
Capt Michael Lees
Lt Tomlinson RE
✞ Lt S.Smith RE
✞ W/T Op LAC H.J. Thompson
Later reinforced by Sgt Faithfull and Sgt Johnson

HACKTHORPE/NECRONIAN
✞ Maj John Sehmer MBE (see WINDPROOF, Hungary)
Sgt Harvey
✞ Sgt F.J. Lindstrom
✞ W/T Op Sgt L. Blackmore
Leban, Slovene interpreter

Others in Yugoslavia
Sqn Ldr Kenneth Syers
Maj John Henniker-Major MC
Capt Robert Purvis MC

Greece/Bulgarian-occupied Thrace
TRIATIC
Maj Donald Riddle
Tpr Kops
(Maj Guy Micklethwaite MBE)

MIZZEN
Capt Ian Macpherson MC
Capt Paul Pike MC
Cpl O'Brien

JAMPUFF
Maj John T. Harrington DSO MBE
Lt Davidson
Cpl Rennie

VAUDEVILLE
(Maj Guy Micklethwaite MBE)

RED HERRING
Maj Guy Micklethwaite MBE
Maj Terence Kitcat DSO MC

SHIPSHED
(Maj Guy Micklethwaite MBE)

BURLESQUE

MI9

INTERVAL
Sgt Joseph
Sgt Joseph (2)

Yugoslavian and Macedonian Partisans

Yugoslav Partisan liaison
General Tempo aka Svetozar Vukmanovic
Djura Zlatkovic – Commander Crna Trava (Serbian) Partisan
    Brigade
Vujo, commander Serb Partisan detachment

Macedonia Partisan commander
General Michaljo Apostolki

Bulgarian Partisans

CPB – Central Committee
Georgi Dimitrov – leader of CPB; later died in suspicious circumstances in a Moscow sanatorium in July 1949
Boyan Bulgaranov – secretary Central Committee and CPB representative in Macedonia 1942–4
Tsola Dragoycheva – member of politburo and General Secretary of OF, 1944–8
Rusi Hristozov – Central Committee instructor, later Minister of Interior

BPA Headquarters
General Dobri Terpeshev, C-in-C BPA
Anton Yugov, member of General Staff, later Prime Minister.
Lt Dicho Petrov, former commander of Botev detachment in Macedonia

1 Sofia Brigade
General Slavcho Trunski aka Transki (arrived September 1943)
Ninko Stefanov – commissar
Misha
Nikolai Stoikov

2 Sofia Brigade
Dencho Znepolski (later Head of Bulgarian Military Intelligence)
Vlado Trichkov aka 'Ivan' – Chief of Staff of the BPA (arrived December 1943)
Yordanka Chankova – Secretary of the Youth Organization
Nikolova aka Nikolina
Georgi Chankov – Organizing Secretary of the Central Committee
Nacho Ivanov
Gorcha (Goco) Gopin aka 'Dragan' – liaison between Mission and BPA
✝ Dicho Petrov – commander Botev Battalion

Trifor Balkanski – CPB wireless operator
Delco Gopin
Jordanka Nikolova
Delco Simov aka 'Gorsho'
Vera Nacheva
Blagoi Ivanov
Valentin Andreyev
Gorazd
Slavcho Lazov aka 'Texma'

SOE in Bulgaria

Prelude: Bulgaria's turbulent political history

The history of Bulgaria is one of shrinkage – an inexorable and inevitable reduction of a territory first won by a comparative handful of warlike tribesmen during the vacuum left by the departing Romans. Hence the Bulgarian thought process about their rightful stature, as with all nation states, is deeply rooted in tales of yore, in a distant yet vital collective memory of triumph, empire and that fleeting epithet, superiority over all opponents. Since the early eighth century, the Bulgars, essentially Onogurs, who were part of the great westward migration of Steppe warriors, had slowly imposed their presence on their chosen territory and bordering lands until, by the early tenth century, they ruled a vast expanse of land from Greece to northern Romania.

During its rise, Bulgaria was in almost constant conflict with its imperial neighbour, Byzantium. The Bulgarian rulers, on the one hand, aspired to conquer Constantinople and inherit its tantalizing empire. On the other hand, the Byzantines regarded the Bulgarian state as an interloper on its territory and tried by various means to subjugate it. The Battle of Belasitsa in 1014 marked a turning point; the Bulgarian army was destroyed in a humiliating defeat that has gone down in the annals of military atrocities. Ninety-nine out of every 100 Bulgarian soldiers captured on the battlefield were blinded; the appalling sight of this pathetic army of 15,000 blind, miserable wretches staggering into his camp gave Tsar Samuel apoplexy and he was dead within two days. A brief revival of the great ninth-century empire of Khan Krum in the twelfth century was not enough to stop the relentlessly expanding Ottomans from capturing the capital of the Second Bulgarian Kingdom, Turnovo, in 1393. Ottoman rule, which was that of an occupying power, was to last for almost 500 years. It was left to the Christian Church, more or less unmolested by Ottoman indifference and expediency, to keep the embers of Bulgar nationalism alight in the darkness of a pan-Islamic Turkey-in-Europe.

In the nineteenth century, Bulgarian national aspirations were more culturally rather than politically driven; this was by necessity since the Ottomans totally controlled the political apparatus of the country. But prosperity had facilitated the funding of a 'national revival' culture and bankrolled a growing self-confidence among the middle classes. This is turn led to the establishment of more militant movements to introduce political objectives into the nationalistic mix. No one better epitomized this new militancy than Vassil Levsky.

Originally ordained as an Orthodox priest – Father Ignati as he was styled – Vassil became restless with his lot and left for Belgrade in 1862, passing by the gruesome tower at Niš where the Turks had set 18,000 skulls of those they had beheaded during the 1816 uprising. In Belgrade he joined Rakovsky's Bulgarian Legion, training hard as a soldier and seeing some action in local street fighting. It was during this time that he acquired the nickname Levsky, which referred to a prodigious jump he had made on a training exercise, a lion's leap or *Levsky skok*.

At the end of 1862, the Legion was disbanded and so he returned to his birthplace, Karlovo, in the foothills of the Balkan Mountains where he threw off his cassock, shaved his beard and became a schoolteacher. But the Turkish authorities now began to show an interest in him, forcing him into exile in Romania. At the age of thirty, Vassil Levsky thus made his final career choice, that of a professional revolutionary.

That summer, he crossed into Bulgaria in a *cheta* of thirty armed fellow revolutionaries. The aim of this infiltration was to make for the high mountains from where it was planned that they should harass and kill members of the Ottoman Army and police. It was a high-risk strategy; the *cheta* was always on the move, living on a diet of nettles and salt, always hungry and thirsty. They had a rule of 'no prisoners' for it was only too easy for a Turkish official or sympathizer to send for the Zaptiahs.[1] The *cheta* never left their wounded or dying: they were given a choice – kill yourself or be killed by us. They took the heads of their dead comrades with them to make it harder for the Turkish authorities to identify the bodies.

Vassil proved a brave and tireless member of the *cheta*, but when he returned to Belgrade that autumn, he conceived the idea of setting up an organization of secret societies as the most effective way to undermine the foundations of the Turkish empire. *Cheta* tactics were too limited to make any meaningful impression. In his view, the key to Bulgaria's freedom was within the country, not from without with bands of exiled soldiers. From this point on, the legend of Vassil Levsky moves into overdrive.

Now the most wanted man in Bulgaria, Levsky was spirited from one hiding place to another, often in monasteries. In April 1869, he issued a proclamation from 'The Provisional Government in the Balkans' and distributed copies of it from village to village. His mastery of disguise was incredible – on one famous occasion, he hobbled past a group of Turkish soldiers as a badly bandaged shepherd on primitive crutches. When it dawned on them that there might well have been something amiss with this sickly herdsman, they charged off down the road and asked a prosperous-looking Turk where the man had gone. The Turkish merchant of course was Levsky. On another occasion, he disguised himself as a missionary from the American Bible Society – so keen was the local governor to make a good impression on the Americans, he gave him an escort of Zaptiahs to see him safe passage.

In the spring of 1870, Levsky based himself at Lovech, the limestone town that lies between Pleven to the north and Troyan to the south. It was a good crossroads from which to set up an organization. Levsky realized that if any progress was to be made, the movement would need discipline and so he published the *Regulation for Workers for the Liberation of the Bulgarian People*. It is a remarkable document, setting out the aims and objectives, the means and the ends. Every layer of the organization had its duties and a strict need-to-know rule was paramount for security. The chapter on punishment for breaking the rules of the organization is draconian; most offences were punishable by death. Yet it was the only realistic option at that time if Levsky was to succeed in creating an underground army, capable of withstanding treachery, betrayal, bribery, torture and all the other black arts of the Turkish intelligence services.

Vassil Levsky was caught by the Turkish authorities on Boxing Day 1873, not far from Lovech. He was taken to Turnovo for interrogation, then to Sofia for trial and hung on 19 February 1873.

This broad-browed, fair-haired man, with twinkling blue eyes, had many facets to him: a devoted son to his mother; a young priest with a strikingly beautiful voice; a non-smoking, non-drinking, tough mountain guerrilla; a sophisticated urban terrorist; a loyal and staunch friend to many.

The generations of Bulgarians who came after Levsky, especially the Partisans of the Second World War, revered him to the point of deification. For them, he was the Apostle of Freedom, a man who risked all to liberate his country, and in doing so acquired immortality. Levsky may not have ascended into Heaven but his memory occupies a corner of every Bulgarian heart, even today, and his face is etched large on the national psyche. For the Partisans, it was a patriotic honour to follow in his footsteps, and for their leaders, he was both the icon and lexicon of revolutionary warfare.

The brutal suppression of an attempted uprising in 1876 brought about the reverse of what the Ottoman Empire had intended. Far from deterring the ambitions of the Bulgars for independence, their savagery precipitated an intervention by the Russians whereupon, once more, legends of military prowess entered the history books. After the declaration of war by Russia against Turkey on 24 April 1877, Russian troops arrived at the Shipka Pass on 15 July. Initially, the detachment consisted of just one Russian regiment – 6th Orlov – and five battalions of Bulgarian Volunteers, supported by twenty-seven guns. Within five weeks, barely having had time to prepare the defences on the rocky hilltops, twenty-four Turkish battalions attacked them.

Although at noon on that day, 21 August, the Russian 35th Briansk Regiment arrived, the odds in favour of the defenders were appalling. Terrible hand-to-hand fighting took place during the night and when they had run out of ammunition, the Russians and Bulgarians chucked anything that came to hand down onto the attacking Turks. At this point, the Turkish commander, Suleiman Pasha, sent what in hindsight was one of the most ill-judged messages in the annals of military history:

August 22, 1877; From Suleiman Pasha to the Sultan.

The Russians can neither resist me nor slip out of my hands. If the enemy does not try and run away tonight, then I will resume the attacks tomorrow and, I hope, I will crush them.

The only redeeming phrase in this message was 'I hope'. Far from giving up, the defenders fought with the utmost ferocity until reinforced by the Russian 4 Rifle Brigade at 6.00 pm the next evening. These troops had made a forced march of many miles in temperatures of 39 degrees without a drop of water. As soon as they reached the top of the peak, they got stuck into the Turks and won the day.

Suleiman retired to lick his wounds and one must suppose to concoct another, somewhat different message to the Sultan. A night attack launched by him in September likewise failed to dislodge the Russians and Bulgarians; then the 'winter of Mount Shipka' began. A surviving diary of a soldier at the time reads: 'Terrible frost and a fearful storm: the number of those with frozen hands has increased tremendously: it is impossible to build a fire anywhere. If a soldier falls in the snow, in 3 to 4 minutes he is buried completely. You cannot hide anywhere from the storm.'

The Russian general in charge of the sector, Radetzi, summed up the battle along these lines. 'Shipka – this was the locked door; it locked Suleiman Pasha and his 40,000 soldiers out of the north of Bulgaria and prevented him linking up with the two other Ottoman armies in the area. In January, we unlocked it and we began our march to Istanbul.' From that moment onward, the Bulgarian nation acknowledged an irrevocable and perpetual debt of gratitude to Russia as its liberator.

The resulting Treaty of St Stefano[2] led to the creation of a huge new Bulgarian state, albeit still a vassal state of the Ottoman Empire. So huge was it that five months later the European powers prevailed at the Treaty of Berlin to have it drastically reduced, including the loss of most of Macedonia and territories adjacent to the Aegean Sea. This was, of course, all about keeping Russia in check rather than penalizing the Bulgarians.

In 1879, a new constitution was drawn up for the fledgling state. A single-chamber parliament, or *sûbranie*, was to be the legislative body and the head of state was to be a prince elected by this assembly. After a shaky start by the courageous but inexperienced Prince Alexander Battenberg, the first elected prince, the new incumbent, Prince Ferdinand ('Foxy') of Saxe Coburg Gotha, proved more than adept at handling the external and internal machinations of Bulgarian politics and by 1900 had imposed his own imprimatur on all aspects of governance. The brutal murder of his first prime minister, Stambolov, on the streets of Sofia in 1895, was attributed to Foxy among others.

Macedonia, that landlocked country in the heart of the Balkans, now became centre stage for the ambitions of Greece, Serbia and Bulgaria, the latter still incensed at its amputation from the body Bulgar at the Treaty of Berlin. Ferdinand encouraged the Army to form ties with pro-Bulgarian Macedonian *cheta* and also turned a blind eye to the activities of IMRO, a group which advocated autonomy for Macedonia.[3] A premature Macedonian uprising against the Ottomans in 1903 – the Ilinden rising – met with a savage reaction from the Turkish authorities and was soon extinguished by the brutal application of overwhelming force.

Bolstered by full independence from the Ottomans in 1908, Foxy Ferdinand, now King of the Bulgarians, plotted expansion and when the First Balkan War started on 8 October 1912, with tiny Montenegro declaring war on the mighty Ottoman Empire, Bulgaria joined with Serbia and Greece and declared war on Turkey as well. After only six weeks, the Turks were beaten and in May 1913 the Treaty of London again made Bulgaria the biggest country in the Balkans – it now bordered the Black Sea, the Sea of Marmara and the Aegean.

But dissatisfied with the portion of Macedonia allotted to her by her allies, Bulgaria turned against them and on 13 June 1913, the Second Balkan War erupted, this time lasting for a month. Bulgaria lost and, under the terms of the Treaty of Bucharest in August that year, was forced to hand back everything she had gained the previous year; Adrianople (Edirne) reverted to Turkey; Romania occupied the southern Dobrudja; and large parts of Macedonia became southern Serbia.

Macedonia was now divided into three portions: Serbia took the major portion of Slavic Macedonia in the north, which roughly corresponds to the present former Yugoslav Republic of Macedonia; Greece took Aegean Macedonia in the south; and Bulgaria was only able to obtain a small region in the north-east, Pirin Macedonia, where IMRO promptly and peremptorily set up a 'state within a state'. Humiliatingly, this last portion was the smallest of the three and the recovery of these losses became part of the Bulgarian national dream once more.

In 1914, Bulgaria, at the outbreak of the new war, saw her chance and after months of reflection, the architect of those disastrous Balkan wars, King Ferdinand, threw his lot in with the Germans; by the autumn of 1915, Bulgaria had regained most of her previous losses. However, it was yet another fatal mistake by this inept monarch, whose actions gave opportunism a bad name. As the feisty US journalist, John Reed, perspicaciously wrote in 1915: 'King Ferdinand is a regular romantic Balkan King. He perpetually sees himself riding into Constantinople on a white horse – the Tsar of an immense, belligerent empire. As I write this, he has again hurled his people against their will into a war from which they cannot emerge except as losers.'

By 1918, her armies, short of weapons and starving, could no longer fight. Bulgaria was the first of the Central Powers to surrender and by the end of that year her allies lay defeated. Once again Foxy had missed winning the prize of Macedonia; this time, the inept architect of Bulgarian defeat abdicated and was succeeded by his son, Boris.[4]

At the Neuilly Peace Conference of 1919, Bulgaria and the hapless Boris were in the dock – she had sided with Germany and frustrated Allied war efforts. Retribution was savage: she lost her granary in the southern Dobrudja to Romania (this was indeed punitive since only 10,000 Romanians lived there compared to the 300,000 indigenous Bulgarian population), her access to the Aegean and many hectares of rich tobacco fields were relinquished to Greece, and some strategic border areas ceded to the new Yugoslavia. Furthermore, the long-cherished prize of re-uniting Macedonia with the Bulgar lands had receded to a mere dream, with a considerable number of Bulgarians now living under Yugoslav rule, for post-1918, Bulgaria held only 10 per cent of this region – the Greeks held 51 per cent and the Yugoslavs 39 per cent. And as in the case of Germany, Bulgaria also had to make heavy reparation payments (£90m) – much of her coal output was assigned to Serbia – and her army reduced to a 'police force' of 20,000.

Joseph Rothschild sums it up in his *History of South Eastern Europe*:

Thus came to naught Bulgaria's prodigious and almost continuous military efforts of 1912–1918, in the course of which her armies had suffered approximately 155,000 killed and over 400,000 wounded, apart from 150,000 civilian dead in the course of cholera, typhus, and influenza epidemics, and not to mention then several hundred thousand 'unborn' of these war years or the loss of a third of her livestock and farm inventory. The military dead alone numbered more than a fifth of the male population between the ages of 20 and 50.

The interwar years of internecine feuding

Interwar Bulgaria was characterized by a level of violence that surpassed even that of its wildest neighbours. Given that it was the most egalitarian society in the region, that it had no aristocracy and no large landholdings, and that its educational system was both excellent and open to all, why was this so? A combination of frustrated nationalism, a king with dictatorial inclinations, the entrenched attitudes of the old *sûbranie* parties, a proud but dangerously sensitive officer class, the presence of the lethal terrorist organization IMRO within her borders, together with a large dollop of anarchist and communist agitators, all contributed to the daily diet of assassinations, bombings, strikes, coups and insurrections.

The monarchy, to date, had not distinguished itself and two political forces, the Bulgarian People's Agrarian Union (BANU) and the Communist Party (CPB), were calling in 1919 for its overthrow and a change of government. One year after Boris's accession, BANU's Aleksandar Stamboliiski was elected Prime Minister. Though hugely popular with the large peasant class through his policies of land reform,[5] access to the legal system and favourable changes in taxation to property, he earned the animosity of the middle class and military, which led to his toppling in a military coup on 9 June 1923; since it was Stamboliiski who had signed the Treaty of Neuilly which had given Yugoslavia most of Macedonia, IMRO were delighted to be a party to the coup and arranged his murder,[6] sending his head to Sofia in a biscuit tin. In a gruesome photograph released by the authorities, his severed hands were shown placed by his corpse. In September that year, the CPB led an uprising against the military government which backfired and resulted in a terror campaign against them. Diplomats put the figure of those killed by the government at around 10,000.

The newly elected government under an academic economist, Alexander Tsankov, muddled on, trying to steer a course through the violent tides of Bulgarian public life, which showed little signs of eddying. In April 1925, two attempts were made on the life of Boris. The King had been in the Balkan Mountains with a small hunting party and, on their return to Sofia on 14 April, they were ambushed by gunmen at Araba Konak; his chief hunter was killed instantly. Boris was extraordinarily brave – he brought the car to a halt, ran under fire towards a passing bus, grabbed its steering wheel and drove to the nearest town, where he commandeered a platoon of soldiers and returned to lead the counter-attack. Two days later a massive bomb planted by the CPB in the roof of Sveta Nedelya Church in Sofia exploded during a funeral service, killing 130 prominent citizens and narrowly missing the royal family. Thousands were consequently arrested; some of them were publicly executed, others disappeared without trace. The CPB no longer existed except in name. These incidents prodded the American journalist, Leigh White, to remark of Boris that he 'owed his life to the poor marksmanship of his would-be assassins rather than to any popularity on the part of his tyrannical regime'.

Tsankov also presided over 'The War of the Stray Dog', which started on 22 October 1925 when a Bulgarian sentry shot dead a Greek soldier who had inadvertently crossed the border in pursuit of his pet dog. The Greeks reacted by sending troops to Petrich, a town well within the borders of Bulgaria. The dispute was finally settled by the League of Nations which fined Greece £45,000.

While successive governments, which shared the twin notorieties of incompetence and corruption, floundered in the fallout of the Great Depression, IMRO careered on out of control, with its heartland at Petrich in south-west Bulgaria a virtual no-go area. Although almost all the killings were internecine, many observers felt that IMRO was the de facto government of Bulgaria, none more than the meddlesome Mussolini who had been bankrolling it since 1926. A destabilized Bulgaria would allow him to exert Italian influence throughout the Adriatic and Aegean region.

So matters stood when, on 19 May 1934, a *coup d'état* brought to power a group of men – the *devetnaitseti* or the nineteenthers –

who had taken part in the Tsankov coup of 1923, and who in 1929 had formed a political organization to demand a new foreign and internal policy, beginning with the abolition of IMRO. This group, led by Colonel Kimon Gheorgiev[7] and Colonel Damian Velchev, called itself the Zveno ('The Link'). Most of its members were honest soldiers who deeply regretted their part in Stamboliiski's overthrow.

The Zveno detested Tsankov, was strongly anti-Italian, and wanted an alliance with Yugoslavia; and it considered King Boris largely responsible for the unwise foreign policy and the intolerable internal situation. Under Gheorgiev as Premier, it set up an authoritarian regime, suspended the constitution, outlawed all political parties and banned all party newspapers. It also outlawed IMRO, and the military and police authorities swooped down to make the ban effective. Its leader Mikhailov fled, first to Turkey and then to Italy, where he was given a hero's welcome by Mussolini and Ante Pavelić, the co-founder of the Ustaše, who also lived under the protection of the Fascists in Rome. Many of his men were arrested and large quantities of arms were seized. To the amazement and relief of everyone in Bulgaria, the dreaded IMRO collapsed overnight. Mussolini had lost his most effective instrument for terrorizing Bulgarian politicians and thereby harassing the Yugoslavian government.

Boris, showing the same ruthless sense of self-preservation as his father, massaged the composition of the new administration over the ensuing year, and by October his own ministers were strong enough to arrest the leaders of the Military League and thus marginalize the Army. The King was now de facto sovereign and ruler of Bulgaria, although he had astutely avoided such provocative measures such as the setting up of a mass political party, the course chosen by his neighbour, King Carol II of Romania. A truncated form of parliamentary rule was re-introduced, but without the restoration of the political parties.

Kosta Todorov, head of the Free Bulgarian Committee, was unambiguous in his analysis of King Boris:

> Although Boris had long been tied up with Hitler and Mussolini, he was careful not to betray his real sentiments before the Fall of France. He even assured the Allies of his

sympathy for their cause. His old trick of compliments and little attentions to the Allied diplomats succeeded marvellously. In extreme cases he played the innocent, and although he was the sole master of the country, he affected to be the victim of mysterious forces, military conspiracy and all kinds of pressure which, so to say, forced his hand. After the Petain-Laval treason, his game became more and more obvious. But, before the British Minister, he continued to lie. To American journalists he would remark, sighing, 'My army is pro-German, my wife is Italian, my people are pro-Russian. I'm the only pro-Bulgarian in this country.' In this cheap rigmarole, one thing was true: the people were pro-Russian. The King had expelled from the army all anti-Axis higher officers. His wife, Queen Joanna, had no influence, while he had been devoted to Hitler since 1937 and to Mussolini since 1923.

The political scene between 1939 and 1942

The situation in Bulgaria on the outbreak of war in 1939 eerily resembled that of 1914. Finding itself alone on the fringes of an all-consuming European conflict, just as its predecessor had done, the government under its pro-German Prime Minister, Bogdan Filov,[8] declared a position of neutrality on 16 September, but in reality was hoping for bloodless territorial gains in the lands occupied by neighbouring countries after the Second Balkan War and the First World War. With 70 per cent of her exports going to Germany, there was also a sense of economic dependency on Berlin.[9] On 7 September 1940, Bulgaria succeeded in negotiating the recovery of the southern Dobrudja – part of Romania since 1913 – in the Axis-sponsored Treaty of Craiova. Marshall Lee Miller in *Bulgaria during the Second World War* neatly concludes: 'As a result of the Dobrudja offer, Bulgaria, which had long looked to Russia as the liberator, now turned to Germany as the benefactor.' This windfall territorial gain reinforced Bulgarian determination to resolve other territorial grievances without direct involvement in the war and on 3 December 1940, Draganov, the Bulgarian Ambassador in Berlin, advised the Führer that Bulgaria''s entrance into the Axis might be considered certain in so far as a solution was reached on 'the minorities issue in Macedonia'. But it was not to be, despite Filov's meeting with Hitler and von Ribbentrop at the Schlöss Belvedere in Vienna on 2 January, when he emphasized to them that the Greco-Italian war had brought the issue of Macedonia into play. Hitler hedged his answers at the time as he still sought Yugoslav entrance into the Axis and any incautious word or promise might have far-reaching consequences.

Two months later, when German troops preparing to invade Greece from Romania reached the Bulgarian borders, King Boris saw no option other than to acquiesce and so Bulgaria officially joined the Axis bloc on 1 March 1941. With the Soviet Union in a non-aggression pact with Germany, there was little popular opposition to the decision.

That April, the Bulgarian government sat on the sidelines as German, Italian and Hungarian troops invaded Yugoslavia and Greece, but after the Yugoslav government surrendered on 17 April, Boris meet with Hitler in Vienna the next day and Bulgarian passivity ended. On 18 April, Ambassador Draganov despatched a telegram to Sofia with the exciting news that 'von Ribbentrop, by order of Hitler, instructed me to advise you of the Führer's wish that we are to enter Serbian Macedonia with three divisions as occupying forces and to take over the administration, in order for German armies to be free from that concern and be ready for action.' On 20 April, the Bulgarian Army entered the Aegean region and occupied territory between the Struma River and a line of demarcation running through Alexandroupoli and Svilengrad, west of Maritsa. Included in the area occupied were the cities of Alexandroupoli, Komotini, Serres, Xanthi, Drama and Kavala, and the islands of Thasos and Samothrace, as well as almost all of what is today the former Yugoslav Republic of Macedonia and much of eastern Serbia. The goal to gain an Aegean Sea outlet in Thrace and to seize eastern Macedonia had been met,[10] although its realization was to prove more difficult.

A number of incidents involving the native population in Macedonia provoked the Bulgarians to turn from a relatively benevolent policy of pacification to a harsher version. Furthermore, relations with their Italian allies were often strained on the Albanian border[11] – Mussolini dubbed Boris as coming from a line of *'regnanti senza fegato'*, or chicken-livered kings. In response, in

September 1941 Prime Minister Filov stated that 'we are not satisfied with the border in Western Macedonia; neither are we satisfied
with the Italian attitude. Such a border is not adequate for us either
in historical, strategic or economic aspect and it is unsustainable.'
Some time later, the Bulgarian Minister of Defence, General
Daskalov, proclaimed that 'we do not recognize the border on Italy
as final; neither are we going to recognize it.' In Greece, where they
felt they were recovering territory lost to the Greeks in the Second
Balkan War of 1913, the policy of the Bulgarians was arbitrary and
severe from the outset of the occupation.

Bulgaria did not join in the German invasion of the Soviet Union
that began on 22 June 1941 and did not declare war on that
country. Boris had argued that the Army was ill-equipped for a
blitzkreig and was better deployed in the Balkan area to deter any
possible Turkish invasion or Soviet counter-attack on the Black Sea
coast. But Hitler was not fooled, remarking that 'Boris is by
temperament a fox rather than a wolf and would only expose
himself to great danger only with the utmost reluctance.' However,
the government was forced by the Germans to declare a token war
on the United Kingdom and the United States on 13 December
1941.

From the beginning, the Bulgarian resistance differed from those
countries invaded and then occupied by the Axis powers. The
historian E.P. Thompson surmised that 'it follows from this that
the Bulgarian Partisan movement must, perforce, engage not in a
national resistance against the occupiers but in a direct insurrec-
tionary action against its own national government, in conditions
of almost-impossible difficulty.' So almost immediately after the
invasion of the USSR by Nazi Germany and her allies, it was
the Politburo of the CPB that decided to prepare for armed resistance against the Bulgarian government. A Central Military
Commission was created to lead the armed struggle, but the arrest
of 244 prominent communists on 3 July,[12] and the lifting of the
immunity of the communist Deputies of Parliament in September
disrupted its plans and general confusion set in. Consequently, the
resistance set up in August was very small in scale, consisting
initially only of a few groups of three to six 'legals', living ordinary
lives during the day and engaging in small-scale sabotage at night.
No actual Partisan bands of 'illegals', living as *cheta* in the hills and

forests, were yet active. The only centrally planned undertaking that took place at this time was an abortive attack on the Gonda Voda concentration camp in the beech forests above Stanimaka, where the arrested communists had been sent along with other Bulgarian political prisoners. A group of communists from southern Bulgaria assembled on 15 August 1941 to spring the prisoners from the camp; scantily trained and poorly armed, the attempt failed, as did a further one a fortnight later.

In order to strengthen the fledgling Bulgarian resistance movement, Russia sent fifty-eight Bulgarian émigré Communists into Bulgaria from August through to October, either dropped by parachute or put ashore from Soviet submarines on the Bulgarian Black Sea coast. The operation was a complete failure; twenty were picked up on arrival and shot and most of the remainder captured within days of their arrival in Bulgaria.

As the year came to a close, King Boris had much to mull over. His strategy of 'wait and see' had proved sensible and events of the early spring had led to cherished territorial gains without any military or financial costs. Yet it was not in the interests of Bulgaria to be fighting on the same side as Russia's attacker – it went against the grain of a strong mutual friendship that had secured the freedom of Bulgaria from its Ottoman suzerain a mere sixty-five years earlier. Nor was it politic to be an enemy of Britain, its Commonwealth and its powerful ally, the USA. At least on the home front, on a positive note, most Bulgarians were able to go about their business with little sign of war, and the Army and Police had crushed all signs of resistance to date.

By the end of 1941, between 700 and 800 communists had been arrested. Initially the CPB had managed to regroup and regain control of its destiny, but a wave of new arrests starting in February 1942 brought the Central Committee and the Central Military Commission to the point of collapse, thereby effectively ending all centrally controlled resistance. Still, Boris was nervous and at the end of March he ordered the arrest of Reserve-General Vladimir Zaimov for treason. A leading figure in the 1934 coup, Zaimov was accused with forty others of being involved in a pro-Soviet conspiracy, and was tried and executed in June.

In the middle of 1942, the CPB came up with a new strategy and, in July, Georgi Dimitrov, the Bulgarian-born Secretary-General of the Comintern, announced the creation of the Fatherland Front (OF), an anti-fascist coalition consisting of the CPB, the Agrarians and the Zveno party. Although the Bulgarian Social Democratic party joined a year later, the OF remained the progeny of the CPB, which jealously guarded its parental role.

Throughout 1942, Bulgaria dabbled in engaging with Allied diplomats, with various ideas of a Southern Slav Confederation and a Balkan Confederation doing the rounds. The former was dismissed as unrealistic since it would be Serb dominated, but the latter was taken more seriously. It was also recognized that the Russians would probably make a determined attempt to exploit pro-Russian feeling in Bulgaria at the end of the war and turn the country into a Russian province. But it was precisely with the objective of setting up a counter-weight to such a move that British diplomats encouraged the idea that Bulgaria might take her place in a Balkan Confederation (along with Yugoslavia, Romania and Greece).

King Boris, 'whose whole policy consists in not fighting but picking up tit-bits for which others have fought', was starting to hedge his bets. Monsieur Jouve, the Free French representative in Istanbul, received a message from the King via a trusted emissary that 'when the Allies enter Bulgaria he will see to it that the Bulgarian army does not resist'. Other messages were conveyed from the King in roundabout ways. A Macedonian of 'good repute' warned the US Embassy that 'should Bulgaria be destroyed by air raids or by other military action, it will then be very easy for the Russians to make use of the despair of the Bulgarian nation and without any resistance the latter will be swallowed up by the Bolshevik element.' In mid-1943, reports reached the British Foreign Office that the Metropolitan Bishop of Sofia, with the King's full agreement, had sent a deputy to Switzerland to get in touch with the Allies. But, for all these feelers, there was little Bulgaria could do to shake off her alliance with Germany.

In April, the FO sent a telegram to the United States, distancing itself from these overtures:

HMG have hitherto received no indication of peace feelers from the Bulgarian government. If any approaches are made in the future, it will be open to HMG to decide on their merits whether or not they should be pursued. It should be borne in mind, however, that any negotiations between HMG and the Bulgarians would at once arouse the deepest suspicion on the part of the Greek, Yugoslav and Turkish governments.

That summer, the message was reinforced with the observation that 'HMG therefore cannot have any dealings with King Boris, whose fate they regard as a matter of indifference, any more than they can have with the present government.'

By early 1943, the OF announced a new tactical doctrine, namely the assassination of prominent government personalities and establishment figures. Given the bloody history of IMRO in this area of activity, it was hardly original and fraught with the probability of rejection and failure from the beginning. During the months of February to May 1943, several police agents and politicians were shot by 'legal' OF units or *'boini grupi'* (fighting group). The first to be shot, on 13 February, was the retired General Hristo Lukov, leader of the pro-German Legionary Movement, and thought by many to be the Germans' choice to replace King Boris. An unsuccessful attempt was made on Lukov's secretary on 6 April, but the failure was made good on 15 April, when Sotir Yanev, the chairman of the Committee of Foreign Relations of the Bulgarian parliament, was assassinated by Violeta Yankova outside his office the day after delivering a pro-German speech. Next was Colonel 'Black Panther' Pantev, the Chairman of the Military Court in Sofia, who died on 3 May at the bloodstained hands of the same team that had killed General Lukov.

The response of the authorities was predictable: on 5 May, the entire city of Sofia was sealed off, subjected to a house-to-house search and police controls were strengthened to the extent that further conduct of urban guerrilla warfare became increasingly difficult. When coupled to the misgivings that the CBP party leadership had had in the first place of assassinating public persons, which was bound to alienate possible political allies, the campaign was wound down in May, though assassinations continued spasmodically (the Deputy Governor of Plovdiv was killed in July 1943).

The successive waves of arrests of communists in 1941 and 1942 led to the creation of the first Partisan bands of 'illegals' living as outlaws in the hills, though growth was slow and at the end of 1942, police estimates put their strength at only 183 men organized in twenty-five *cheta* in the country at large, discounting the areas acquired by Bulgaria in 1941.

Soviet successes on the Eastern Front and Yugoslav Partisan successes in the West, as well as a continuing domestic clampdown (6,700 communists were arrested between 1941 and 1943) led to more recruits joining the OF, bringing the Partisan strength to 650 in forty-seven *cheta* by June 1943. However, this should be compared with the September 1943 German estimate of guerrilla forces in the Yugoslavian and Albanian theatre of operations at 145,000, the bulk of them, some 90,000, under Tito's command.

Increasing numbers brought about the need for a reorganization of the OF command structure, and consequently all Partisan units were incorporated into a new People's Revolutionary Army of Liberation (NOVA), led by the General Staff of the Resistance, formerly the Central Military Commission. During March and April 1943, Bulgaria proper (including a few small areas of Greek Thrace and Macedonia, and Yugoslav Macedonia) was divided into twelve Insurrection Military Zones (VOZ), numbered I to XII.

More recruits led to more activity: the number of Partisan actions rose from twelve in January 1943 to twenty-eight in February, eighty-three in March, seventy-two in April, 125 in May and 145 in June. The drop in April can be attributed to the twenty-day blockade of Sredna Gora[13] imposed by Bulgarian police in cooperation with Regular Army units. The second half of 1943 saw further expansion of the Partisan forces. The old Partisan detachments spawned off new units, among others the 'Vassil Levsky' Partisan unit that was expanded into a brigade in 1944, and fourteen entirely new units came into being around Pleven, Jambol, Pasardshik and Varna. Hence, the number of Partisan actions increased too, from 174 in July to over 187 in August, 214 in September, 274 in October and 280 in November. Though these actions included burning factories and sawmills, and attacks on mines, most were of much less significance, and the impact of the Partisans on the economy and internal security of Bulgaria remained miniscule. The *cheta* were on average only a dozen men strong, who were mostly concerned with their own survival in a harsh and hostile environment.

In August 1943, King Boris flew up to Poland for a meeting with Hitler at the Wolf's Lair, deep in the Polish forests, and died unexpectedly on his return a few days later in Sofia. All manner of rumours abounded: did he die of a coronary thrombosis, as stated in the official communiqué? Was he murdered by poison or by some other means? If so, who committed the crime? Or did King Boris commit suicide as suggested by some? There is no conclusive answer, but the death of the Bulgarian head of state and its de facto ruler made little difference to the everyday business of government; his heir, King Simeon II, was a minor and a regency council was quickly formed by the Germanphile Filov, with Prince Kiril, the brother of the late King, and General Mihov. Filov's political poodle, Dobri Bozhilov, became Prime Minister.

SOE: the early days in Bulgaria

So this then was the political situation in Bulgaria in September 1943 as SOE made last-minute preparations to send in their first Bulgarian Mission. Their strategy, developed by Captain Hugh Seton-Watson, an eminent Balkan historian, and Colonel Bickham Sweet-Escott, a former executive of the Courthauld textile company, had begun some three years earlier. In their first assessment, the key element for SOE was to contact the three illegal political parties – the Protogueroffs, a faction of IMRO named after its founder, General Protogueroff, a Macedonian general in the Bulgarian army; the Agrarian Movement (BANU); and the secretive and shy Military League headed by Colonel Damyan Velchev. However, it was acknowledged that they were all under surveillance and their members saw little advantage in taking risks.

After a somewhat shaky start when SOE operative Julian Amery, the son of Leo Amery, the Secretary of State for India, had infuriated the FO by his antics in Sofia promoting his unauthorized initiative of a Bulgarian-Yogoslav union,[14] in late 1940, Colonel Bill Bailey, who was part of the expanded SOE desk in Belgrade,[15] met with Dr 'G.M.' Dimitrov,[16] the leader of the 'Pladne'[17] left-wing Agrarians, who agreed to form a number of small groups to be trained in the use of explosives and other devices. When enough material had been assembled in Belgrade by the end of February 1941, Dimitrov and his associates were unexpectedly arrested, though it turned out that the arrests were more of a routine than specific nature. SOE lamented that 'the lateness of our start and the long delays in obtaining supplies later had fatal consequences, for the amounts left behind was enough to incriminate their possessors but too small to be of much use.' Dimitrov managed to escape from police custody and was spirited by Colonel Bailey across the Yugoslav border in a crate of documents. Emerging from the box none the worse for wear, he was joined by Professor Ivan Kostov who had also escaped from the police, though his journey in walking across the frontier had been more arduous than hazardous.[18] The Yugoslav authorities allowed them to recruit twenty Bulgarian émigrés under Nesho Tumangelov, best known for taking a pot shot at King Boris in 1925, and soon they were ready to return.

On 12 March, ten days after Bulgaria had joined the Axis camp, the British Minister, Sir George Rendell, and his staff managed to leave Bulgaria, leaving behind Mr Greenwich, a Passport Control officer, whose whereabouts was unknown.[19] It was a far from fraught journey that culminated in disaster when a bomb planted in their luggage exploded in their Istanbul hotel, killing two female typists and two Turkish policemen.

Alas events overtook the nascent revolutionaries. On 25 March, the Yugoslav government signed the Tripartite Pact in Vienna and in doing so threw its lot in with Germany and Italy. It was an act of surrender but for those in power at the time, infinitely preferable to a hopeless armed resistance. Urged on by the British, a group of air force and army officers staged a successful *coup d'état* the following night and the signatories of the pact, Prince Paul and Prime Minister Cvetković, were summarily dismissed. General Mirković, the architect of the *coup*, and General Simović, the new Prime Minister and Chief of Staff, proclaimed the seventeen-year-old Prince Peter as King and, at the same time, ordered Prince Paul into exile in Greece.

Although Churchill declared that 'early this morning the Yugoslav nation found its soul', the significance of the revolt was that Yugoslavia's accession to the Tripartite Pact was in doubt. Despite having urged on the plotters, British aid was suddenly non-existent – 'praise, advice and promises' were all that were on offer.[20]While Britain's 50,000-strong Expeditionary Force remained in Greece, Hitler's Directive No. 25 declared that 'Yugoslavia must be destroyed as quickly as possible.' He meant it since his cherished invasion plans for Russia would be impossible without a secure Balkan flank. On 6 April, the Axis[21] onslaught began with a massive air raid on Belgrade, and as Tumangelov and his band of saboteurs headed for the Bulgarian border, they met German troops of the First Panzer Group coming in the opposite direction bent on invading Yugoslavia. By 17 April, the invasion was over – it had been a spectacular demonstration of German military prowess, with German casualties of only 151 killed, 302 wounded and fifteen missing in action. The fate of Tumangelov's small force has never been ascertained but Dimitrov and Kostov managed to leave Belgrade with the British Legation and arrived in Istanbul via a Sunderland flying-boat journey to the Middle East. Unfortunately, during the first arrests of Dimitrov's group, security had been broken and the police arrested a further twenty-five members and seized most of their explosives and money. For SOE, their Bulgarian cupboard was now bare.

In late 1942, SOE had asked for guidance from the FO about their proposed plans for sabotage and subversive operations in Bulgaria. Sir Alexander Cadogan replied on 4 January 1943, that:

It is quite impossible for us to give you even our views on the future of Bulgaria, let alone a definitive clearcut policy. Our policy towards Bulgaria must at present in the very nature of things be fluid and opportunist. We have no vital interests in Bulgaria and no moral commitments towards her. We are therefore in a position to wait on events and to exploit any turn they may take. We consider it essential to maintain this freedom until such time as it can be shown beyond all doubt that a definite commitment on our side will bring real advantage. Before undertaking such a commitment, we should in any case be obliged to consult the Soviet Government, and this we have no wish to do at present.

Cadogan finished by reneging on an earlier undertaking that SOE could contact the Protogueroffists. 'Our feeling is that it is playing with fire to encourage these bandits, and we should therefore much prefer to have nothing to do with them.'

The last remaining option was the OF, although it was well known that the CPB had been instrumental in founding it. In SOE's 1942 country assessment, the assassination of King Boris was discussed but subsequent events ruled this out. As to the potential level of Partisan recruitment, very little was known other than that Bulgarian military and police morale, although low in some border areas, was nowhere near the point of collapse. Little emphasis was placed on the likely attitude of the Bulgarian people, especially the peasant farmers who populated the Partisan areas of operation. In hindsight, this was a glaring and costly oversight.

The choice to contact the communist-dominated OF bears an uncanny similarity to the failure of SOE and its agents in Greece to appreciate from the first that they were confronted with the Greek Communist party (KKE) in their dealings with EAM and ELAS. In his *Struggle for Greece 1941–1949*, Christopher Woodhouse, the commander of the Allied Military Mission to the Greek guerrillas in 1943–4, writes:

> When the first British parachutists landed in mainland Greece on the last night of September 1942, they knew nothing of EAM or ELAS and there had been no mention of the KKE in their briefing. The first reference to EAM was in a telegram from SOE Cairo to Myers in Greece,[22] dated 21 December 1942, asking if he had any contact with a Greek organization of that name . . . On 24 January 1943 . . . he stated 'EAM represent many parties but controlling party extremely left-wing with headquarters in Athens radiating strict control civil groups throughout country' . . . and on 24 February 1943 . . . added for the first time: 'I believe Communists control EAM unknown to most members.'[23]

In the summer of 1943, the immediate priority was to send a mission to establish contact with the OF. Colonel Bill Bailey, the SOE officer in Istanbul and a former mining engineer in Serbia, asked General Mihailović to provide a secure reception area since his forces were nearest to the Bulgarian frontier; hardly surprising, this turned out to be a non-starter since Mihailović had no intention of supporting any communists, let alone Bulgarian ones. Instead Bailey had to enlist the help of Tito's Partisans who were a long way from the border areas. A reception area was chosen in Albania and General Tempo, Tito's commander in Macedonia, agreed to provide an escort to take the Mission up to the Bulgarian border. This circuitous infiltration plan, ambitious as it was on paper, was to turn out to be even more extreme in its execution.

The officer selected to lead the mission was 33-year-old Major Mostyn Davies. Educated at Charterhouse and Magdalen College Oxford, where he read law, Davies trained as an accountant with Coopers and then joined the Civil Service as a deputy accountant for Trinity House, the lighthouse organization. Although visiting lightships and remote lighthouses appealed to his sense of adventure, the work began to seem insignificant in the light of the worsening international situation and Davies applied to join one of the new Ministries being set up in expectation of war. He became Private Secretary to John Llewellin MP[24] and followed him to various ministries, such as the Ministry of Information, Ministry of Aircraft Production and Ministry of Transport and Shipping. However, life in a reserved occupation proved frustrating when many of his contemporaries were fighting, so Davies sought a more active role in the prosecution of the war and soon found himself in Lagos, working for the West African Governors' Conference Secretariat reporting to the banker Louis Franck. In fact, Davies was now a fully fledged SOE operative.

It was here that he met his wife, Brenda. 'I can only say that I suppose it was a question of love at first sight and we decided to get married,' Mrs Davies recalled years later and they married on 6 August 1942. After a five-day honeymoon, Davies was posted to New York to join the SOE liaison mission headed by Colonel Stephenson. Here he worked with other SOE high fliers like Bickham Sweet-Escott, Tom Masterson and John Keswick who all went on to become senior SOE officers. It was clear that, from the start, SOE had seen in Davies an officer of exceptional talent and potential.

His brief in New York was to see whether anti-Axis operations could be mounted in South America,[25] and hence he was away for much of the time. Brenda managed to join him from Lagos before Christmas and they resumed married life, albeit sporadically due to his hectic travel schedule. In June 1943, recalled to England, they sailed in a convoy across the Atlantic, a hazardous voyage made worse when Davies developed pneumonia and was saved by his wife's careful nursing. On arrival in England, they booked into the Savoy Hotel for two weeks and spent the time meeting their respective in-laws and other relations. Davies then went straight to Force 133 in Cairo, where his close friend from New York days, Bickham Sweet-Escott, was running the SOE Balkan desk, to start preparing for a mission to contact the Bulgarian Resistance. The choice of someone to lead the mission as senior and well connected in the upper echelons of SOE as Mostyn Davis reflected the importance attached to it – the hope must have been to replicate the success of William Deakin and Fitzroy Maclean in Yugoslavia. After a brief period of training to prepare for the drop into Bulgaria, Davies was ready. Brenda's last letter from him was that September; after that, she received the standard monthly SOE telegram, 'Am fit and well. All my love.'

On 20 September 1943, the four-man MULLIGATAWNY Mission dropped into the Monasteris Hills in Albania, bringing the number of SOE missions in the Balkans to over eighty. The other members were Sergeant John Walker, a demolitions expert from the Royal Army Service Corps, Sergeant Nick Munro, Pioneer Corps, a Canadian-naturalized Croat who was to act as interpreter, and Corporal James Shannon, Royal Signals, their wireless transmitter (W/T) operator.

Their brief was as follows:

- To make their way with the aid of Yugoslav Partisans to the Bulgarian border.
- To establish relations with the Bulgarian Partisans who were believed to be in large numbers in the frontier regions and to contact the Fatherland Front Organisation (OF).
- To equip and organise Bulgar Partisans in the Frontier regions.
- Eventually to proceed into Bulgaria and, in conjunction with the OF, to prepare dropping grounds and reception areas for stores, equipment and other missions; and to organize and coordinate such activities against the Germans and the Fascist war machine in Bulgaria.

Although they would have been aware of the Italian surrender earlier in the month, they probably did not know about the establishment of the Albanian National Committee under German sponsorship, on 15 September, which governed Greater Albania until a formal Albanian government under a Regency Council was established on 3 November that year. If they had, they may well have chosen a different route.

The following précis is from a detailed narrative lodged in the SOE MULLIGATAWNY files. Although this narrative is mysteriously written in the first person, Major Davies never returned from Bulgaria, so possibly it is best construed as a composite report based on signals sent and received, and debriefs from other SOE teams who were in contact with the mission. There are some curious discrepancies in it which suggest that the author was not completely au fait with the political geography of the time, especially the post-1941 borders of Albania, Serbia and Bulgaria.[26]

The MULLIGATAWNY Mission:
20 September –13 October 1943

The first ten days of the Mission were spent in establishing W/T contact with Cairo, purchasing mules to carry its radio equipment[27] and hiring the all-important mule men. On the evening of 30 September, it set out for Macedonian Partisan HQ with a mule train of twelve animals, carrying the equipment of the DONKEY-WRENCH Mission (an Albanian country section mission consisting of Captain Macdonald and operator) which had gone ahead earlier travelling light, in addition to its own.

The first night the mission bivouacked at Trebinje and on 1 October, after a twelve-hour march, it arrived in the late afternoon at Balauci, a village just south of the Struga-Elbasan road. Here it cautiously crossed the road about one mile from a German post.

After bivouacking in a small village in the hills, it crossed the Albanian-Macedonian Frontier[28] at an altitude of about 2,000 ft and after a bad march of nine hours over rough mountain tracks finally reached Belica. The villagers at Belica were nervous lest the Germans at Struga should be attracted by the Mission's presence and so, taking four local guides, the Mission set off again that same night. The route from Belica lay through Vevcani and then straight up the main Struga-Debar road to a village just short of Lukovo, where the party arrived all in at 0400 hours on 3 October and went to sleep in the local school.

On 5 October, the Mission reached Macedonian Partisan HQ at Crvena Voda. Here Davies met Svetozar Vukmanovic, better known as 'Tempo' (one of Tito's Partisan generals, later to be his chief representative in eastern Serbia), and established his HQ in a school overlooking the Botun-Godivje road. He spent the next few days in conference with Tempo for it proved impossible to reach Bulgaria by the route originally contemplated (Prilep to Kyustendil), and therefore it was eventually decided to go via the longer route over the hills north of Skopje to Trn.

Three days after its arrival, news reached the Mission that Kičevo[29] had been retaken by Fascist Albanians stiffened by German troops, and that atrocities had been committed. There was also a report that Germans were arming Moslems to the north of Struga and on 12 October firing broke out near the Mission, which continued intermittently throughout the night. Tempo decided to return to Bosnia to explain the whole Macedonian situation to Tito.

The Mission's departure was brought forward by a more determined attack on the night of 13 October when steady MG fire broke out about a mile from the school. Sergeant Walker and Major Davies had to give first aid to a Partisan with a badly wounded leg and the whole party, with an escort of thirty Partisans, accompanied by Tempo and his staff, moved off about midnight.

The account of Davies's march to Crvena Voda given by Stowers Johnson, the author of *Agents Extraordinary*, is so entirely different as to call in question either its veracity or that of the SOE files. According to Johnson, MULLIGATAWNY was dropped at Tservena Voda on 20 September and met by Partisan guides before being taken directly to the HQ of the Macedonian Liberation Army where Tempo and General Apostolki, the military commander of the Macedonian Partisans, were waiting for them. Later that month the British Military Mission supposedly attended a 'Freedom Parade' in Kićevo, a garrison town on the main Titovo-Skopje road; this event is supported by Johnson with a photograph attributed to the Belgrade historical archives.

On the same day as MULLIGATAWNY had dropped, Major

Rootham in the Homolje area of eastern Serbia had been joined by a 'Capt Patterson' – in reality Captain W. Petro-Pavlovsky of the Bulgarian Army – whose brief was to infiltrate into Bulgaria and make contact with the OF. However, Colonel Pavlović, the local area commander, insisted on obtaining Mihailović's permission, which for obvious reasons was not forthcoming. Whether Davies knew of this concurrent attempt to touch base with the Partisans is not recorded.

The MULLIGATAWNY Mission: 14 October–7 December 1943

After three hours' march, the party rested in a disused school. The following day a forced march of fourteen hours through the mountains brought them to Debar, where they lodged in an hotel despite the fact that the town itself was full of Italians.[30] The occupation of Kičevo by the Germans[31] had necessitated a change of route since Davies had originally planned to go via Kičevo, and then to skirt Gestivar and Tetovo on the way north. He now decided, on Partisan advice, to keep to the mountains to the north and north-west, a route which included the passage of the Sar Planina, only once before negotiated by the Partisans. With summits stretching from south to north of 2,753m, 2,582m, 2,748m and 2,615m respectively, this is one of the most rugged and remote ranges in the Balkans, prone to the vicissitudes of the Balkan weather.

On 16 October the mules were sent ahead with a small Partisan escort, which returned that evening with the story that they had only reached the village of Maqellare where all the mules and mule men had been captured. Fortunately it turned out that the mule train had been forwarded under an escort of Bali[32] (Albanian *chetniks*) to the INFLATION Mission (one of the Albanian Country Section missions under Squadron Leader Hands) but only after much of the kit had been pilfered.

The next three days were spent in highly charged negotiations with the Bali and Partisans to secure a route through Peshkoplje and on to Silove, where the Mission arrived on 20 October, having first made contact with Hands, who had warned it on no account to march through the area between Fshat and Bicaj as it was controlled by followers of a local warlord in the pay of the

Germans. The only way forward therefore lay through the wild mountains west of Silove and then north to Shistevo.

From Silove the Mission moved to Radomir and from there a steep climb east brought them across the Albanian-Yugoslav frontier[33] at a point just short of spot height 2,105m where it found four sheep disembowelled by a timber wolf. Continuing their march, the Mission arrived at 1700 hours in a valley north of spot height 2,174m where they decided to spend the night. They then descended to the outskirts of Shistevec where a band of about 100 ruffians suddenly poured over the hill, 'running, shrieking and waving firearms'. After conferring with the village chief, the Mission was able to spend the night in the village, but when they finally moved out Davies knew that he had to avoid inhabited areas as much as possible, and for the next eighteen days the Mission had to stick almost exclusively to a cross-country route where 'sheep tracks were considered a luxury'.

Passing close to Dikance where they were given sour milk and apples, and then Kukoljane, at about 0400 hours they reached a point just short of a pass between spot heights 2,204m and 2,369m where Davies decided to bivouac until daybreak. It was very cold and, although the members of the Mission put on their flying suits and huddled between the rocks, they were unable to keep warm. On 24 October, in a well-concealed dip just over the pass, Corporal Shannon erected an aerial between two rocks and worked a successful 'sked'. This was the last time that MULLIGATAWNY had contact with Cairo for twenty-six days.

Early in the morning of 25 October, the Mission arrived exhausted in a small wood 2 miles north of Bozuvec. Concerned that their route would take them too near to Tetovo,[34] they headed into the moonless mountains. Each mule was supported by Partisans holding head rope and tail, but several pitched over, chucking their loads. One got stuck between two rocks from which it took over an hour and a half to extricate the animal. At 0900 hours on 26 October, the Mission arrived at a small lake 3 miles north of Vejce where it hid all day.

At 1700 hours the column moved off in the direction of spot height 2,640m in rapidly worsening weather and as it travelled along a knife edge at 2,000m, a bad blizzard developed and there was a serious danger of the mules being blown over the precipice.

Indeed, this is what happened the next day when the mule carrying the W/T lost its footing and somersaulted 200 feet down the hill. The rhomboid containing the wireless equipment was pitched another 300 feet, crashing through two clumps of trees en route. Much to the Mission's surprise, there was no serious damage to the set apart from one transmitting valve broken.

From 25 October to 1 November the Mission and their escort stayed in the wood north of Vraniste, eating nothing but meat from the dead mule, apart from one dish of flour soup. Unless a Partisan base was found quickly, their prospects looked bleak. Fortunately, news arrived of a Partisan camp in the area, and on 1 November, after a difficult march in bitterly cold conditions across precipitous country during which a horse fell over a cliff and was killed, the Mission arrived tired and hungry at the Partisan base situated in a wood.

The next five weeks were spent reaching the Crna Trava area of eastern Serbia. The first part of the Mission's route lay across very difficult country to Urosevac, the base of the Kosovo (JANL) Partisan Brigade, and the Lethohija Partisan Brigade, which they reached in the third week of November after making their way along mountain tops with very little food; the valleys were infested with Bulgarian troops and Gendarmerie.

At this point the Mission joined up with BUMBOAT (one of the Yugoslav missions under Captain Dowd) which was operating in the Kosovo area and remained with it until the Crna Trava area was reached. On 2 December, Davies decided to move to a new base to the east of his position and with an escort from 1 Partisan Battalion, made for Kriva Palanka via the Crna Gora Hills. The journey was a hazardous one and involved crossing two valleys, both with roads and railway lines heavily patrolled by enemy troops. On one occasion the Mission was surrounded and nearly captured by the Bulgarians at Kriva Feja but, due to the efforts of their Partisan escort, they managed to avoid the trap.

Yet again, Stowers Johnson's account differs, almost in its entirety. Between 1 and 9 November, a German division reportedly occupied Kičevo, and Tempo and Apostolki, together with the British Mission, were forced to move out of the Ilinden valley; for the next thirteen days they marched across the southern frontier of

Yugoslav Macedonia, skirting north of Lerin and Edessa until they reached Fustani in the Kožuv Mountains near Gevgelija. On 18 December, under pressure from Bulgarian police and militia units, and from the German Eberloss Brigade and 91 Kotpusa, they continued their forced march over the Tserna Reka to the Kozjak Mountains, north-east of Skopje, from where they finally made their way to Crna Trava. How they covered a distance of 130 miles across country in two days is not made clear.

MULLIGATAWNY arrives in Crna Trava area: [35] 8 December 1943–9 January 1944

Eventually the Mission reached the Lepeneal and Morava Rivers and after trouble-free crossings, arrived in the hills north of Kriva Palanka. It was now about 7 December and, after a few days rest, the Mission moved off again in a northerly direction keeping to the west of the Bulgarian border and making for the Crna Trava-Trn area. On 13 December, it finally arrived there, having once more barely escaped capture in another engagement, during which the Partisans used up all their ammunition.

It had been an epic journey by any measure. Eighty-four days on the march, sometimes up to fourteen hours a day (or more usually at night), in heavily patrolled, hostile territory, inhabited by an untrustworthy and cowered populace, was an astonishing achievement. Dodging Albanian, Bulgarian and German troops and Gendarmerie, moving mainly at night across wild and inhospitable country, battered by rain and snow, constantly hungry, always tired and dirty, with blistered feet and louse-ridden uniforms, much of the time out of radio contact, the members of the MULLI-GATAWNY Mission carved themselves a unique chapter in the valiant annals of SOE

Davies's immediate and most pressing needs were supplies of arms, clothing and food, and after urgent requests had been sent to Cairo, sorties were flown on 20 December. The Bulgarians, who had seen and heard planes overhead, made a small drive[36] on 23 December, and in the ensuing battle the Partisans severely mauled the Bulgarian force. But in spite of their victory the Partisans wisely decided to relocate their base and, after burying the bulk of

Hitler with
Admiral Horthy,
Schloss
Klessheim, April
1943.
*(Permission IWM
HU/39515)*

Hitler greets Slovakian Foreign Minister, Vojtech Tuka, April 1943.
(Permission IWM HU/62524)

Lieutenant Colonel Harry 'Perks' Perkins. *(Permission SFC)*

Colonel Bickham Sweet-Escott. *(Permission SFC)*

Lieutenant Colonel Tom Masterton DSO. *(Permission SFC)*

Lieutenant Colonel Peter Boughey OBE. *(Permission SFC)*

Major John Sehmer MBE. *(Permission Jamie Sehmer)*

Major John Coates DSO, Bucharest, 1945. *(Permission Ms Frances Cooley)*

Hitler and King Boris, June 1941. *(Permission IWM HU/39550)*

Major Mostyn Davies DSO. *(Permission Hugo Yorke-Davies)*

Major Frank Thompson MC. *(Permission Dorothy Thompson)*

Bulgarian Partisans in action, September 1943. *(Permission NHM Sofia)*

Bulgarian Partisans from Sredna Gora detachment, 1944. *(Permission NHM Sofia)*

Hitler and Marshal Antonescu, June 1941. *(Permission IWM HU/39556)*

Captain David Russell MC.
(Permission Griselda Cuthbert)

Colonel 'Chas' de Chasterlain DSO OBE.
(Permission SFC)

Major Ivor Porter with Princess Nadia Cantacuzino. *(Permission Ivor Porter)*

their equipment and stores, moved off to Dobropolje where the Partisans began to formulate ambitious plans for attacking the Sukovo bridge of the Nis-Sofia railway line. After a wait of several days in deep snow at Dobropolje the Mission moved nearer towards Bulgaria and, after a short engagement with some 280 Bulgarian troops and paramilitaries, they arrived on 30 December at Crvena Jabuka, less than two hours' march from the Bulgarian frontier. The next day a further drive was launched against the Partisans and the Mission found themselves surrounded by a force of approximately 3,000 troops and Gendarmerie.

Although there had been previous courier contact between the Mission and OF, real contact was not established until the arrival on 4 Januar of two delegates from Sofia using the cover names Ivan[37] (Vlado Trickov) and Gorsho.[38] Gorsho was a wireless expert and both represented the military HQ of the OF in Sofia. Long and detailed conversations took place between the delegates and the Mission but, as the Bulgarians were continually 'on the prowl', the Mission was unable to open any pinpoints and, when Cairo suggested to Davies that Major Thompson of CLARIDGES Mission should be infiltrated to assist him, he was not in a position to accept the Mission. By 9 January, Davies and his men had reached a point half way between Rarovdal and Dobropolje, and were moving by night to avoid the Bulgarian security forces.

SOE files contain a report on these 'conversations' between Trickov and Davies but it bears little semblance to the SOE paper on political problems in Bulgaria which had been circulated two months earlier around key ministries, including the FO. 'The work of this department,' wrote the author, 'would be easier if more was known of the views of the FO on Russian influence in Bulgaria . . . there are rumours about Britain abandoning Bulgaria to the Russian sphere of influence.' On 3 December, the FO came back with a note: 'Our people in Moscow are of the opinion that this programme [that of the OF] is Russian-inspired, as indeed it may well be. Incidentally the OF Committee, so our people inform us, control the scattered bands of resisters within Bulgaria, the leaders of which provide the driving force behind the movement and are undoubtedly Communist.'

Judging by the extracts from Davies's report on his meetings with Trickov, little of this had been passed on to him.

The first information given by Ivan about the composition of the OF indicated that it was divided into a political and military group; the political group, he claimed, was representative of all the Bulgar opposition parties with the exception (at that time) of the Democrats and right-wing Agrarians, since these two parties, though anti-fascist, disapproved of sabotage and similar activities. All the political activities of the OF had been underground since all opposition parties were illegal; the military group consisted, in the weaker areas, of groups of saboteurs and in the stronger areas of Odreds which existed subject to the hazardous life of the mountains, since there was inside Bulgaria no liberated territory.

Up until the beginning of 1944 the chief activities of the movement . . . had been confined to attacking town halls, to destroying records and incriminating documents, and to attacking one or two specific targets etc. For example: the machinery of the Trn gold mines blown up in December '43; the sawmills destroyed at Asenovgrad in November '43; and a munitions dump exploded at Kazanluk in mid December '43. Attacks on communications had been hampered by lack of explosives but a number of trains had already been destroyed by the simple expedient of tearing up the tracks. According to the delegate the whole of Bulgarian was divided into nine zones . . . The delegate assessed their total military strength at 12,000 . . . They stated that they had first-line Odreds (i.e. groups of approx twenty armed men) in the areas of Trn, Botevgrad, Karlovo, Panagyurishte, Troyan, Sevlievo, Haskovo, Asenovgard, Peschera, Razlog and Dupnitsa.

The delegate further stated that the OF enjoyed the backing of such well-known political personalities as Georgiev . . . Mushanov, Staynov, Velchev and Shardanov. The latter, with Georgiev, had been under detention late in '43 but had been set at liberty at the end of the year. One of the key notes of the movement's policy was that, though it was a united front against fascism, each constituent party, within the framework of the organisation, maintained its own separate identity. Ivan listed the activities of the organisation in the following order: first, recruitment of personnel and sabotage in industrial areas;

secondly, penetration and subversion of the Army and police forces; thirdly, action in country villages.

Ivan reported that the finances of the OF were centrally administered from Sofia HQ. Intercomm, however, between Sofia and the various zone HQs or between the zone HQ and the various Odreds was of the most primitive type, usually courier. For example, it took anything up to fifteen days at that time to reach the Yugoslav frontier from Sofia since the couriers had to contend not only with the vigilance of the police but also with the rigours of the winter. The political policy also of the OF was laid down in Sofia and transmitted to the various zone HQs by clandestine press and couriers and thence on to the separate Odreds by word of mouth, zone delegates or covertly printed sheets.

The foreign policy of the OF, said Ivan, was based on the principle of friendship with all peoples. With the USSR, the OF had no direct link since the USSR was still maintaining diplomatic relations with the official Bulgarian government . . . With Tito's HQ, the OF had no official link but there was a permanent delegate, Sergei, who was attached to Macedonian Partisan HQ and he had a voice in all the decisions of the Macedonian Partisans . . . Ivan also claimed that the OF had a delegate stationed at ELAS HQ at Zanthe.

It would appear that SOE, despite the warnings from the FO, chose to take the contents of this report at face value and to gloss over any apparent contradictions. By accepting the OF as a pluralistic, democratic, independent movement rather than the creature of Moscow it was, and by endorsing its strength as 12,000, SOE was able to justify its decision to work alongside it. The truth, as would soon become apparent, was very different.

'Winter is a bad season for guerrillas; the lack of leafy cover, the tracks left behind in the snow, and the difficulty of finding a roof at nights are all against them,' wrote Lieutenant Colonel Jasper Rootham in Serbia in 1943. Mostyn Davies, only a hundred kilometres to his east, experienced identical difficulties.

MULLIGATAWNY waits: 10 January–24 January 1944

By 14 January 1944 the Mission found itself again badly in need of stores and supplies as no sorties had been received since 20 December and it was doubtful if it could remain in that position after 16 January. Cairo explained that everything possible was being done to fly food, clothing and arms, and that the planes were waiting at Bari on top priority but that unfortunately 'met' was still keeping them grounded.

Davies managed to maintain his position for a few more days and on the night of 18/19 January Bari was successful in getting four planes into the air. Unfortunately, there had been confusion about fire signals between the mission and Cairo, and the result was that no fires were lit and the planes therefore returned to their base without making any drops. For the next seven nights, 'met' again kept them grounded and, although the Partisans agreed to remain where they were until 28 January unless attacked, the intention was to move on 29 January to a new pinpoint which would be opened the next night.

At this stage in the narrative, it is worth asking what, if anything, did Mostyn Davies know of the activities of the *chetniks* and their British Mission 20 miles to his west. For the previous six months, Captain Michael Lees had been supporting three brigades of *chetniks* – about 1,000 guerrillas in all – in the area of the Kukavica Mountains, albeit with drops from only four sorties. Several successful sabotage operations had been carried out by Lees on the Belgrade to Slavonika railway line and on the road MSR from the Reich to German forces in Greece. This activity had resulted in the deployment of additional security forces in the area and an increase in the number of fixed installations such as watchtowers, pillboxes and guard posts. Even direr was the impact of the signal Lees had received on 10 December: 'It has been decided to discontinue all support of Mihailović and his forces. Cease all operations. BLOs should plan to evacuate if possible, or make their way to Partisans. Mihailović has not yet been informed. We will instruct you of date to move.'

As to what Tito's Serbian Partisans had been doing in the area, Captain Lees is most illuminating: 'Those on Mount Radan had certainly done little except hinder my operations. If they had carried out any sabotage I should certainly have heard of it. So far I had received only one such report, when they burned the wooden bridge on the Lescovac-Lebane road; a singularly useless operation, as this was only a by-road going no further than Lebane.' It was hardly surprising therefore that Davies entered the area escorted by a group of Macedonian rather than Serbian Partisans. The latter were simply not a force to be reckoned with in this part of Serbia.

In effect, Davies had been sent into a hornets' nest of Wehrmacht troops, *Nedics* (members of General Nedic's security forces), Bulgarian army units and Gendarmerie with the additional hazard of disaffected Chetniks, who had been so summarily dismissed as Allies by the British. Worse still was the fact that it was run by the Germans for although on 17 January 1942 the Bulgarian I Occupation Corps had been ordered by OKW to be responsible for security in the newly annexed zone of eastern Serbia, it remained under the command of the German military commander in Serbia. The Bulgarians' task was to safeguard the railroads, particularly the Belgrade-Nis-Sofia track and the Nis-Skopje track, highways and main industrial centres including mines and supply depots. Any major operation was to be cleared by the Germans.

Around this time, the operational role of MULLIGATAWNY was revised and refined:

Stage One
- The Mission to be established in eastern Serbia or western Bulgaria with a senior representative from OF HQ Sofia attached to it as adviser.
- W/T intercom to be established between the Mission HQ and Sofia, and Sofia and Plovdiv.
- Sorties of arms and ammunition dropped to the Mission as and when conditions allowed and the stores so obtained to be distributed to the Bulgar Partisans.
- The Bulgar Partisans to select from their own ranks certain intelligent men and to send them to Mission HQ to be trained in demolition work.
- Bombing raids by the RAF to be arranged against targets specified by OF HQ Sofia.

Stage Two

- The elementary W/T communications envisaged above to be expanded by the provision of sets to operational zones other than Plovdiv.
- The Mission to move into the interior of Bulgaria as soon as 'liberated territory' near Sofia was in Partisan hands.
- As and when other operational zones inside Bulgaria were sufficiently strong, further Missions to be dropped into those areas for the purpose of speeding up the organization of those zones by direct communication with Cairo.

However in early January, SOE heard that AFHQ had received a telegram from Washington telling them that the OSS representative in Istanbul had reported that a Bulgarian banker, Kouyoumdjeff,[39] had arrived from Sofia to put out feelers about bringing Bulgaria out of the war. The response from SOE was that this would be premature since Bulgaria would be immediately overrun by the Germans. This contradicts the SOE strategy at the time of advocating the bombing of Bulgaria as 'the quickest way to promote resistance in Bulgaria and possibly bring the country out of the war.'[40] A massive raid by 101 US Flying Fortresses on 10 January met with approval by Churchill,[41] who had pronounced that 'the Bulgarians are a peccant people to whom a sharp lesson should be administered.' Far from promoting resistance, the bombing unified the Bulgarian people against the Western Allies and drove them towards their old allies, the Russians.

The advent of these heavy raids over Sofia prompted MI9 to start making plans for the escape of Allied aircrew.[42] Operation INTERVAL, consisting of two sergeants, both by the name of Joseph, in civilian clothes and furnished with all the necessary Bulgarian documents, was to be infiltrated across the Turkish/Bulgarian frontier. However, constant difficulties were met both in procuring the documents and in crossing the frontier, and they did not make it across until September 1944 when they reported to the Allied War Crimes Commission.

At around the same time, American intelligence received a report that the architects of the successful Zveno military coup in 1934, Colonels Velchev and Gheorgiev,[43] were contemplating a *coup d'état* to oust the Regency and its government, and put in its place a government of national unity. This information was passed to Nicholas Momtchiloff, the permanent delegate to the League of Nations in London, but nothing more was heard.

SOE was trapped between the bellicose noises emanating from General Wilson, Commander MEF, and the FO. On 3 February 1944, MEF policy was one of 'giving the maximum possible assistance to all Bulgarian units or individuals who wish to fight Germans' and was duly passed as an instruction on 24 February to Force 133. SOE/OSS operations in Bulgaria were tasked by Wilson 'to stimulate and encourage partisans with maximum possible support, having regard to forces available'. Yet that same day, the Foreign Office sent a memo to Wilson:

> In these circumstances it will not be our advantage either to secure the overthrow of a government which is willing to negotiate or to embarrass its efforts to resist German occupation by creating conditions which will necessitate the employment of troops on internal security duties . . . The OF partakes of the character rather of an instrument of pressure against the present government than of the party with whom we hope ultimately to negotiate.

With such conflicting aims, it was no wonder that Thompson, Davies's successor, was later unable to get the clarification on policy he asked for from Sweet-Escott.

A further hitch occurred when, on 21 April, SAC (Algiers) put all Balkan operations on hold. There were to be no further actions outside Yugoslavia and Albania without prior approval. Thus the decision, which had been endorsed by Wilson, to build up the Bulgarian Partisan movement was reversed; future supplies were to be limited to maintaining existing missions and for intelligence purposes only. In signal traffic between SOE Cairo and SAC Algiers, this policy was reaffirmed both on 10 and 20 May. The fact that this appears never to have been explicitly communicated to the SOE teams on the ground suggests either a light touch on the reigns of command or a deliberate oversight designed to hamper the Partisans and discredit them as a fighting force.

CLARIDGES arrives but so do the Bulgars: 25 January–18 March 1944

The commander of the CLARIDGES mission, Captain Frank Thompson, was a very different character to Major Davies – both in background, age and temperament. Educated at Winchester and Oxford, Thompson had been brought up in a rarefied intellectual atmosphere at the family home at Boars Hill outside Oxford. His father was a respected poet and socialist with a wide circle of friends and neighbours such as Robert Bridges, John Masefield, Gilbert Murray and Sir Arthur Evans. Frank himself showed promise as a poet and his early work had catapulted him into the Oxford undergraduate literary world of the young Iris Murdoch. They were said to have been lovers and certainly a strong affection developed between the two of them, judging from their endearing wartime correspondence.

Like many of his contemporaries, Thompson had been at first enthused and then appalled by the Spanish Civil War and politically traumatized into the Right/Left divide. In 1939, with his disaffection with the political status quo aggravated by the death of his friend Anthony Carritt in Spain, he joined the Communist Party of Great Britain as a disillusioned nineteen year old, hungry for an idealism that would bring radical change. This new affiliation did not prevent him from quitting a glittering university career to join up and, after enlisting on 5 October, he was commissioned on 2 March 1940 in 118 Field Regiment of the Royal Artillery. After two months of regimental duty on the South Coast, Thompson transferred to the top secret Phantom (GHQ Liaison) Signals Squadron and within the year found himself in North Africa with the Eighth Army. It was the start of a peripatetic Army existence which took him to the Levant in May 1942, with tours in Syria and Iraq, then back to North Africa in July before disappearing to Hamadan in the hinterland of Persia for four months. As a gifted linguist, Thompson thrived in these exotic postings, spending much of his time engaged with local characters rather than homesick British officers whose mood was generally maudlin and invariably xenophobic.

In July 1943, Thompson landed in Sicily with the first wave of the Allied invasion force and experienced the horror of coming under artillery and mortar fire on the beachhead at Zig Green.

The mortar shells continued to fall fairly regularly, most accurately. I remember noting one tall lance-corporal striding past me on the left. Just as he overtook me he reeled, his trousers suddenly turning bright red, and a couple of comrades helped him into cover. The blood, touching his sea-drenched slacks, turned them red in an instant, as though with a magic wand. It was an unpleasant sight. Half a minute later the same thing happened to a fellow a few paces in front of us. His trousers turned a bright red, he limped forward, groaning, for a yard or two, then fell on his face . . . I can't honestly say I was frightened during all this – nothing like I have been on other occasions.

He acquitted himself with distinction, although his attitude did not fit with that of a stereotypic Army officer.

In September 1943, Thompson volunteered for service with SOE and was accepted for recruitment training. After completing his parachute training, he was posted to Cairo where he worked on the staff of SOE. Much has been subsequently made of his supposed vocal dissatisfaction with Allied policy towards the Greek communist Partisans – ELAS – but this remains pure conjecture and simply serves to fit the post-war lionization of Thompson by the CBP as a fellow traveller.

Frank Thompson was dropped on the night of 25/26 January 1944, along with W/T Op Watts. Mostyn Davies, who had argued that his arrival was premature, cordially greeted him.

On 29 January, the Mission moved as planned to its new pinpoint (Ruth) and Gorsho returned to Sofia whilst Ivan remained. On the night of 4 February, two planes were able to fly, and all loads were recovered by the Mission and found to be in good condition. The explosives were split, some going to the Sofia zone of the OF for sabotage in the capital, and some being cached for future Bulgar-Serb operations. The Mission then moved to a new pinpoint called Clara, some 5 miles to the south of Ruth, where the next ten days were spent waiting for further sorties which were on priority but unfortunately, once again owing to 'met', the planes were unable to fly.

On 17 February, Gorsho returned from Sofia accompanied by Kamenov, commander of the Sofia zone of the OF. Their journey had taken eleven days.[44] On Gorsho's return, Ivan decided to go back into Bulgaria and stated that he would be replaced by a permanent delegate of the OF. Later Davies heard that he had been killed by a police patrol whilst crossing the frontier. By 25 February it became fairly clear to Cairo that it was very improbable that they would be able to fly the sorties outstanding for February and on the following day they duly informed the Mission.[45] This decision was received with displeasure by the Partisans who still did not appreciate all the difficulties entailed in supplying stores to them; furthermore, their displeasure had been increased by a broadcast from London on the night of 26/27 February, which reviled the whole Bulgarian people as being completely inactive and branded the Bulgarian Army as the passive tool of the Germans.

On 28 February, a further drive was opened by the Bulgarians against the Mission and the Partisans, forcing them to keep on the move. On 4 March, Dragan, the new permanent delegate to the OF, arrived at Mission HQ.[46] His mid-winter journey from Sofia had taken him fifteen days and he was suffering badly from frost-bite. Although Davies explained to him the position about sorties and the difficulties involved in flying under adverse weather conditions, by 8 March bad flying conditions still kept the planes grounded and relations between the Mission and the delegates were becoming strained. Meanwhile the snow was melting fast and enemy groups were marshalling for a big attack.

On 9 March, a Partisan versus police battle broke out at Bistrica and ended two days later with the withdrawal of the Bulgarian police who lost eight men killed. The only Partisan casualties were two men badly wounded. At last, on 14 March, two planes arrived overhead and dropped their supplies. The Mission continued to stand by at the same pinpoint to await the arrival of more and on the night of 17 March one further sortie was successful. From these three sorties all stores were recovered intact. This was in the nick of time since on 18 March the Bulgarian offensive based on Brod opened.[47] The Partisans later estimated the total enemy forces involved, including Chetnik, *Nedic* and Bulgarian troops, was about 25,000 men. In the first phase of the battle, the Partisans achieved some measure of success, but it soon became clear that the strength of the enemy was far greater than had been appreciated.

Late in the afternoon of 18 March, Davies and Thompson decided that the MULLIGATAWNY and CLARIDGES Missions must move at nightfall without their horses. All stores and equipment were buried, with the exception of the W/T set, which was to be carried on the back of a Partisan. On the evening 'sked' of 18 March, Davies informed Cairo that they were likely to be on the run for some days. It was to be his last signal.

The reality of the insidious position of the Missions must have now struck home to Davies, for not only was there no 'liberated territory' in Bulgaria proper for the Partisans to dominate but also there was no resting place here in the newly annexed area inside Serbia. If Mostyn headed west, he would find himself in country controlled by *chetniks*, who had been cut loose by the British the previous September; the nature of any welcome there would be dubious to say the least. To the south and north lay German and Bulgarian army ambushes. To the east, a hostile country stretched into the far distance, with little cover and few supplies.

The last days of MULLIGATAWNY:
19 March–24 March 1944

The events of the next few days were reported to Cairo by Major Thompson over the CLARIDGES set. According to Thompson, at dawn on 19 March the party reached Ruplje where they remained hidden in buildings until noon. Their Partisan escort, nearly 200 strong, concealed themselves in the neighbouring woods but were soon attacked by a large force of Bulgarians and *chetniks* who had succeeded in surrounding their position. The Partisans managed to hold off the enemy until dark and after waiting for about three hours in intense cold, the column, thinking that the enemy had retreated, decided to slip away. They walked straight into another ambush.

The column scattered in complete disorder and Corporal Shannon became separated from the remainder.[48] The Partisan carrying Major Davies's haversack dropped it but Sergeant Walker, though already heavily loaded, had the presence of mind to pick it up, thereby saving the money and maps it contained.

By dawn, the party now about thirty strong, succeeded in

reforming in the area of Bankovce. Corporal Shannon failed to report to the rendezvous and, owing to the proximity of the enemy, the party was forced to go on without him. After reaching a village near the Serb frontier, the march was resumed on the evening of 21 March. Almost immediately after setting out, they ran into an ambush and, after an exchange of MG fire, the column scattered into the woods.

The party was again split up – Sergeants Walker and Munro went off in one direction while Major Davies, Major Thompson and Signalman Watts went off in another. As the latter knew it would be hopeless to cross the Morava without a guide, they decided to head for Crna Trava and lie low there. By the morning of 22 March, they had reached a village where they lay up for the day.

By this time Davies was on the verge of complete exhaustion and his feet were in a very bad condition. Signalman Watts was also exhausted and suffering from acute diarrhoea. Just before dark Davies called Thompson's attention to the fact that the house was being surrounded by armed men who had crept up unobserved in the gathering gloom. The only escape route seemed to be by the windows at the back of the house which looked out on woods some two to three hundred yards away.

Thompson was the first to leave the building and ran for it. Though he was fired on several times, he managed to reach the wood unscathed; there he waited for five minutes during which shooting continued. He watched the window carefully but no one else came through it. Judging from the noise, he later said he thought an attempt was being made to force in the door on the other side of the building. There was a sound of a bursting grenade, followed by silence. This was the last he saw of Davies and Signalman Watts and, being unable to wait any longer, he continued to Crna Trava.

Stowers Johnson's account of the last days of MULLIGATAWNY is considerably more detailed than the SOE mission report. When the German-Bulgarian offensive opened on 15 March, Davies was at Dobropolje. Bulgarian Army units captured Gornje Gare to the north of Dobropolje and destroyed it, thereby forcing the Mission up to the Cemernik massif. From its commanding heights, they soon realized that the enemy's tactics were to encircle the Partisans with a view to their total destruction. The Mission decided to break out and followed the Rupska River to Stojmirova below Ruplje. Here they were ambushed but managed to break contact and headed towards Novo Selo and Dadinica. Finding themselves completely encircled in the Ostrozub valley, Davies ordered his group to dump the heavy equipment and the Mission cached its radio at the opening to the Novo Selo valley by the Rupska River.

Now split into pairs, although Watts stayed with Davies and Thompson, Davies's group with its escort of eight partisans was ambushed a second time 100 metres from Bucje hamlet. Wading chest deep through the river, they successfully extricated themselves and spent the night in a hayrick outside Novo Selo. That day, 21 March, they hid in a cottage in the hamlet of Lesko Palina cottage until moving out at 2200 hours towards the frontier in thick fog. The next day they found shelter in a house at Palojca, where they assessed that the main danger was posed by the *chetniks* in the forests, Bulgarian soldiers and police being more inclined to stick to the roads. On the evening of 24 March, they arrived at Delina Bara and after spending the night in a house, pushed on towards the frontier at Kozarackoj.[49]

It was at this point, according to Stowers Johnson, that Davies decided to return to Novo Selo to retrieve the W/T set. After reaching the area, they lay up in a watermill on the Rupska River and it was here that they were attacked by unknown elements. Thompson was the only member of the Mission to escape. The next day, Partisan forces found Davies wounded and Watts dead. Putting him on a litter, the Partisans carried Davies to Dadinca but he died en route in a ravine at Gerdelicka,[50] near Ruplje, where the Partisans buried him.

In assessing the failure of the Mission, the SOE report states:

One thing above all hampered it – bad weather. For bad weather meant no planes; no planes meant no arms; no arms meant no partisan fighting force and no fighting force meant no achievement against the German or Bulgar forces. One thing is abundantly clear that given arms, under the inspiring and heroic leadership of Major Davies, the mission could have formed a formidable Bulgar partisan force which would have undoubtedly been capable of liberating territory inside

Bulgaria and thus provided a base for future SOE operations. The failure of the mission to do this is the story of the hapless struggle of man against the Gods of the heavens.

Ironically, on 15 May 1944, Davies received a letter from General Paget, C-in-C Middle East Forces: 'I am writing to let you know that I have conferred on you an immediate DSO for your outstanding services in enemy occupied territory.' On 4 May, three days after Thompson's report of the demise of MULLI-GATAWNY had been received by Cairo, Davies was officially reported missing. It came as a great shock to his friend and colleague, Bickham Sweet Escott, who rued the loss of 'a man of great charm and immense dedication'. On 22 November 1944, his category was changed to 'missing believed killed'. His wife was later presented with his DSO by the King at an investiture at Buckingham Palace in 1946.

What had really happened to Corporal Shannon, Major Davies and Signalman Watts? In all likelihood, Corporal Shannon was captured and then shot by Bulgarian security forces.[51] It is apposite to recall what had happened to Lieutenant Smith who had dropped in with Captain Lees six months earlier. Badly wounded in a battle with Bulgar troops, Smith had been rescued by local peasants and hidden in a miller's hut. When the Mission recovered him, they gave him a shot of morphine and he was then able to recall lucidly what had happened to him.

He had been asleep with the rest of the Mission . . . on being awakened by the alarm . . . they came out of the house by the front door . . . [and] saw the last of the Chetniks disappearing into the woods below. They tried to follow but at that very moment the first Bulgar MG opened fire and, catching them bunched together outside the house, had mowed them down. In the first long burst, [Sgt] Thompson was killed outright and Blackmore, Smith and one of the New Zealand sergeants from Sehmer's party were hit, the latter two only in the legs . . . the niceties of war, however, were lost upon the Bulgars. Rushing upon the wounded men they ransacked their pockets and tore off their boots. Smith's leg had been broken by a bullet and, when they tugged at his foot, he fainted with pain.

He came to a few seconds later to find a sergeant leaning over him. As he opened his eyes he heard two single shots followed by a rattling groan from Lindstrom lying just behind him. Before he could open his mouth to say a word, the Bulgar reached down and, taking the automatic from his pocket, spat in his face and fired a shot at his heart. After that Smith could remember nothing else . . . Smith's story was plainly the truth. Contrary to all the rules of war, the Bulgars had murdered our men in cold blood as they lay wounded.

As the sun sank below the horizon Sehmer came out of the cave to tell me that Smith was dead.[52]

SOE concluded that Davies and Watts had most likely been killed by a grenade at the watermill. However, it should be remembered that they had an escort of eight partisans with them and Thompson, when he reached the edge of the wood, recalled hearing firing. So it is possible that either one or both survived the attack, only to die later of wounds or be captured and shot. Major Dugmore of ENTANGLEMENT signalled Cairo in late April that he had received a report that Davies and Watts had been captured by the Bulgarians, held under armed guard and, though seriously wounded, had been shot. Other Partisan rumours current at the time tended to agree with this report.

Mostyn Davies's achievements were little short of heroic. The long march in through some of the most desolate mountains of Southern Europe, in conditions of constant hunger and consistent cold, all the time skirting Albanian, Bulgarian and German security forces and avoiding bands of brigands and *chetniks*, was a test of leadership which Davies magnificently responded to. Once in the Crna Trava area, Davies and his mission were in daily contact with enemy forces and were continually on the move in a bitterly cold and harsh winter landscape. He was not a professional soldier, yet he held the torch of military virtues high. As an amateur diplomat, he excelled in building a vibrant relationship with General Tempo. Above all, he gained the confidence of the Bulgarian Partisans and preserved it, despite the difficulties and vagaries of aerial resupply. His unwitting mistake was to pass on to Cairo the figure of 12,000 Partisans which, in hindsight, proved fictitious. Had the OF given him the correct figure of 2,000, SOE policy makers may well have restrained MULLIGATAWNY and CLARIDGES from ever entering Bulgaria proper.

During Davies's stint in Bulgarian-occupied Serbia, the overall picture of Bulgarian Partisan activity had been disappointing. Although the level of armed resistance increased during the latter part of 1943, and additional numbers of communist émigrés were sent from the USSR, they were too small in number to matter militarily and brought no supplies with them. During this same time, the first so-called large-scale desertion of soldiers of the Bulgarian Army took place, with seventy-five soldiers joining the Partisans in the Yugoslav free zone as the 1st Soldiers Battalion of the Bulgarian Resistance. This however was a trickle and not a flood, given that the Bulgarian Army's manpower was in excess of 800,000.

In trying to remedy the general lack of weaponry among the Partisans (the Partisan armoury at the end of 1943 only consisted of 563 rifles, 314 pistols, thirteen sub-machine guns and nine machine guns), only three of Davies's fifteen requested supply drops during February and the first half of March, materialized. Consequently little changed.

In Bulgaria proper, the Partisans did not enjoy any of the advantages that those in Macedonia did. They had no free zones to flee to, received no supplies from abroad and were subjected to repeated attacks. In early 1944, a special Gendarmerie with its own cavalry and mechanized units was formed with the sole purpose of exterminating the Partisans. Police reprisals against suspected Partisans and their helpers did produce a numbers of new recruits who fled into the mountains, but at the same time the police actions also scared the populace away from helping the Partisans – increasing numbers of Partisans therefore competed for smaller and scarcer sources of food, and hunger became their constant companion. Morale plummeted, with some Partisans deserting and trying to return to their villages. Partisan leaders had to resort to summary execution on charges of desertion. In the 'Anton Ivanov' detachment, Partisans were even executed for having stolen food from one another.

The 'Anton Ivanov' detachment itself was annihilated in March, when 135 of its 153 men were lost in a matter of days, either being killed in action, or captured and executed by the Gendarmerie. At the same time, two members of the Central Committee of the Politburo of the CPB, Hristo Michailov and Vlado Gheorgiev, were killed. That winter saw the number of Partisan actions dwindle to ninety-five in January, although it picked up and increased to 159 in February. As 1944 began, Partisan strength lay at around 2,000 men, a far cry from the grossly inflated number of 12,000 bandied around.

CLARIDGES takes over

After escaping from the watermill, Thompson had waited for five minutes in the wood but, hearing nothing, continued on his own to Crna Trava. He marched all night and at dawn hid in a deserted barn. The next night he approached a village in the Bistrica area where a friendly villager hid him in a mill and put him in touch with the Partisans.[53] For the next two weeks, Thompson's routine alternated between resting and being chased through snow by Bulgarian forces. As his brother, E.P. Thompson, concluded over thirty years later: 'It is my firm impression that the major part of all Bulgarian partisan activity was concerned with a desperate effort at mere survival, at being able to eat, to sleep, to stay – for a day or two more – alive.'

Whilst in Bistrica, Thompson succeeded in contacting Sergeants Walker and Munro on 24 March.[54] With no means of communication with HQ in Cairo, CLARIDGES now moved to the HQ of the ENTANGLEMENT Mission, at that time established to the south of Radovnica (28 miles SSW of Crna Trava), to link up with its new W/T Operator, Sergeant Scott,[55] who was dropped to the ENTANGLEMENT pinpoint on 7 April.[56] Reaching ENTANGLEMENT around 12 April, Thompson and his team remained in the Radovnica-Trigoviste area until the end of April, developing contacts with the Partisans and with the Partisan General Staff.[57]

Towards the end of April reports reached CLARIDGES that Bulgarian troops previously concentrated in the Vranje and Kumanovo areas were about to open an offensive in considerable strength. The Mission therefore decided[58] to move north to the Kalna area, where strong Partisan groups were reportedly established, and reached Kalna ten days later, having passed through the villages of Crna Trava and Dobropolje en route. Here it could supply Bulgarian refugees with arms, clothing and other stores whilst also acting as the supply base to 2 Sofia Brigade.[59]

Early on 12 May, the Bulgar Partisan Chief of Staff[60] informed Thompson that the Partisans were leaving immediately for the Kom area with the intention of moving into central Bulgaria via the Sredna Gora when the moment was opportune. With orders from Cairo to remain with Partisan HQ, it was clear that CLARIDGES would be accompanying the Partisans, including Dragan,[61] who had acted as liaison delegate between the Bulgarian Partisans and CLARIDGES when the Mission was still in Serbia, Ivan, the political leader of the group, and Dencho,[62] the military leader.

CLARIDGES moved out of Kalna village on 13 May and reached Kom two days later. On the night of 13/14 May the column was ambushed by a party of about twenty Bulgarian policemen armed with knives, who had been lying in wait across the track on which the Partisans were moving. In the skirmish that followed, one Partisan was killed and Dencho received three knife wounds; one policeman was stabbed and another taken prisoner. This prisoner stated that he had been recently conscripted into the Bulgar Gendarmerie, adding that he was a married man with children. Since his papers showed him to be unmarried and a member of the Regular Forces, the Partisans smashed his head in with a rifle butt.

The Iskar River was reached early on 17 May at a point due west of a cluster of villages known as Lavatnik. In spite of the constant threats from police patrols and the danger of moving across an open valley in daylight, the river was crossed without incident and the party reached Lavatnik at about 1000 hours. Although it was intended to rest there for a few days and to purchase sufficient food to continue the march, CLARIDGES had been in Lavatnik for less than an hour when reports reached it that one of the police patrols which were known to visit the area daily was already approaching. The Mission was therefore forced to leave the village immediately and throughout the rest of the day was continually on the move with the Partisans, unable to disengage completely from the police patrol, with rearguard actions continuing until dusk.

By evening it was clear that a small company of Bulgarian troops with mortars had outflanked the Partisans to the south and was now lying in wait across their path. Partisan scouts warned the column commander, who was able to by-pass the enemy force and once the Mission and General Staff considered themselves to have outdistanced the enemy, they lay up in a thick wood until about noon the following day. It must be understood at this point that the Mission was without guides and travelling in unfamiliar country. They had been harassed constantly throughout their march from Kom and had had no opportunity for rest or resupply. Moreover, the groups of Partisans which the Mission had banked on contacting had not materialized, and there was the constant danger that wherever the party moved its position might be disclosed by villagers to the Police or Army.

At noon the party was surprised by accurate MG fire from the surrounding hills. It was clear that in spite of the posting of sentries the position was completely encircled and an attempt must be made to break out in force. The General Staff had already moved to the southern edge of the wood,[63] but on account of a large rocky promontory, which was precipitous on its southern edge where it projected from the wooded slopes,[64] CLARIDGES became separated from the main company. In the confusion which followed, Walker and Munro were separated from the rest of the Mission, who moved along the riverbank for approximately half a mile. CLARIDGES was now composed of Thompson, Scott, approximately twelve members of the Bulgarian Partisan staff, and five or six Partisans including three women. Thomson was struck in the back by a bullet whilst making his getaway, but fortunately he was unharmed since the bullet lodged in a dictionary which he was carrying in his pack.

The river was crossed at about 1230 hours and the party succeeded in reaching the cover of a wooded spur some hundred yards further east. From this new position CLARIDGES was able to survey the country in which the ambush had taken place. Whilst in this position the Mission was joined by a Partisan, who said that Walker had crossed the river shortly after the ambush, together with Dencho and one woman Partisan, but no further news was received as to the fate of this party.

At about 1800 hours a Bulgar policeman, walking alone on the far bank of the river, stopped opposite the Mission's hideout to scrutinize the hillside. At that moment one of the Partisans with CLARIDGES had the misfortune to slip from his position. The sound of the falling gravel immediately attracted the attention of the policeman, who raised his rifle and pointed it in the direction from which the sound had come. At once, well-aimed MG fire was opened on the position from many directions, forcing the party to climb the hill and continue eastwards until a suitable hideout could be found. As the bottom of the eastern slopes was reached, a party of Bulgarian troops was seen marching northwards, along a track which the Mission would have to cross. By now considerably exhausted, the Mission and those accompanying it spent the night in thickets on the hilltop.

The following day, 19 May, CLARIDGES remained in hiding, but since it was essential to get food and as some of the members of the party had been wounded, at nightfall the entire party entered a village which lay half a mile to the north. Up to this time the only food with the Mission had been a small quantity of cheese, the remainder of the booty taken from a village just east of Kom some days previously.[65] (The Partisans, on entering this village on the Sofia-Ferdinand road, were informed by the villagers that all the milk in the neighbourhood was commandeered for use in the dairy farms which were employed in making cheese for the Germans. The installations were completely wrecked by the Partisans, and large quantities of cheese were carried off.)

After some provisions had been purchased and the few remaining weapons distributed evenly throughout the party, the Mission and those of its escort still remaining continued their move eastwards with the intention of contacting the Murgash Partisans, with whom they could reorganize and rest. It was soon realized that the group had travelled far too far south and Thompson discussed with Scott whether to return to Kom or continue to move east. In view of the difficulties of recrossing the Iskar River, and since the mission had already penetrated so far into Bulgaria, he decided he should proceed to the Sredna Gora area. To make best possible speed, he and Scott planned that during some subsequent skirmish with the Army or police, they would separate from the remainder of the party and then lie low until it was safe to continue.

At dawn on 31 May, a police post was spotted on a hill 300 yards away, and it was therefore considered unadvisable to make any further movement during daylight. At approximately 1400 hours, a twenty-strong police patrol was seen to move out of the village where bread had been purchased by the Partisans on the previous day and to advance in the direction of the Mission's hideout. Fortunately, it did not attempt to cross the river or approach the place where the Partisans lay hidden.

At 1600 hours, the first bullets fell into the wood. As was their practice on such occasions, the Partisans moved rapidly downhill. Thompson decided that this was the moment for him and Scott to separate from the Partisans – they therefore climbed for a short distance and then moved round the eastern slope of the hill about halfway down its face.[66] Here they were fortunate to find good cover provided by four trees growing close together,[67] surrounded by considerable quantities of dead leaves and broken branches. Thompson and Scott concealed themselves in this position, believing they had a reasonable chance of escaping detection, especially since the Partisans had now become involved in a battle with the Bulgarian troops who had closed on the Partisan position from the north, but were still some distance from the Mission hideout.

Above the noise of small-arms and mortar fire, Thompson and Scott could hear the excited cries of Anna, one of the three women who had remained with the Partisans since the ambush of 18 May. It was later learned by Scott that in spite of painful shrapnel wounds received in this battle, she had shown great courage and had killed several Bulgarian troops with grenades.

Although CLARIDGES did not know it at the time, a small force of enemy troops had entered the copse in which the Mission was sheltering, and were now converging from the east, while a second force advanced from the north, in order to surprise the Partisans in the rear. These troops advanced nearer and nearer without changing direction and when only 10 feet away from the hide, one of the Bulgarian soldiers saw Thompson and Scott. As Scott stood up, the nearest soldier, raising his rifle to his shoulder, took aim at him and fired. Scott saw a small flash in the muzzle piece and the puff of escaping gases but did not feel the bullet strike him. He stood for some moments feeling cautiously over his body for any wound, but was incredulous to find he had not been hit.

Thompson and Scott were then dragged from their hiding place and each was surrounded by an escort of four soldiers. Both men were brutally kicked, punched and hit with pistols and rifle butts until a senior NCO arrived to take charge. The prisoners were led to a military post on the hilltop, where one Partisan was already tied up. Both prisoners had their hands tied behind their backs, Thompson with a belt and Scott with a rope, their wrist being so tightly bound that in a few moments the bonds had cut almost to the bone and the flow of blood to their hands had ceased.

With their hands still tied behind them, the two British prisoners were taken down a hill and led towards the village where the bread had been purchased the previous day.[68] On the way local villagers turned out to swear and spit upon the prisoners. Moreover, those who could get near enough struck Thompson and Scott with their fists. It was later realized by the captives that this attitude of the population and the Army was largely due to the loss of life caused by the Allied bombing of Sofia. It was an attitude with which Thompson and Scott had to contend at all times.

On reaching the village Thompson, who was extremely weak through lack of food and exhaustion, and the ill-treatment he had received since his capture, lost his balance and collapsed. Hauled to his feet, he was led with Scott to a small building where a cursory search and brief interrogation was carried out. At this interrogation, the prisoners were asked their name and rank. They were then taken down to a disused cellar under the house where they were beaten with a rubber truncheon.

Their next interrogation was carried out in the presence of a Bulgarian army officer by a lance corporal who had learnt some English in one of the American schools in Sofia and by means of Thompson's scanty knowledge of Bulgarian.[69] Neither of the two prisoners gave any details but their names, ranks and numbers, and Thompson stressed that in view of the fact that they were both members of HM Forces and were wearing British uniforms,[70] they must be treated as prisoners of war. The military commander assured them this would be so.

After being returned to the cellar for a further two, they were taken in a vehicle to a commandeered school on the outskirts of Sofia.[71] Shortly after their arrival, a Gendarmerie officer, apparently of high rank, came into the room and started the now familiar routine of spitting, kicking and beating. When this formality was over, the officer turned towards a seedy looking man who appeared to be a Russian prisoner and said: 'There you are – what do you think of your ridiculous Allies now?' In the middle of the night, Thompson was taken away for further interrogation. He returned about three hours later and Scott in his turn was taken upstairs to the room which Thompson had just left. Scott noticed before being led upstairs that Thompson looked extremely haggard and was hardly able to stand.

The interrogation which followed was clear-cut and military. There were several men in the room, three of whom were clearly Gestapo representatives. Scott was shown a W/T set which he recognized as his own. There was also a second wireless set which Scott had not seen before, but which his interrogators insisted had been captured in the ambush on 18 May. The question which most interested his interrogators concerned the SOE Signal School in the Middle East. Scott was repeatedly questioned on the whereabouts of the school, who was in charge and the nature of the courses which were being held there. A second point which caused the interrogators much interest concerned the whereabouts of the outstation to which Scott had been signalling, for it was clear from the low frequency shown in his signal plan that the station could not be Cairo or any other area in Egypt. A third question which was often asked during the long interrogation concerned the whereabouts of other British missions operating in the Balkans. Scott avoided replies to all these questions by pointing out that his operation, and all those of the organization to which he belonged, were carried out with the highest degree of secrecy, and that owing to these security measures he was totally ignorant of the activities of other missions.

The following day, 1 June, Scott's request for medical attention for his poisoned arm was granted and he was taken with a small escort to see a military doctor about a mile away. The doctor, who spoke reasonable English, slipped into his conversation a query as to where and how Thompson had learned to speak Bulgarian.[72] Since Scott had been asked this question several times at the interrogation in the early hours of the morning, he realized that the Bulgars attached some importance to the answer and he replied evasively. For the next twenty-four hours the two prisoners were detained in the school.

The following day, whilst being marched to the doctor, a car drew up behind Scott and a German officer instructed the escort to put their prisoner in the back of the car. Scott was then driven to a house about 4 miles south-west of Sofia on the Sofia-Pernik road, where, on arrival, he was taken straight upstairs to the bathroom, which was to be his prison for the next fourteen weeks.

Scott realized that he would almost be certainly ordered to carry on operating his wireless set and reckoned that his best plan would be to accede to this command but not until he had shown disapproval and some resistance. His reasoning was that by operating his set, he stood a good chance of warning Cairo that the Mission had failed, that he and Thompson were being held prisoner, and that the Partisan General Staff had been captured or scattered. By including subtle changes in the writing and sending of his messages, he would indicate to Cairo that he was operating his set under duress.

On 3 June, his fears proved well founded and over the next few days he was subjected to various threats unless he got in wireless communication with Cairo without delay. In order to prevent an appearance of being over-eager, Scott initially refused but by that evening he decided that he would acquiesce, provided that all signals sent and received by his set were shown to him.

About a week later, during which time his set had been operating spasmodically, a Bulgarian officer announced to Scott that Thompson had been shot. When Scott demanded the reasons for shooting a prisoner of war, the officer replied that Thompson was a rebel and that he, Scott, would also be shot unless the reports on his behaviour and cooperation were satisfactory. In an attempt to get further details, Scott asked a Feldwebel to try to obtain some details which might substantiate the story but the NCO would only tell him that Thompson had 'died bravely'.

Until the middle of June,[73] Scott worked his wireless set at spasmodic intervals, after which time the Germans took over the transmissions. Scott continued to be held prisoner in the same house until approximately 5 September 1944 when he was transferred to a civil prison in the western suburbs of Sofia. On 9 September, he was removed from Sofia and sent to join the Allied POW party being evacuated to Turkey.[74]

The shocking fate of CLARIDGES' commander

After Scott's departure, Thompson was taken to the town of Litakovo on 4 June, where after what can only be described as a mock trial, he was taken to the hillside at the top of the village along with a number of Partisans and executed by firing squad under the command of Captain Stoyanov of the Bulgarian Gendarmerie.

The only account of this event is Stowers Johnson's. From 2 to 4 June, Thompson was kept in the village cellar, but on the morning of 5 June, he and the other Partisans were driven through Botevgrad to Litakovo, where he was placed under guard in a side room off the porch of Litakovo town hall, while a trial was in progress in the main hall. Thompson was then brought in and arraigned. After 'the platitudes of so-called justice', the death sentence was read out, and the prisoners were taken away and lined up in front of a special firing squad that had arrived from Sofia. To a man, they raised their clenched fists in 'defiant proclamation of the defeat of Fascism' and then fell before the bullets of the firing squad.

The remains of Frank Thompson were interred with those of the Bulgarian Partisans in a common grave on a hilltop above Litakovo. On 12 November 1944, 'The Litakovo Partisans' were given a ceremonial reburial before a crowd of over 50,000 villagers and peasants from the surrounding countryside. The thirteen men and women were disinterred from their hillside graves and borne in coffins to the top of a hill above the village. Today, an imposing obelisk marks this spot.

A year later, a tablet was erected on the site of the grave, inscribed with the words of Christo Botev, Bulgaria's national poet:

> I may die very young
> But I shall be satisfied
> If my people later say:
> 'He died for justice,
> for justice and for liberty.'

What happened to Sergeants Walker and Munro? Feldwebel Kunchev told Scott in the third week of July that Walker was dead but did not go into any detail. No one told Scott that Munro was dead – merely that he had been found with a W/T transmitter on him in the area of the ambush. A later Partisan report of 5 August stated that the body of Sergeant Munro, together with those of nine Partisans, had been found in the vicinity of the 18 May ambush.

There followed a considerable press and parliamentary campaign by Thompson's parents in an endeavour to induce the WO and the FO to press for drastic action against those Bulgarians responsible for the execution of their son.[75] They also wanted to get hold of his final effects (not possible until the owner was officially 'dead') and to implement his will. On 4 November they placed a 'Missing' notice in *The Times* and later that month, a lengthy article in the *London Evening News*. This caused some consternation with SOE and on 5 December, Lieutenant Colonel David Talbot-Rice wrote to calm the Thompsons: 'Firstly, I do want to assure you that your son's life was not thrown away uselessly . . . It is certainly true that the Partisan effort in Yugoslavia has been far more spectacular in its results, and has indeed produced much more actual activity against the Germans, but the Bulgarian Partisan movement was not a forlorn hope and your son's task was not a hopeless one.'

It transpired after the war that those deemed responsible had indeed been punished. But it was a selective list. Professor Petko Stainov's report of 23 January 1946 to Colonel General S.S. Biriuzov, Deputy Chairman of the Allied Control Commission, stated that 'during the first days of July', Thompson, Munro and Walker and five Partisans were shot at Litakovo on the orders of Captain Stoyanov, commander of a Gendarmerie battalion. This infers that more than a month elapsed since Thompson's capture.[76] If so, where was he held? Likewise, the report indicates that Walker and Munro had both been captured alive. Where were they held? What were the circumstances of their capture?

According to this same report, Captain Stoyanov was executed by 'local administrative authorities' on 11 September 1944.[77] Who gave the order for his execution and, more to the point, who gave the orders to Stoyanov to shoot SOE personnel in the first place? It is extremely unlikely that Stoyanov was acting independently, especially since Tseno Tsoakoff, the mayor of Litakovo, proclaimed Stoyanov 'an honorary citizen' and gave him 30,000 leva from municipal funds. Furthermore there were many senior

Army officers and Gestapo agents involved. The actual 'trial' was conducted by Lieutenant Colonel Manov, the Area Commander, First Army Headquarters, who had interrogated Thompson and Scott at Gorni Bogrov; Stoyanov was ordered to carry out the sentence of the court at Litakovo. Manov was never tried, unlike Stoyanov's five subordinates, who supposedly did the actual shooting. They were tried by the People's Court at Botevgrad in early February 1945, sentenced to death on 7 February and executed the same day.[78]

Was the march of 2 Brigade and its British mission viewed as a precursor to a communist uprising led by an Englishman? If that was the case, then it is understandable if the Bulgarian government saw a need to send a clear message to the British, 'no more missions, no more arms drops to the Partisans'. However, this remains speculation for the Bulgarian authorities have steadfastly denied access to government archives. Maybe it was Dimitrov in Moscow all along; after all, the Russians did not want any SOE-trained partisans in Bulgaria for they had been busy infiltrating their own. We know from Tempo that it was Dimitrov who ordered the Partisan HQ to Plovdiv and put a lieutenant in charge,[79] much to his amazement. We also know it was Dimitrov who urged both brigades to set out from Serbia on what can only be described as vainglorious expeditions. And we know both were destroyed. Even Dimitrov must have known that the sheer numbers of troops, security forces, police and scared villagers were always going to make the plan impossible. How can you take a band of 200 people through enemy territory like that, particularly so close to Sofia? E.P. Thompson summed it up thus in his book *Beyond the Frontier*:

> In fact, of course, no 'explanation' of the defeat is required at all. The explanation, if any, must be as to how the Partisans ever allowed themselves to get into that utterly exposed position. No signals intercept was needed for the Bulgarian authorities to plot their movements. Some two hundred Partisans were threading their way through a countryside thick with informers and police posts; sometimes they moved openly by day, even entering villages for meetings; they had no guides; they had no food; they were only an hour or so

away from Sofia by motorised transport; in the immediate district through which they were passing were some 12,000 troops and armed police. It was a military folly of the first order, justifiable only in terms of a symbolic confrontation.

After the war, in November 1945, a commemoration service was held at Litakovo, attended by senior Bulgarian Army officers and members of the British Military Mission. Seven graves had been laid out, containing the remains of fifty Partisans, and those of Thompson and an American officer. However, in 1947, despite the previously acknowledged fact that he had been fighting with the Partisans, the Bulgarian communist government decided to portray Thompson as an agent provocateur and Mostyn Davies as an 'imperial villain', bent on ensuring the failure of the march of the OF Sofia brigades. If it wasn't Thompson himself, then it was his masters at SOE, suggested General Trunski when he turned to E.P. Thompson in 1979 and pronounced: 'It is said that 2 Sofia Brigade was defeated because the British Mission were reporting daily to Cairo and Cairo was then sending messages to the Bulgarian army as to the route of the march and the locations of the partisans.'

This preposterous stance was later radically revised and Thompson was rehabilitated as a hero of Bulgaria, with his uniform going on display in the Museum of the Revolution and a railway siding near Novi Iskar named after him: 'Tompsun'. A monument to him and a group of Partisans was duly erected at Batuliya village to complete the process of recognition. Much was made of his fleeting membership of the Communist Party of Great Britain, his pronounced and vehement dislike of fascism, his youthful infatuation with fellow communist undergraduate, Iris Murdoch, and his supposed last words, 'Death to fascism', as he clinched his fist in the communist salute; all these epithets served their purpose in creating a legend whilst concealing the truth. Just like Lieutenant Smith, Corporal Shannon, Sergeant Walker, Sergeant Munro, and most likely Major Davies and Signalman Watts, Thompson was shot because he was a British soldier and that was the official policy of the Bulgarian government.

In all likelihood, there wasn't even a 'trial'. Brendan Simms's explanation in his review of E.P. Thompson's *Beyond the Frontier* is speculative: 'The royal Bulgarians executed this captured officer in uniform because they saw him not primarily as an enemy soldier – like Sergeant Scott – but as an ideological warrior and an agent of international communism, akin perhaps to a Soviet commissar.' But as Sergeant Scott himself had realized halfway through his interrogation, if he had refused to operate his set without Thompson being present, then he might have bestowed his own 'usefulness-to-the-enemy' status onto his Commanding Officer and thus saved his life. For sure, if no radios had been recovered by the Bulgarians, Scott would have been shot out of hand.

The fact was that the Gestapo and the Bulgarians saw in Scott a golden counter-intelligence opportunity, which in hindsight looks amazingly naive. They believed that they could 'run' Scott to feed false information to SOE and that his signals to Cairo would be read as genuine. On 12 June, Force 133 advised Istanbul and London that:

> CLARIDGES has come up on air again after a lapse of over three weeks, and given location as Murgash rpt Murgash which is some thirty-five miles North-East of Sofia. Story briefly as follows: CLARIDGES left Serbia for Bulgaria about 19 May with Partisan Bde and was apparently badly ambushed and split on 21 May. Capt Thompson became separated from main body and only Sgt Scott remained with Partisan HQ which eventually fought way through to Murgash. Whereabouts of others is not known.

While it is not possible to state for certainty that SOE rumbled Scott's transmissions from the word go, it is highly likely since Scott had been trained for exactly such contingencies. The CONSERVE Mission signalled Cairo on 14 July that they were in contact with a group of Partisans who had been with Thompson in Bulgaria, and that Thompson and Scott had been captured by Bulgarians, questioned and handed to Gestapo agents.

In one of his letters home in early 1942, the 22-year-old Thompson wrote:

> Indulging in a little introspection myself, I can see how little that practice, when I have given way to it, has affected my life.

How for the most part I have been strolling, with a straw between my teeth, down a winding English lane of impulse and instinct, while in the hedgerows, Scar top and Bledlow, the Dragon School, Winchester and Oxford, memories of Greece and America, were at once the determinants of my course and the friendly onlookers – the goosewort, stitchwort, groundsel and ground ivy. How very rarely have I found myself marching down the streamlined Autobahn of my Socialist theory. In this way I am sure my contribution to life will be more individual if not so forceful . . . I look at it this way. The only thing important, 'immortal' if you like, about a man is his individuality. And his individuality is only of value if it is a spontaneous growth, not messed about by continued psychological kit-inspections.

Unquestionably, Frank Thompson was extraordinarily gifted: a classics scholar, a talented linguist, a passionate and nascent politician and a poet of immense promise. Had he lived, he would most probably have made a lasting contribution to Britain and indeed to Europe as a social democrat. His statement 'that freedom and fascism can't live in the same world, and that the free man, once he realizes this, will always win' would almost certainly have had to be revised to extend to the post-war world of Russian hegemony in Eastern Europe. But this is speculation and a more proper and fitting assessment of Frank Thompson is his service as a British Army officer. His record was exceptional by any standards, with courage and determination his watchwords as a young officer with Phantom Squadron, first in North Africa, then in the Levant and Persia, before culminating in the hazardous and dangerous landing in Sicily in 1943. But it is his service with SOE in Bulgaria that stands out as truly remarkable.

After the dreadful debacle of MULLIGATAWNY and his subsequent escape and evasion at the very limits of human endurance, Thompson showed exemplary fortitude in leading his Mission into Bulgaria proper. He knew the odds were stacked against them, yet as all good soldiers, he obeyed his orders from Cairo to accompany 2 Sofia Brigade to Sredna Gora. The immensely experienced General Tempo tried to dissuade him (Vukmanovic, *Struggle for the Balkans*):

I tried at least to persuade the leader of the British Military Mission, Major Thompson, of the folly of the decision to set off for the interior of Bulgaria towards the Sredna Gora Mountains. I told him that I frankly did not believe the arrival of a brigade in Bulgaria would provoke a general armed uprising. I suggested that his Mission should come along with us and promised that we would be returning to this area within a month at the least, thus enabling him to continue his Mission. He turned down my suggestion, not only because, as a British Army officer, he had to obey orders [his task was to link up with the Bulgarian HQ and the OF which were somewhere in the mountains near Plovdiv] but also because he believed that the situation in Bulgaria was such that the appearance of Bulgarian brigades would set in motion a mass armed uprising.

Nearly thirty-five years later, Major John Henniker-Major[80] wrote to E.P. Thompson:

When I met him, Frank was desperately tired – physically and emotionally; little wonder, after the marches, uncertainties and then Mostyn Davies' death and his narrow escape. So tired that one night when we had to move he went to sleep on the march and fell over a small cliff into a river . . . I liked him very much; he'd suddenly been saddled with the whole responsibility; he was, I think, very exhausted; he had to put up a constant fight to avoid being taken over by the Yugoslavs and to steer a middle course between this and being led off on a lunatic mission by the Bulgarians. I remember meeting the Bulgars with him and forming the impression that I was glad that they were not my prop and stay – a pretty inexperienced and low-level mixture of individual deserters and Communist civilians from the towns . . . Compared to the Yugoslav army they had an unreal and slightly horror-comic air of a brigand army, boastful, mercurial, temperamental and [with] an inexperienced yen to go it alone.

Along the way, he and his men experienced constant danger from enemy patrols, desertion and treachery by their own ilk, instant betrayal from intimidated villagers and peasants, extreme hunger, verminous lice, vicious sores and scratches from moving at night, bleeding, blistered and calloused feet, bitter cold and pernicious wet; yet, not once did he turn back despite ample good reason for doing so after the first ambush on 18 May. He pressed ahead indomitably to complete his task, however remote and impossible it must have seemed on many occasions. Thompson's immortality was indeed his own individuality as he assumed the mantle of leading his mission into the heartlands of Axis Bulgaria, an erstwhile T.E. Lawrence of the Balkans or not.

The other aspect of Thompson's short life which demands recognition is his poetry, which follows the legacy of the First World War poets. In 2003, Trent Editions published *Selected Poems of Frank Thompson*, an anthology put together by his niece, Kate Thompson, herself a poet.

The swansong of SOE in Bulgaria

An objective assessment of Partisan and SOE operations in Bulgaria makes gloomy reading. Thompson and his mission, like that of Davies before him, had achieved little. From the outset, the spring of 1944 had not looked promising for the Partisans: the fate of the 'Anton Ivanov' detachment had been a precursor to the Bulgarian Army's major offensive against the main Partisan groups in the Kalna area in eastern Serbia in late March, when Davies's Mission was destroyed.

The formation in May 1944 of the two Sofia Partisan brigades was more of a propaganda exercise than a military reality. 1 Sofia Brigade, commanded by Trunski, was formed from a few members of the old Trn *odred* and had a strength of about 300. 2 Sofia Brigade, commanded by Dencho Znepolski, comprised the rest of the Trun *odred* and was about 200 strong. Brigades in militaryspeak are meant to be 2,000 to 3,000 strong.

These brigades were expressly raised to let the Bulgarians go over to the offensive, and the British, in cooperation with the Bulgarians and Yugoslavs, came up with an operational plan to establish a free territory that would stretch from Kratovo and Kumanovo in northern Macedonia to Kiustendil in western

Bulgaria, thus giving the Bulgarians a critical 'free zone', on their own soil. It was launched on 25 April 1944, but though the Yugoslavs initially made some gains around Kratovo, the operation ended in total failure and had to be aborted. Without a free zone, any serious incremental expansion of the frontier Partisan brigades became impossible and attention switched to the Partisans in Bulgaria proper. A new brigade, the Chavdar, was formed in April in the Murgash region, north-east of Sofia, and by the end of May had supposedly reached a strength of 437 men, being the largest partisan unit in Bulgaria.

Thus, a slim opportunity for creating a free territory in the Sredna Gora Mountains to the east of Murgash presented itself to the Partisan leadership in Plovdiv – or this may well have been an order from the CPB's Dimitrov in Moscow – and 1 Sofia Brigade under Trunski ('Vassil Levsky' and 'Khristo Botev' battalions) set out for the Rhodopes and Mount Rila area, while 2 Sofia Brigade left the Kalna free zone on its 'Long March' on 13 May, together with Thompson's Mission. The plan was that the Brigade would penetrate into Bulgaria, steer north of the capital, Sofia, then meet up with a number of partisans' detachments in the Sredna Gora Mountains and establish an area of liberated territory where they could receive arms and supplies from British-directed airdrops.

It was a half-baked idea as the outcome demonstrated. When 1 Brigade reached the Yelovishna Mountains by 9 May, its numbers had dwindled. Eighty-five went off with Demirevski and some with the 3rd battalion; the rest were killed, wounded or melted away during intense attacks. As for 2 Brigade, having lost any vestige of surprise, its critical link-up with the Botevgrad Chavdar Brigade was never a credible idea, for its three battalions, without a single automatic weapon between them, had been wiped out in early May. As the SOE account vividly records, 2 Brigade was easily intercepted by Bulgarian Army and Gendarmerie units. Most of the Partisans were killed during the ensuing skirmishes, others being captured and shot over the following days, Frank Thompson among them.

No further efforts were made by SOE to support the Partisans within Bulgaria proper with one curious exception. In the SOE archives, there is the following account.[81] On 3 May 1944, Major

Harrington and his W/T operator – the JAMPUFF Mission – were dropped into the mountains south of Plovdiv.

> All through May, June and July, Harrington searched for the elusive Bulgarian partisans . . . final success came on 27 August. That evening at dusk, Harrington and his companion advancing with caution – for they were on Bulgarian soil – came upon a man and two boys armed with rusty Turkish rifles and bandoliers, who said they were the outpost of a Bulgarian Partisan brigade . . . (who were on inspection) a tattered and valiant band of outlaws.[82]

Delighted by the arrival of the British, the Partisans soon became disillusioned when no weapons or rations were dropped, courtesy of the change in HMG policy. Meanwhile Harrington and his W/T operator continued to subsist on a diet of beech-nut stew. The Mission supposedly ended up in Sofia.

In August 1944, a two-man OSS team was dropped into Bulgaria near the Greek border where they joined the *andartes* in harassing withdrawing German troops. They reached Sofia in mid-September, linking up with another OSS team which had arrived by road from Istanbul. They were then able to arrange the evacuation of over 300 airmen before being given their own marching orders by the Russians on 24 September.

In Bulgarian-occupied Thrace, there were a number of SOE Missions, JAMPUFF (Major Harrington), MIZZEN (Captain MacPherson), RED HERRING (Major Kitcat) and VAUDE-VILLE (Major Micklethwaite who had originally been dropped into Epirus in Greece). Micklethwaite recalled that 'the Bulgars are not a gentle people' and that 'one had to sleep out and keep moving'. When he finally returned after eighteen months behind enemy lines, he weighed in at 9 stone compared to the 13 he had left at. They were joined by TRIATIC (Major Riddle) on the night of 9/10 August, who met up with Harrington and MacPherson at Ailias, where they all promptly came under heavy attack from Bulgar troops and split up.

TRIATIC embarked on a five-day march with its escort of

Greek *andartes*, 'subsisting on the occasional maize (cooked on the cob) found in some of the fields, and also a small bag of oatmeal, a bag of sugar and two tins of bacon which [I] shared out among the party of twenty-six'. Vigorous Bulgarian counter-Partisan operations continued until 7 September, forcing the mission to hide up in a forest south of the Nestos River. But events had now overtaken the Mission and on 3 September it received instructions from Cairo that no further arms dropped were to be flown. After Riddle joined Micklethwaite at Drama, the two officers found themselves on a mission to Sofia on 16 September as representatives of Capetano Antones,[83] the leader of the 2,000-strong Greek Nationalists bands (known as '*capetanos*') east of the Strymon River.

Their task was to broker an agreement between the Greek nationalists and the Bulgarians, who by this time had changed sides and were fighting the Germans, yet continuing to harass the *andartes*. For the next three weeks they played a virtually impossible game of keeping the two sides apart, for since 18 September the Bulgarians had been under orders from the Russians who were supporting communist-only resistance movements. At the same time, a power struggle had erupted between EDES and ELAS in Greece. Before long, a chorus of complaint from the FO had reached SOE that its officers were exceeding their authority and Riddle and Micklethwaite were extracted on the night of 8 October. The 'C' military mission, whose task was to oversee withdrawal of Bulgarian troops from Greek territory, withdrew on 24 November, signalling the end of all British military activity in Bulgaria. Micklethwaite had been in the field in enemy occupied territory for a staggering 480 days.

Macpherson's MIZZEN Mission eventually reached Plovdiv but there was little to do. 'So ended our mission in Bulgaria. It is unlikely that anything we did altered the course of events in that tip of Europe and, to that extent, we achieved nothing.'[84]

Guy Micklethwaite put it bluntly: 'We failed to subvert any Bulgarians.'

Norman Davies, the author of a number of internal SOE historical reports and himself a distinguished member of the organization, wrote:

In the strictly military field the Partisans cannot be considered to have done much, as their contribution consisted rather in the propagation of general internal disorder than in fighting the Germans or sabotaging war material or industry. The effect of their activities on the government was, however, immense. The savage reprisals carried out against them became a constant subject of controversy and played a considerable part in the fall of the Bozhilov government. The limited support which we were able to give them was therefore amply repaid.

In her study on *British Policy in South-East Europe in the Second World War*, Elizabeth Barker's conclusion is somewhat different:

The British efforts to arm and develop a Bulgarian Partisan force with Yugoslav Partisan help was therefore a failure. But the fault did not lie with the Yugoslav Partisans or the British – except in so far as they imagined, quite wrongly, that the Bulgarian partisans would turn out to have the same qualities and fighting capacity as the Yugoslavs. The cause was to be found in the internal Bulgarian situation and the internal dispute inside the Bulgarian Communist party.

The outcome of the Second World War in Bulgaria

Reliable sources show that by the early summer of 1944, the Partisans had increased in strength to around 4,000 men, armed with 2,026 rifles, 190 sub-machine guns, 885 pistols, 1,000 hand grenades, 129 light and medium, and sixteen heavy machine guns. German suggestions that the Partisans had 12,000 men by 1 July 1944 can more or less be dismissed as probably based on deliberate Bulgarian overstatement. For example, the 'Vassil Levsky' Partisan detachment (one of the most active units) in the Varna region was estimated at 3,000 men, whereas its real strength was 150. To put these numbers in perspective, the strength of the Bulgarian Army was nearly one million, excluding that of the Gendarmerie and police.

After the death of King Boris, the Bulgarian government had put out a number of feelers to the Americans in October 1943, but the Allied terms were deemed to be too harsh, namely unconditional surrender, the evacuation of all occupied territory and an Allied occupation. The loss of Macedonia and Thrace was unthinkable and Filov responded by saying that Bulgaria would join the Allies when the Allies joined Bulgaria by landing in the Balkans. Such wishful thinking soon petered out when the Soviets started to apply pressure on Bulgaria to leave the Axis. The message was stark – if she did not break with Germany, then she would ultimately be occupied by the Russians; yet if she did go along with the Russians, then she would suffer German occupation like the Hungarians in March 1944. Prime Minister Bozhilov sensibly resigned at this point and his successor, Ivan Bagryanov, began the delicate process of extricating Bulgaria from the war.

The formation of a new government on 1 June 1944, together with events on the front line (the Normandy invasion on 6 June 1944, for one) led to negotiations between the government, the OF and the other official opposition parties as to how to take Bulgaria out of the war. In the end, Soviet successes on the Eastern Front against Romania, and the fact that the government continued to crack down on the Partisans, brought a halt to the negotiations. From the OF's point of view, the end was in sight and the result a foregone conclusion.

Consequently, the level of Partisan activity greatly increased, averaging 500 incidents in both July and August, though most on a tiny scale. Nothing had really changed since 1941 – the Partisans remained more a potential threat than an actual one. For instance, in their most dramatic raid during June 1944, when Partisans stopped a train on the Kazanluk-Plovdiv railway line and ordered all the crew and passengers to detrain (among them Peter Kioseivanov, vice president of the *sûbranie*), they were interrupted and put to flight by soldiers sent out to rescue the train. The relief force consisted of four soldiers and one lieutenant!

During August, the Bulgarian government tried to save itself as best it could. While peace envoys were sent to the Western Allies, the only ones with whom Bulgaria was at war, Bulgaria declared herself neutral in the war between the Soviet Union and Germany. At the same time, determined to remove the Partisans from the post-war political equation before the Soviets turned up on the

Bulgarian northern border, the government came up with a twin-track initiative. A general amnesty was announced for all Partisans, while simultaneously a massive anti-Partisan offensive by the Army, police and Gendarmerie, named 'Operation Bogdan', was launched during August. It was far too late.

On 20 August, the Soviets launched their Iasi-Chisinau offensive and steamrolled through the Sixth German and Third and Fourth Romanian Armies. Russian troops rolled south, and on 30 August the USSR announced that it did not recognize the Bulgarian declaration of neutrality, at the same time requesting permission to enter Bulgarian territory. Soviet planes dropped weapons to the Bulgarian Partisans for the first time in late August, thus making it possible for the Partisans to form their first so-called division, the 1st 'Sofia' People's Liberation Division.

On 2 September 1944 the government of Ivan Bagryanov, threatened by the Red Army's arrival on Bulgaria's doorstep, stepped down and the new pro-Western government under Konstantin Muraviev, the nephew of the famous Agrarian Stamboliiski, ordered the Army not to resist advancing Soviet forces, demanded that the Wehrmacht leave, broke the union with Germany and started negotiations with NOVA commander Dobri Terpeshev. The right-wing Agrarians, who controlled the government, offered the OF some ministerial seats. In the meantime, the police and the Army continued to pursue the Partisans, unchecked by the civil power. But the advance of Soviet troops gave the communists confidence and they reject the Agrarians' offer.

A Bulgarian declaration of war against Germany was considered on 5 September, but was postponed when the Prime Minister was advised by Minister of War Marinov, who was secretly in league with the communists, to wait seventy-two hours to enable him to withdraw Bulgarian forces from the occupied areas. This gave the OF the time it needed to organize a coup and take over the government. Communist-organized demonstrations had already begun the day before and Partisan units now began converging on the capital. Between 6 and 9 September 1944, 170 Bulgarian towns and villages were 'captured' by the Partisans. On 9 September, Terpeshev ordered all Partisans to descend from the mountains and seize power across Bulgaria.

While communist-led strikes and demonstrations multiplied, the

'Shopski' Partisan detachment was smuggled into Sofia and placed directly under the Partisan General Staff. All over the country, army units were proving to be increasingly unreliable – not surprising considering that Marinov was in cahoots with the communists. Under the impression that Soviet troops were massing on the border, the Chief of Police was also quickly won over. By now, on the eve of a coup that would bring the communist-led OF to power, the Partisans probably had around 10,000 men, up from 4,000 only three months earlier.

As the last German units rolled west out of Bulgaria, the government finally declared war on the Reich at 6.00 pm on 7 September, effective as from 6.00 pm the next day. But it was too late, for the Soviets had by now declared war on Bulgaria and their tanks were crossing the Danube. As Bulgarian troops, surrounded by German forces in Macedonia, fought their way back to the old borders of Bulgaria, the Partisans struck with surgical skill. Most of the Sofia garrison had been dispersed to outlying towns as a result of Allied bombing, leaving the capital dangerously undefended. Early on 9 September, Partisans and sympathizers from the Sofia Military Academy and army units led by Zveno officers occupied key points throughout the city, and with the help of Marinov, the Partisans were let into the War Ministry, where the government was gathered. Its ministers were arrested and a new government of the OF was appointed on 9 September with 'the old coup maker' Kimon Gh eorgiev as prime minister, five Zveno, four agrarian, three social democrat and four communist ministers.

Three Bulgarian armies (some 455,000 strong in total) under Russian command deployed from Sofia to Niš and Skopje with the strategic task of blocking the German forces withdrawing from Greece. Southern and eastern Serbia and Macedonia were liberated within a month, and the 130,000-strong Bulgarian First Army continued on into Hungary, crossing into Austria in April 1945. Contact was established with the British Eighth Army in the town of Klagenfurt on 8 May 1945, the day the Nazi government in Germany capitulated. Over 32,000 Bulgarian soldiers had been killed in this campaign.

Soon after the OF's seizure of power, former Partisans were placed in key positions in the Bulgarian military to ensure its loyalty, including the formation of a new all-Partisan force, the

People's Guard, which was restricted to operations in Bulgaria only. They also created a People's Militia, which replaced the Bulgarian police, and, together with local OF committees, allegedly participated in mass retaliation which took the lives of thousands of former civil servants, policemen and gendarmes.

In February 1945, the former regents, royal advisers, all members of the last *sûbranie*, and all who had served in government since 1941, were arrested. Most were found guilty, and over a hundred were taken out and executed in groups of twenty on the same night that the verdicts were announced. A year later, after a journalist had revealed at a staged trial that there had been a military conspiracy, 2,000 officers were purged from the Army list. Though it would take them another two years with People's courts, the grotesque trial and judicial execution of Nikola Petkov, the leader of BANU, and rigged elections before they had completely eliminated the democratic opposition, the communists were in power and were not to relinquish it for forty-six years.

But there was another twist to the story. Georgi Dimitrov, the *eminence gris* behind the OF, who had returned from Moscow on 7 November 1945 and instantly 'won' the elections of 18 November, spoke at a press conference in Bucharest at the end of January 1948 at which he extolled the idea of an eventual formation of a federation comprising Albania, Yugoslavia, Bulgaria, Romania, Hungary, Poland, Czechoslovakia and even Greece. Stalin was appalled and *Pravda* swiftly denounced Dimitrov's 'problematical and fantastic federations and confederations'.

As with the other resistance groups who fought the Germans and their allies in the Second World War, the courage and heroism of the Bulgarian Partisan has never been in doubt. Indeed it could be argued that given Bulgaria's status as an ally of Germany and to all extents a non-combatant party, thus freeing up its army for internal security duties, the challenge facing Bulgarian Partisans was commensurately harder. Meagerly armed, poorly provisioned, always on the run, facing relentless hardships and virtually guaranteed a short life span, Bulgaria's Partisans demonstrated a fatalistic, almost crazy courage, similar to that of their revolutionary icon, Vassil Levsky. Post-1989 research comes out with a number of around 9,900 Partisans.[85] In clashes with government and German forces, and as a result of torture and executions, 9,140 Partisans and

20,070 *yatatsi*[86] died between 1941 and 1944; 1,590 people were sentenced to death for revolutionary activity. Frank Thompson would have been proud to be one of their number, irrespective of the outcome.

Notes for Part Two

1. Turkish soldiers.
2. Yeşilköy, 11 kms to the west of Istanbul on the Sea of Marmara.
3. Founded on 1 November 1893 in Salonika by three young men, whose aim was to rid Macedonia of Ottoman rule. In 1895, the movement split into the Supremacists (or EO – External Organization) who wanted to liberate Macedonia and join it with Bulgaria and the Internal Organization (IO) who wanted an autonomous self-governing Macedonia (the IO then split again with Sandanski's Social Agrarians).
4. Ferdinand went to live in Germany and died in Hamburg in 1948.
5. 85 per cent of the population were subsistence farmers.
6. IMRO had murdered Alexander Dimitrov, the War Minister in 1921.
7. Gheorgiev became known as 'the old coupmaker' because of his involvement in the coups of 1923, 1934 and 1944.
8. Described in one of Allen Dulles's telegrams as 'a little known archaeologist who strayed into politics'. In fact, he had been the Rector of Sofia University and President of the Bulgarian Academy of Sciences.
9. 6 per cent to Italy and a mere 1 per cent to France.
10. To maintain order in their new territories, the Bulgarians despatched their V Corps, composed of three divisions, to Yugoslav Macedonia, and their I Corps to Thrace. A subsequent reassignment of units, with the movement of Bulgarian troops into the German zone in Yugoslavia, brought the I Corps to south-eastern Serbia and a provisional 'Aegean Corps' to Thrace. Later in the war, the Aegean Corps was relieved by the II Corps.
11. Armed clashes were recorded on 13 August, and 16 and 30 October 1942.
12. The police 'most wanted' CPB list had 291 names on it in total.
13. A small mountain range in central Bulgaria. Its highest peak is around 5,000 ft.
14. Amery was peddling the agenda of the Serb Peasant Party, who were close to Banu.
15. Alongside Tom Masterson, Julius Hanau, Bill Hudson, Bill Bailey, Hugh Seton-Watson and Julian Amery.
16. Dimitrov used his initials to differentiate himself from his namesake, G.M. Dimitrov, the leader of the CPB who was based in Moscow during the Second World War.
17. The name of their newspaper, in English 'Zenith'.
18. The Agrarian politician Dimitri Matsankiev also left Bulgaria with SOE help.
19. He disappeared without trace on 26 February.
20. Tomasevich, *The Chetniks*.
21. Germany, Italy and Hungary all invaded Yugoslavia.

22. Brigadier Eddie Myers DSO.
23. By May 1943, it was estimated that there were about 17,000 *andartes* of whom most were affiliated to ELAS.
24. John Jestyn Llewellin, 1st and last Baron Llewellin, was Member of Parliament for Middlesex, Uxbridge Division, between 1929 and 1945 and held the office of Lord of the Admiralty between 1937 and 1939. Made Privy Counsellor in 1941, he was chairman of the British Supply Council between 1942 and 1945.
25. Davies had taken up Spanish when he was at Oxford and attended a course at Saragossa University. He was a member of an Oxbridge delegation which visited Buenos Aires University.
26. Hitler and Mussolini created a Greater Albania during the Second World War. Western Macedonia, or Illirida, as the Albanians called it, was annexed to Greater Albania, with Debar, Tetovo, Gostivar, Struga, and Kičevo being the key Macedonian towns and cities. From 29 June 1941 to October 1944, Debar remained part of Greater Albania. The Italians placed the town under Italian and Albanian occupation, and civil and military administration. The Macedonian Slavic population fled to the Bulgarian base in Struga due to the terror and intimidation by local Albanian and Italian occupation forces. Indeed, they established their own neighbourhood in Skopje called Debarsko Maalo. [Close up lines in this note]
27. Although the Type 3 Mk.II (also known as B2) radio set was delivered in a small suitcase/containers with a total weight of 14.5 kg, the battery charging equipment including a generator and fuel cans needed up to sixteen pack animals to transport it.
28. For some reason, the author of this report is referring to the pre-1939 Albanian-Macedonian frontier. When the Italians took control of Albania in 1940, they extended the frontier into Macedonia in order to mollify those Albanians with aspirations for a Greater Albania. All border crossings and customs/police posts were consequently adjusted and remained in place until 1944.
29. First captured by Partisans on 11 September 1943, it changed hands six times before the end of the war.
30. Debar had been in Italian-controlled Greater Albania for two years and from 8 September 1943 to November 1944, German forces occupied the Italian areas once Italy surrendered. Debar thus would have come under German occupation around this time. The security forces there consisted of: [Close up lines in this note]
    - 16 Police (Albanians). [Close up bullet point lines/bullet points to be aligned vertically, as per Note 34]
    - 300 German occupation troops.
    - 500 members of the Balli Kombëtar.
    - 200 Albanian gendarmes.
    - 7 German Gestapo agents.
31. The Germans did not retake Kičevo until the first week of November 1943.
32. Presumably this refers to the Balli Kombëtar (National Front). Formed in

September 1942 as an Albanian anti-Italian movement, they were soon switched into an anti-communist one and worked alongside the Germans. It seems odd that they were prepared to work with the British.

33. The author is referring to the pre-1941 frontier.

34. Tetovo:
   - The Italian military intelligence service, OVRA (Opera Volantario per la Regressione Dell' Autifasismo), formed the 'Ljuboten' Battalion in Tetovo made up of ethnic Albanians from the region. The unit was given the task of uncovering, questioning and annihilating any resistance to the occupation. After the surrender of Italy on 8 September 1943, the German forces retained it, allowing its members to keep their Italian-issued uniforms and weapons. Members of the Balli Kombetar later joined the battalion.
   - Police force (Albanians): 16.
   - Balli Kombetar: 2,000.
   - 250 Albanian Gendarmerie units (armed police).
   - An 800-strong Albanian Security Battalion.
   - 80 Albanian troops and border guards.
     (The total number of Albanian police and paramilitary units in Tetovo during the German occupation was 4,646].

35. In Slavic, Black Valley. Crna is sometimes spelt Tserna in English.

36. A 'drive' was similar to a pheasant shoot. Blocking forces were deployed, i.e. the 'guns', and then a line of troops would sweep across the hills or fields like 'beaters', driving the Partisans into the gun line and cut-off groups.

37. Vlado Trickov.

38. Delcho Simov.

39. Also spelt Kouyoumdjian (Armenian), Kuyumdjiski or Kuyumdzhiisky, he was badged as a colonel in the US Army by OSS.

40. There were seven bombing raids on Sofia during the time of the British Missions:
   - 14 November 1943: 91 Mitchell bombers destroyed 47 buildings and killed 59 people.
   - 24 November 1943: 60 Liberator bombers destroyed 87 buildings and killed 5 people.
   - 10 December 1943: 120 aircraft bombed the industrial zone and airport. 11 people were killed.
   - 20 December 1943: Over 113 buildings were destroyed and 64 people were killed.
   - 30 December 1943: Sofia railway junction was bombed; 70 people died.
   - 10 January 1944: Sofia bombed round the clock by Allied bombers.
   - 17 April 1944: 350 bombers destroyed over 749 buildings in the city. The results of this aerial bombardment were 12,564 buildings damaged (2,670 completely destroyed), 1,374 people killed and 1,743 injured.

41. On 25 December, Churchill informed the Deputy PM and the Foreign Office that 'we have decided to make the heaviest possible air attack on Sofia at first favourable opportunity with a view, inter alia, of influencing political reactions in Bulgaria.'

42. In September 1944, 303 US aircrew arrived at Aleppo by train from Bulgaria.

43. Later became Minister of Defence in OF 1944 government.

44. When Gorsho returned, he brought a request for 20 million leva for mobilizing the OF militia, subversion in the Army and similar tasks. SOE Cairo decided that the full amount should be sent. 7 million leva were successfully dropped to the Mission in March but a further 12 million leva, dropped later, fell over the wrong area and was irretrievably lost.

45. Davies had asked for 30, which were scaled down to 20: he received 2.

46. Dragan requested official recognition of OF by HMG. Major Davies endorsed it, stating he was confident that the OF represented the only really strong resistance movement in Bulgaria and that, in view of its wide platform of democratic aims (especially as they asserted that their intention was merely to set up a provisional government until such time as full democratic elections could be held), official support would not run counter to the aims of the Atlantic Charter. The decision of HM Minister Resident ME was that the FO could not commit themselves to the support of any one political party and the Mission was duly informed.

47. Operation Radan, a joint German-Bulgarian offensive, was launched on 15 March. The Bulgarian Fifth Army under General Bojdev at Vranje and 14th Infantry Division under Colonel Nedev at Skopje combined with 600 German troops at Surdulica and Belo Polje with tanks and AA batteries to encircle the Partisan forces in the Cemernik massif area. Source: Stowers Johnson.

48. Both Dugmore and Saunders sent reports to Cairo from Partisans that Corporal Shannon had been shot/executed around 20 March by Bulgarian police/Army. However, Thompson stated that he heard from a courier on 26 March that Corporal Shannon was safe with a Partisan column in Vranje area. So Thompson sat tight and sent for him but no trace was found of him despite repeated Partisan patrols.

49. This makes little sense since, once across the frontier, the Mission would be in Serbia where the Chetniks controlled the forests and the valleys were garrisoned by Germans and Bulgarian troops.

50. A Partisan column returning from Jablanica reported that two Englishmen, one of whom was wounded, had been seen under guard at Gerdelicka.

51. Signal to Cairo from Thompson, 21 April: a British soldier and 150 Partisans had been shot in Crna Trava area. On 2 May, Major Dugmore reported that Shannon had been captured by the Bulgars in the Ruplje area and executed by them on or about 21 March.

52. Lees, *Special Operations Executed*, pp. 66–7.

53. Stowers Johnson's account relates that on 24/25 March, Thompson lived in a snow-hole until he was found by a shepherd who fetched a Partisan patrol. They took him to Dobrotina across the South Morava River and, avoiding

Bela Breg, went on to Tula village close to the rallying point at Kukavica Mountain. News then came that Munro and Walker were at Bistrica, so Thompson and his party recrossed the Morava, moved to the north of Predejane and they all met up not far from Dobro Polje.

54. This outline of the history of the CLARIDGES mission is based on field signals and the evidence of Sergeant Scott, mission W/T operator.

55. Kenneth Scott, as a member of the TA, had been mobilized in 1939 and became a signals sergeant in the King's Royal Rifle Corps. Volunteering for special duties, he was transferred to the Royal Signals and trained for behind-the-lines operations at the SOE Middle East Training School for wireless operators. CLARIDGES was his first Mission. He died in 2008.

56. From a Force 133 signal from Major Seton-Watson on 7 May 1944, we know that Scott was dropped on 8 April without his ciphers or signals plans. As at 7 May, CLARIDGES had been unable to contact Cairo direct. It turned out that Scott's signal plans were dropped to the JAMPUFF Mission on 3 May.

57. Johnson has Thompson already at Radovnica on 1 April where he met Squadron Leader Kenneth Syers, a former journalist working for Military Intelligence HQ MEF. Syers had apparently brought a briefing for Thompson with him.

58. On 29 April, Thompson sent a request to Captain Seton-Watson in Cairo for a 'general directive soonest'. It was not forthcoming.

59. Thompson, worried about the amount of equipment the British missions needed to operate their radios, thereby slowing down movement and exposing Partisan forces to needless risk, made the point: 'We have eight Englishmen here now which is thought maximum handicap for any Partisan unit entered for Spring gallop.'

60. Vlado Trichkov.

61. Gorcha (Goco) Gopin.

62. Dencho Znepolski.

63. Marina Murtvina (*Long Wood*).

64. Kamen Kurvav.

65. The Partisan column had ransacked the milk factory at Berkovitsa and then destroyed it. This precipitous action would have alerted the police and Gendarmerie and ruined any chance of a covert approach march.

66. This is a patch of woodland to the north of Eleshina village.

67. Near village of Sarantsi.

68. Eleshina.

69. In a letter to the Thompson family dated 16 August 1946, Stefan Vimitriff claimed he was the interpreter when the British pair was interrogated by the commander of the Gendarmerie. Thompson, very weak, collapsed and had to be given water to revive him. When he was searched, they found he had forty-two gold sovereigns, maps, and two hand grenades. The questioning went on for three hours and Vimitreff interpreted throughout (Thompson did not speak in Bulgarian). From there the prisoners were taken to Bohovo (8 kms from Eleshina); Vimitriff volunteered to come along as interpreter but was told they had one waiting.

70. The British Army issue battle dress (BD) uniforms worn by Thompson since 5 January and by Scott since 7 April in all likelihood would have had serious wear and tear and would have either been augmented or replaced by locally sourced clothing.

71. Gorni Bogrov.

72. Letter to his parents, 21 January 1943: 'The last half-hour I've been listening to a communist station, probably Russian, talking to Bulgaria. Bulgarian is, of course, nearer to Russian than most Slavonic languages. I can understand about as much of it as I can Ukrainian, and the language of communists is much the same in all Slavonic languages.' This, of course, was before he dropped into Bulgaria.

73. There is a note from Force 133 dated 12 June which says that 'CLARIDGES has been on air again after a lapse of over three weeks.' It states:
    - Left Serbia about 19 May with Partisan Brigade.
    - Badly ambushed and split up on 21 May.
    - Thompson separated from main body.
    - Only Scott remained with partisan HQ which got through to Murgach.

74. Scott was awarded a well deserved DCM (Other Ranks equivalent of DSO).

75. Their sponsor was Lord Vansittart. Coincidentally he had it in for Kenneth Syers (*Hansard*, April 1950): 'I come now to the daisy of the bunch (of communists), Kenneth Syers. Mr Syers, in the early stages of the war, was Secretary of the Oxford Regional Committee for the Education of His Majesty's Forces. Curiously enough, I heard some complaints that they were getting only Communist stuff and Communist lecturers. I was not surprised; I thought that other people might have shared that view. From there he went to Cairo, and from Cairo he went to Yugoslavia. Now he is a pamphlet writer for the Bureau of Current Affairs at No. 117, Piccadilly. As late as April, 1949 – again, please note the date – this Mr Syers wrote a pamphlet, which was published by the Bureau, on Eastern Europe. I went through the stuff – I wade through an awful lot of muck every week – and this really was an extraordinary compound of ignorance and mendacity.'

76. General Apostolski told Major Strachey that he had received a letter from Bulgaria which indicated Thompson was still alive about the middle of July.

77. Johnson says he committed suicide.

78. Stoyan Lazarov, Angel Tzanishev, Boris Vassilev, Ilia Tupankov, Gorcho Mladenov, Ilia Dushanski. There are six names in all.

79. Lieutenant Dicho Petrov, former commander of the Botev detachment in Macedonia, was well known to Tempo.

80. Later Lord Henniker.

81. This account is contradicted by the diary of the TRIATIC Mission which records that JAMPUFF and MIZZEN decided to head north from Polygrephyrion into Bulgaria on 14 August.

82. This account may or may not be true but the TRIATIC mission reported that in mid-August it made contact in the Batak region, south-west of

Plovdiv, with the Partisans; of an alleged strength of 500, no more than fifty to sixty had firearms.

83. He was actually a Turk but described by SOE as 'a good Greek patriot'.
84. Macpherson, *Blurred Recollections 1939–1946.*
85. On the evening of the 9 September 1944 coup, functioning units were one Partisan division, nine Partisan brigades, thirty-seven Partisan detachments and an unknown number of *cheta* and combat groups.
86. Village supporters.

Part Three

Romania

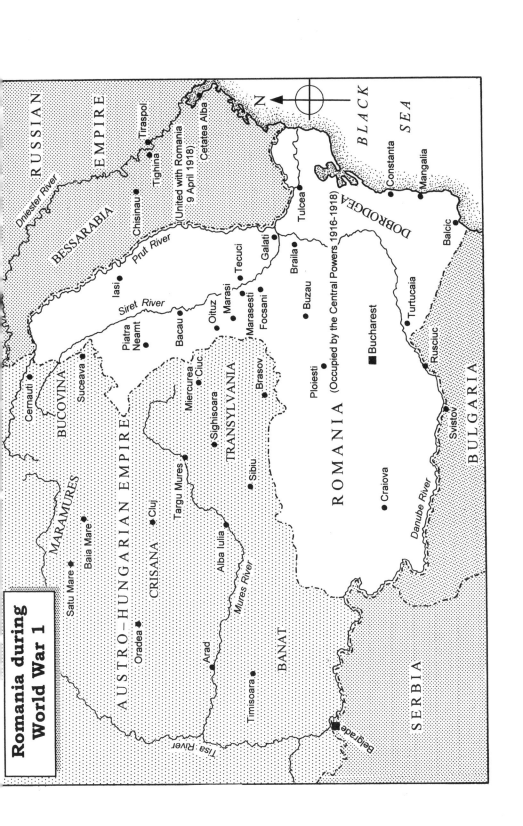

Romania during World War 1

RUSSIAN EMPIRE

Dniester River

BESSARABIA

Tiraspol

Tighina

Chisinau

(United with Romania 9 April 1918)

Cetatea Alba

BLACK SEA

Prut River

Tulcea

DOBRODGEA

Constanta

Mangalia

Iasi

Siret River

Galati

Braila

Balcic

Cernauti

BUCOVINA

Suceava

Piatra Neamt

Bacau

Oituz

Marasi

Tecuci

Marasesti

Focsani

Buzau

Turtucaia

Rusciuc

N

Satu Mare

MARAMURES

Baia Mare

Oradea

CRISANA

Cluj

Targu Mures

Miercurea Ciuc

Sighisoara

TRANSYLVANIA

Sibiu

Brasov

Ploiesti

ROMANIA (Occupied by the Central Powers 1916-1918)

Bucharest

Svistov

BULGARIA

AUSTRO–HUNGARIAN EMPIRE

Arad

Alba Iulia

Mures River

Timisoara

BANAT

Tisa River

Belgrade

Craiova

Danube River

SERBIA

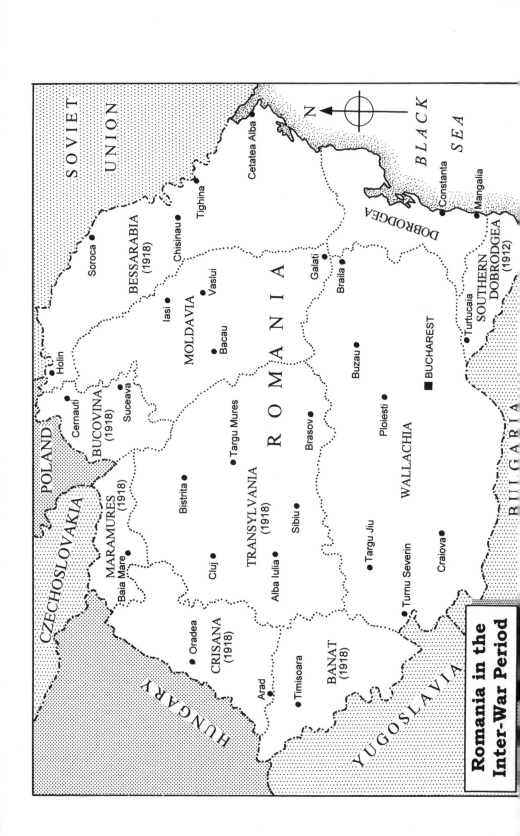

Romania in the Inter-War Period

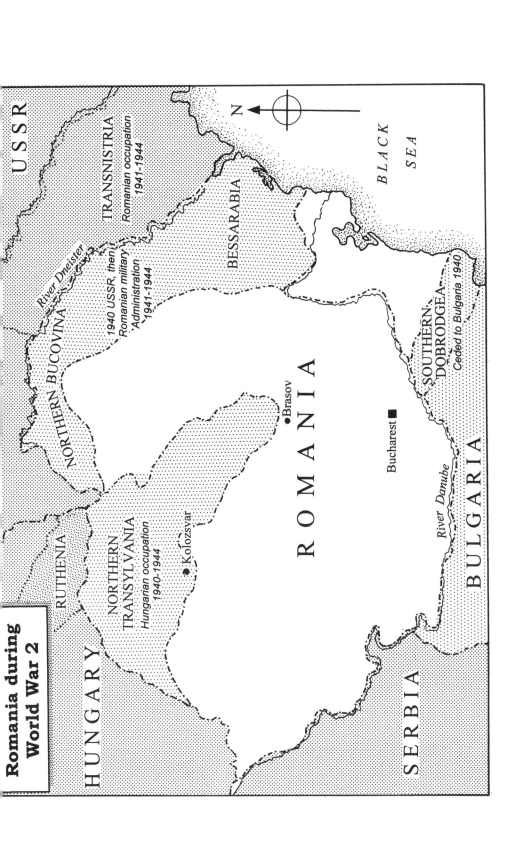

Romania during World War 2

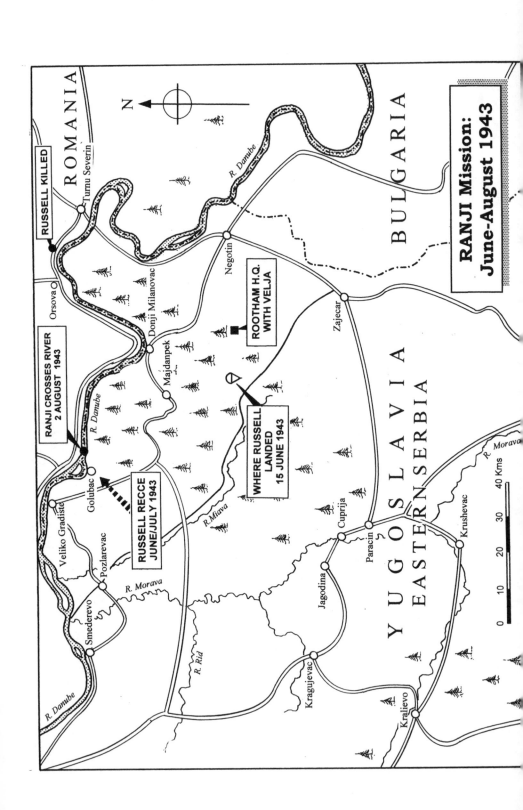

RANJI Mission:
June–August 1943

ROMANIA

BULGARIA

RUSSELL KILLED

Turnu Severin

R. Danube

Orsova

Negotin

Donji Milanovac

RANJI CROSSES RIVER
2 AUGUST 1943

ROOTHAM H.Q.
WITH VELJA

Majdanpek

Zajecar

R. Danube

WHERE RUSSELL
LANDED
15 JUNE 1943

Golubac

RUSSELL RECCE
JUNE/JULY 1943

Veliko Gradiste

R. Miava

Pozlarevac

Krushevac

R. Morava

Cuprija

Smederevo

R. Morava

Paracin

Jagodina

40 Kms

R. Rid

Kragujevac

30

20

Y U G O S L A V I A

E A S T E R N   S E R B I A

10

R. Danube

Kraljevo

0

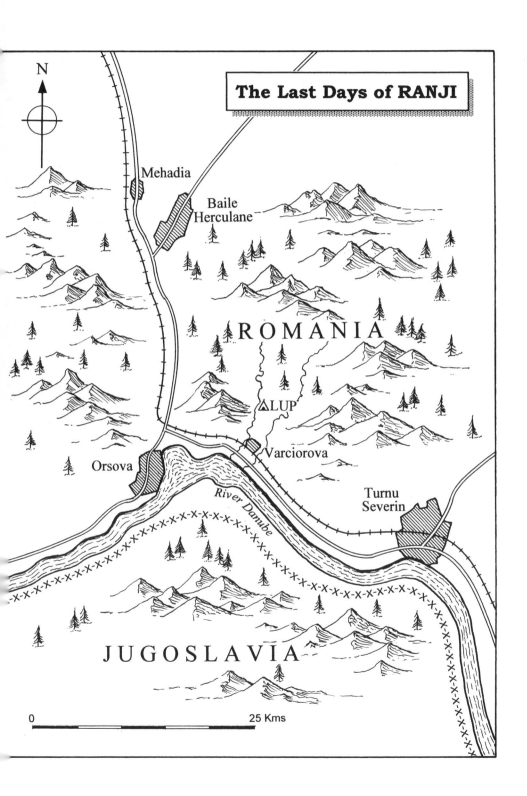

The Last Days of RANJI

N

Mehadia

Baile
Herculane

ROMANIA

△LUP

Varciorova

Orsova

Turnu
Severin

River Danube

JUGOSLAVIA

0   25 Kms

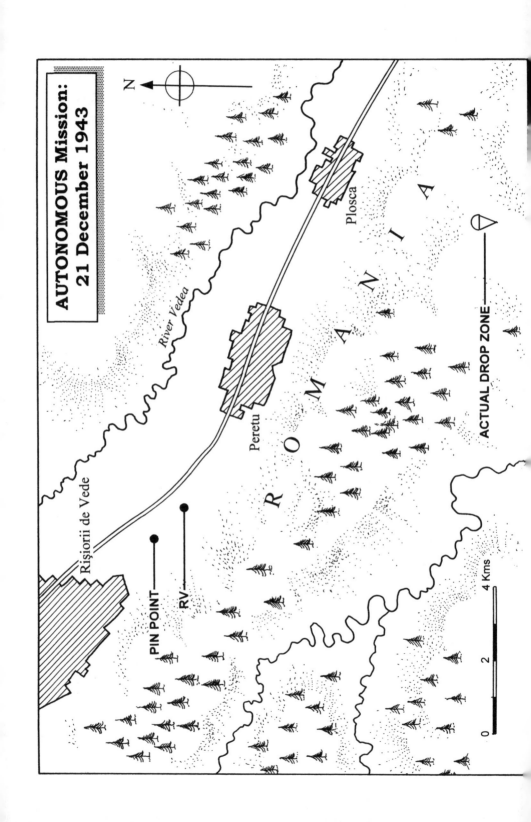

AUTONOMOUS Mission: 21 December 1943

N

River Vedea

Rişiorii de Vede

Peretu

Plosca

R O M A N I A

PIN POINT

RV

ACTUAL DROP ZONE

0   2   4 Kms

SOE Personnel in Romania

✞ *Killed in action/executed/died of wounds*

The early saboteurs

Lt Col William Harris-Burland OBE
Capt Max Despard DSO RN
Major W.R. Young (Section D)
Maj James Davidson-Houston
Messrs Treachy and Anderson
Hon Col George Taylor CBE, formerly Section D Balkan desk.
John Toyne

SOE Missions

RANJI
✞ Capt David Russell MC
W/T Op Nicolae Țurcanu (REGINALD)
Sgt Maj Petre Mihai

Drop zone reception at Homolje:
Lt Col Jasper Rootham
Lt 'Micky' Hargreaves
Sgt C.E.Hall W/T Op

AUTONOMOUS
Lt Col 'Chas' de Chastelain DSO OBE
Maj Ivor Porter
Maj Charles Maydwell (withdrawn by SOE London)
Capt Silviu Mețianu

Trained by not deployed:
George Georgescu
Victor Moldovan

SOE Romanian network

Rica Georgescu (JOCKEY)
Lygia Georgescu
Gheorghiu

Popovici's original wireless network:
Bălan
Jean Beza
Augustin Vişa

Constantin ('Dinu') Mircea
Prince Matei Ghica – the pilot
Alecu Ionescu
Capt Radu Protopopescu
Alecu Ştefănescu
Alexander Cretsianu
Sandu Racotta (STEFAN)
Sandu Ioan ([SORIN)

MI9 in Romania

Operation MANTILLA (1943)
Sgt Liova Bokovsky
Sgt Arich Fichman

Operation GOULASH (May 1944)
Sgt Isaac Măcărescu
Sgt Levy/Raico Depesco

Operation SCHNITZEL (June 1944)
Shaika Trachtenberg
Isaac Ben Ephraim

Operation RAVIOLI
Sarah Braverman

Operation DOINER

SOE in Romania

Prelude: the Resurrection of a Nation

The emergence of Romania as a modern nation state began in 1859 when the two Principalities of Wallachia and Moldavia merged to form the United Principalities. Both had been Ottoman vassal states since the fifteenth century,[1] and had been governed by princes whose first allegiance was to the Sultan, next their pocket and lastly their people. Walking this political tightrope involved balance and cunning, for the Ottoman Empire was but one of three that collided against each other in the Romanian lands; the Habsburg Emperor and the Russian Tsar both regarded the Principalities as within their sphere of influence.

Separate to the Principalities was Transylvania which lay behind the Carpathians to the north-west. Part of Hungary since the twelfth century, it had achieved semi-autonomy in the seventeenth century as a result of the Ottoman occupation of Hungary proper, although like Wallachia and Moldavia it was trapped between conflicting empires, in its case the Habsburgs and the Ottomans. For a fleeting moment in the summer of 1600, the Wallachian Prince, Michael the Brave, had united the three principalities, a result of opportunism and luck rather than of design. Nevertheless, this brief 'reunification' of Romania became a symbol of Romanian nationalism over the coming centuries, particularly after the eighteenth century when Romanians accounted for the majority of the Transylvanian population. Ruled by a firm hand from Vienna after the expulsion of the Ottoman armies in 1699, and by an even firmer hand from Budapest after the *augsleich* of 1866, Transylvanian secession from Austria-Hungary became the focus of Romanian nationalism.

As the 1866 constitution was being drawn up, Prime Minister Brătianu went in search of a suitable candidate for *Domnitor* (Head of State), a position which required the occupant to 'rule but not govern'. It turned out that there were few takers and he returned with the unimportant 27-year-old Prince Karl, younger brother of the Prince of Sigmaringen-Hohenzollern, whose small but not insignificant state had recently been absorbed into the Kingdom of Prussia in 1850. But he had chosen well for King Carol I, as he became in 1881 after the Treaty of Berlin,[2] was a man of courage, principle and integrity, the very characteristics that were needed as an antidote to the centuries of corruption and self-interest that had been the hallmark of previous rulers. In his forty-eight years of rule, Carol helped the nascent Romanian state grow into a prestigious and economically successful country, despite the setbacks of rural unrest in Wallachia in 1888 and Moldavia in 1907, which were symptoms of the economic stranglehold still exerted by the land-owning ruling classes.

Towards the end of his reign, as war clouds gathered over Europe, Carol's inclination was to enter the coming war on the side of the Central Powers, even though the Romanian government sided with the Triple Entente.[3] Carol had previously signed a secret treaty in 1883 which had linked Romania with the Triple Alliance (1882)[4] and although the treaty was to be activated only in case of attack from Imperial Russia towards one of the treaty's members, Carol was convinced that the spirit of the treaty required him to support Germany.

An emergency meeting was held with members of the government where Carol told them about the secret treaty and shared his views with them. In the event, Carol I's death shortly afterwards postponed any decision and his heir, Prince Ferdinand, under the influence of his English wife, Marie of Edinburgh, chose the more prudent path of neutrality. However, pro-Allied voices prevailed and on 27 August 1916, with the prize of Transylvania dangled in front of her,[5] Romania entered the war against Germany and Austria-Hungary. It was a disaster. Battlefield defeat led to the loss of Bucharest in December 1916 and, following the defection of Russia in 1917, there was no option left other than to sign a humiliating peace treaty in 1918,[6] including handing over the leases of its oilfields for ninety years. Although ratified by the Senate and Chamber of Deputies, King Ferdinand obstinately refused to sign it, an act which later on exonerated Romania on the grounds that an unsigned treaty was not binding.

Fortuitously re-entering the war on 10 November 1918,

Romania emerged twenty-four hours later on the winning side and though some voices were raised about her dismal performance which breached both the spirit and the letter of the agreement with the Allies, Romania emerged triumphant. The union of the regions of Transylvania, Maramureş,[7] Crişana[8] and Banat[9] with the Old Kingdom of Romania was ratified in 1920 by the Treaty of Trianon, which recognized the sovereignty of Romania over these regions and settled the border between the new independent Republic of Hungary and the Kingdom of Romania. The union with Romania of Bucovina, formerly part of Austria-Hungary, and Bessarabia, a province of Russia since 1812, was ratified in 1920 by the Treaty of Versailles. Romania had also recently acquired the southern Dobrudja territory from Bulgaria as a result of its participation in the Second Balkan War in 1913; this award was allowed to stand. It was an extraordinary turnaround. *România Mare*, the dream of a Greater Romania, was now a reality, but at a cost – over 250,000 Romanian soldiers gave their lives,[10] and a further 120,000 were wounded, a high price for a country of just 7.5 million people.

The interwar years and a Playboy King, Carol II

The addition of these new provinces, as well as the adoption of universal suffrage in 1919, revolutionized Romanian political life. The Conservative Party disappeared, a victim of its former pro-German policies, and its place on the right was filled by two parties: the Liberal party of Ionel Brătianu, a staunch defender of the urban middle class; and the People's League led by General Averescu. Beginning in 1920, several fiercely anti-Semitic and ultra-nationalist factions broke away from the People's League to form the National Christian Party led by Alexander Cuza, and the National Christian Defence League of Corneliu Codreanu. In the centre of the political spectrum sat the Peasant Party of Ion Mihalache and the former Transylvanian Romanian National Party, led by Iuliu Maniu. On the left, the Socialist Party enjoyed brief popularity due to the post-war economic difficulties and a failing currency, but it fractured in May 1921, when a large number of its members joined the Third International and formed the Romanian Communist Party.

Until the death of King Ferdinand I in 1927, Romania was subjected to a series of governments that distinguished themselves by rigging elections and using violence to exert pressure on any opposition. The elections of November 1919 were the first and the only elections to take place under almost fair conditions, even though the Hungarian, German, and Macedonian national minorities – making up over 20 percent of the population – could not participate. The elections resulted in a majority for Mihalache's Peasant Party and Maniu's Transylvanian Party. The Transylvanian, Alexandru Vaida-Voevod, a former deputy to the Hungarian parliament, formed a mixed cabinet, but the King dismissed it after three months because of growing peasant and worker unrest.

Power passed to General Averescu of the People's League, who quickly dissolved the Chamber of Deputies, and organized new elections which, after careful preparation, gave his party 224 of the 369 seats. Despite a successful programme of rural land reform, the General's style was increasingly dictatorial, causing unease with the political classes and faint alarm with the King, who removed him in January 1922 and appointed Ionel Brătianu's Liberals in his place. The new government promptly organized new elections that resulted in an overwhelming majority for the Liberals, who took 260 of the 360 seats. The new parliament, with the connivance of Ferdinand, adopted a revised constitution in 1923, which allowed the King to retain sweeping executive powers. Parliament was divided into two chambers exercising legislative power: the Senate was elected by a two-step ballot and included hereditary members; while the representatives of the Chamber of Deputies were elected to four-year terms by universal male suffrage. The same parliament passed a new electoral law which automatically gave half of the seats to the party obtaining 40 per cent of the votes, with the rest distributed proportionally among the other parties, including the majority party. This assured the party with 40 per cent of the vote of gaining at least three-fifths of the seats. The electoral law went into effect in time for the 1927 elections, and propelled the Liberals to a resounding victory, aided by unprecedented heavy-handed police tactics at the hustings and the ballot box. These methods shocked Maniu and the other Romanian politicians of Transylvania, who were accustomed to the honest and efficient

Hungarian administration of only a few years before. They began to rue the day they had thrown their lot in with Bucharest.

The authority of the Royal Family had begun to slip due to the antics of Crown Prince Carol. In flagrant disregard for the constitution, he had eloped with a commoner, Zizi Lambrino, and married her in Odessa in 1918, deserting his military post in the process. After the marriage was annulled in 1919, he fell into line and married Princess Helen of Greece in Athens in 1921, but soon reverted to his old ways and began an affair with a divorcee, Magda Lupescu.

Once more he abdicated and renounced his rights to the throne in favour of his six-year-old son, Prince Michael, who became King on the death of his grandfather in 1927, under the Regency headed by his uncle, Prince Nicholas. Carol divorced Queen Helen in 1928 and retired to France to plan his return, this time on his own terms rather than his mother's, whom he viewed with filial loathing. For it had been Queen Marie who had sent Prince Stirbey, reputedly her lover, and Colonel Joe Boyle, reputedly another lover, to remonstrate with the love-struck Carol after his elopement with Zizi Lambrino. And it was the Queen who referred to King Michael as 'Our Tender and Lovely Hope', a phrase that seriously irked Carol.

The National Peasant Party chose to use the Regency period to move against the Liberals, given Ionel Brătianu's death on 24 November 1927. But little changed since his brother, Vintil, seamlessly succeeded him. The Brătianu dynasty, at the centre of Romanian politics since the inception of the new country, was not leaving the stage without a fight. Persecution of the opposition continued to intensify and in January 1928 the National Peasant deputies boycotted parliament and later organized large demonstrations in the streets of Bucharest. At the same time, the nationalist far right increased its activities, most notably the brutal attacks on Jews. The streets became a Roman circus, staging bloody clashes between various political groups. The Regency reluctantly agreed to dismiss the Liberal cabinet and, on 10 November, Maniu formed a National Peasant cabinet, with Transylvania prominently represented by Vaida-Voevod as Minister of the Interior, and Popovici in charge of the Finance Ministry. 'Ours is the triumph of Constitutionalism over Despotism. We shall immediately call for the dissolution of Parliament and hold new, honest elections,' proclaimed Maniu. Having learnt a trick or two from the opposition, on 15 December 1928, Maniu's supporters emerged victorious from the elections, with 78 per cent of the votes and 348 seats, compared to the Liberals' ten.

His manifesto was admirable and ambitious. First, to convert Romania into an Anglo-Saxon democracy, retaining a constitutional monarchy. Second, to accord to Romania's national minorities a just and lawful share in government. Third, to de-bureaucratize and decentralize the government, granting more authority to provinces and municipalities. Fourth, to reform the notoriously corrupt and unscrupulous police, Gendarmerie and Secret Service. Fifth, to reconstruct the national economy, providing broad measures of agricultural and industrial assistance. Sixth, to reverse the previous government's policy of shutting out foreign capital, and welcome inward investment under appropriate and lenient restrictions.

Such a programme needed at least a decade to take root and time was not on Maniu's side. The Wall Street crash of 1929 heralded the start of the Great Depression and Maniu, bent on shoring up the weakening position of his cabinet, proposed to Carol that he should return to Romania and lead the nation through the dark and difficult days that lay ahead, with the proviso that Maniu would remain in office at his side. The story of Carol's arrival had a Ruritanian twist to it as *The Times* reported on 8 June:

The events of the last forty-eight hours have succeeded one another with bewildering rapidity. On Friday evening Prince Carol's arrival was still unknown, today he is not only here but has already been proclaimed King instead of his son. The coup d'Etat has been completely successful . . . What had happened was that Prince Carol had left Paris on Thursday nominally for Sigmaringen, the home of his father's family, but instead of going to Sigmaringen he had gone to Munich, where on Friday morning he embarked in a French aeroplane for Romania. It is believed that the pilot did not know the identity of his passenger. The aeroplane had to come down for petrol at Oradia in Transylvania. Meanwhile, Colonel Precup, a Carolist artillery officer at Cluj, warned by telegram of his coming, informed the Commander of Military Aviation at Cluj, who sent out two aeroplanes to meet the Prince. One of them discovered his aeroplane near Oradia and took up the Prince as passenger. In this way he arrived at Cluj about 8.00 pm. Here he embarked in another military aeroplane, which landed him at the Bucharest aerodrome soon after ten o'clock. The Prince immediately went to Cotroceni, a suburb of Bucharest, where there is a Royal residence, and visited the barracks of the two battalions of Chasseurs which are stationed there. Here he was enthusiastically welcomed by the officers, and at the head of both battalions, with band playing and colours flying, the Prince went to the Palace, where Prince Nicholas was waiting to receive him. The two brothers embraced on the steps of the Palace, while the troops drawn up in the courtyard cheered frantically. Soon after Dr Maniu, the Prime Minister, arrived.

The timing of his arrival may well have been last minute for it was on the same Friday that his mother, Queen Marie, had left Romania for Oberammergau. Should she have still been inside the country, it is highly unlikely that Carol would have risked a return. With Magda Lupescu soon installed in Cotroceni Palace, Romania now entered a period of intense uncertainty, drifting ever closer to the extreme Right. As Hugh Seton-Watson saw it:[11] 'Superficially brilliant and basically ignorant, gifted with enormous energy and unlimited lust for power, a lover of demagogy, melodrama and bombastic speeches, he [Carol II] was determined to be a Great Man, the Saviour and Regenerator of his country.'

High on the list of Carol's priorities was revenge, that dish traditionally best served cold. He had had three years to plot the comeuppance of his family. Almost as soon as he was installed, he embarked on an orgy of persecution and harassment of all those he hated. Barbu Stirbey was exiled. His ex-wife Helen was spied on, her house ransacked and searched and she, too, was thrown out of the country. His mother, the Dowager Queen, was deprived of the money and property Ferdinand had left her, and when Carol turned on Princess Ileana, the sister who had always been closest to him, Marie fled to France and Germany taking Ileana with her. In April 1937, Carol struck yet again and exiled his brother Nicolas, together with his wife. In the summer of 1938, when Queen Marie was dying of liver cancer in a Dresden sanatorium, Carol refused to send an aircraft to collect her so that she could die at home in her beloved Romania; instead, she had to go by train, almost dying when the lurching of the carriage brought on a haemorrhage, but she survived and reached the Royal Palace at Sinaia where she died on 18 July. When Stirbey, living in exile in Switzerland, asked for permission to return for Marie's funeral, Carol refused to let him come. Revenge had indeed been sweet.

Maniu, who had been the architect of King Carol's return in a deal that had specifically excluded Lupescu, peremptorily resigned in October, and a succession of cabinets headed by the diplomat Titulescu, the historian Iorga, and the Peasant Party's Vaida-Voevod, proved as inept as the next in solving the country's seemingly unending list of problems, including falling prices in agricultural commodities and land, growing industrial unemployment and several bank failures.

Before long, a new, sinister and uniquely Romanian political movement emerged on the national scene, the anti-Semitic and anti-communist Corneliu Codreanu[12] and his Legion of the Archangel Michael (Iron Guard). After years on the lunatic fringe, the Legion had manoeuvred itself into the mainstream of national political life. Now, with five seats in the Chamber of Deputies, Codreanu started what was to become almost a decade of non-stop political violence. The new government of the National Liberal Party under Prime Minister Ion Duca ordered the arrest of large numbers of Legionnaires after Codreanu had publicly expressed his full support for Hitler and Nazi Germany. On 29 December, Duca was assassinated in broad daylight at Sinaia railway station by a Legionnaire death squad.

No report gives a better feel of the sense of cold-blooded farce that surrounded these Balkanesque events than *Time Magazine*'s 8 January 1934 article.

Because of cold and snow the 9:45 express train from pine clad Sinaia into Bucharest was delayed one night last week. A fair-sized crowd was on the station platform, for nearby is the extravagantly turreted palace that is King Carol's country home. Impatiently awaiting the train were Premier Ion Gheorghe Duca, hurrying back to the Capital after a conference with the King, former Mayor Costinescu of Bucharest and Secretary General of the Legislative Council Michel Vlashide. Frugally all three bought third-class tickets. They did not notice a group of university students at the other end of the platform.

Suddenly there was a yellow flash, a loud explosion. One of the students, Nicholas Constantinescu, had pulled a smoke bomb from his pocket and hurled it. Before the smoke had cleared he walked slowly up to the unscathed Prime Minister, placed one hand on his shoulder and fired four shots into his head and body. Ion Duca turned at the second shot, made the sign of the Cross, dropped with blood oozing from his mouth.

King Carol, told by telephone of the tragedy, had Premier Duca's body brought to the royal palace and placed in state in one of the drawing rooms. Twice during the night His Majesty tiptoed into the room to look at his dead Prime Minister, still in his bloodstained travelling clothes.

Next afternoon Premier Duca's body was sent back to Bucharest. Assassin Constantinescu, who after police hustled him to safety, had spent several hours puffing out his chest and posing for photographs, was taken the same day to Ploesti near Bucharest for trial. The murdered Premier's brother-in-law, Radu Polizu, took the morning train out from Bucharest and burst wild-eyed into the Sinaia stationmaster's office where Assassin Constantinescu was held. He whipped out a small revolver and sent two bullets whistling round the prisoner. Bang! Bang! Neither of them took effect. Radu Polizu was disarmed and hustled out of the room. Another bomb, apparently a spare left over from the evening assassination, burst in the station waiting room wounding a small child who stepped on it by accident. The engineer of the funeral train pulled out with a sigh of relief.

Premier Duca was a member of the Liberal Party, old time machine of the famed Brătianu family and long bitterly opposed to the restoration of King Carol. Lately he was won over to the King's side and set valiantly to work suppressing anti-Semitism and a terrorist organization known as the Iron Guard. Beyond question it was the Iron Guard that killed him. Martial law was declared throughout the country; all army leaves were cancelled; an iron-clad censorship was clapped on the Press. Detectives went out in squads, picking up every known member of the Iron Guard, 1,400 in all. A special bodyguard was set over King Carol's Jewish mistress, Magda Lupescu.

Codreanu immediately went into hiding on the imposition of martial law but was later arrested and tried. Once again, he was acquitted of any involvement and under the new government of Gheorghe Tătărescu, a suave Liberal politician known for his anti-communist and anti-Russia views, was given free rein which he used to eliminate his opponents within the Legion and its splinter groups. King Carol, faced with a decline in the appeal of the more traditional political parties, made a bold offer to Codreanu as Tătărescu's term neared its end, demanding leadership of the Legion in exchange for a Legion cabinet; he was refused for Codreanu had changed tack.

After the consequent ban on paramilitary groups, the Legion turned itself into a political party, running as 'Everything for the Fatherland' in the 1937 elections. To the consternation of Carol, it received 15.5 per cent of the vote, making it the third largest political party in Romania and by far the most popular fascist group. The Legion, in its new political clothing, was specifically excluded from entering into coalitions with other parties by King Carol, who was busy creating the National Christian Party with the support of a blue-shirted Fascist paramilitary corps called the *Lăncieri* ('Lance-bearers'), who were either involved in fighting street battles with the Iron Guard or in violence against the Jews. It began to look like Carol, borrowing the tactics of the Legion and initiating an official campaign of persecution of Jews, was attempting to win back the interest the public had shown in the Iron Guard.

After an orgy of street violence, Codreanu was approached by the new Prime Minister, Octavian Goga, a stooge of Berlin's Foreign Affairs Bureau with only 9 per cent of the vote, to withdraw from campaigning in the 1938 elections. Believing that the regime was in terminal decline and that Goga's and the anti-semitic academic Professor Cuza's crude attempts[13] to steal the Legion's political clothes were never going to undermine the Iron Guard's popular support, he agreed but his plans were stymied by Carol, who sacked Goga in February 1938 and introduced a Royal dictatorship backed by big business and several prominent politicians from the traditional parties.[14] Observing the niceties of a referendum, Carol felt vindicated when 4,289,000 voters accepted his plan, with only 5,483 dissenting. As well as head of state, Carol now controlled the legislative and executive bodies, although he retained a veneer of collective governance by appointing the aged patriarch, Miron Cristea, as Prime Minister and Tătărescu as Foreign Minister. Soon all political parties and associations were abolished by decree. The ban on the Guard was again tightly enforced, this time by the one-eyed Wallachian lawyer, Armand Călinescu, who had been made Minister of the Interior – when Carol felt he was on top of the situation, he ordered its brutal suppression and had Codreanu arrested together with forty-four other high-ranking members of the movement on the evening of 16 April 1938. Codreanu was first tried for slander and sentenced to six months in jail; then the authorities indicted him for sedition and other political crimes. He was eventually sentenced to ten years of hard labour and moved to Doftana prison, where, despite the sentence, he was not required to perform any form of physical work.

In the late autumn of 1938, following the successful Nazi annexation of the Sudetenland and the Axis gains reflected in the Munich Agreement and the First Vienna Arbitral Award,[15] Carol accepted an invitation for a state visit to London. The day he arrived coincided with the State funeral in Germany of Ernst von Rath, whose assassination in Paris by a Jewish youth had triggered the infamous *Kristallnacht*, when over 200 synagogues were burnt down and thousands of Jewish homes and businesses ransacked. It was ironic that Britain was welcoming a ruler who had also passed draconian discriminatory laws against the Jews. The timing could not be helped but it certainly accounted for the lukewarm tone of proceedings.

On 16 November, with the British government under more and more pressure to take some sort of action in response to

Kristallnacht, there had been a full meeting of the Cabinet as several ministers felt that by doing nothing Britain was seriously damaging her reputation in the United States, which was being pressurized to take more Jewish refugees. One possibility discussed was making land available to Jews in one of the colonies, British Guiana being the front runner, but no large-scale immigration could be possible until the IGC efforts to enable Jews to bring a significant amount of money out of Germany succeeded. Meanwhile it was decided to increase the scope of temporary refuge in Britain and the office dealing with applications for entry visas received a much-needed increase in staff. On 21 November, Chamberlain made the first public speech to the House of Commons on the refugee problem, and it was finally agreed to allow Jewish children into the country without having to go through the process of gaining passports or visas, as had been the case before.

Given that the stakes were high, *The Times* gave Carol the benefit of the doubt, verging at times on a rather rosy version of events:

From Our Bucharest Correspondent: King Carol II of Rumania, who arrives in London to-day on his state visit to the King and Queen, has led his country, so far with success, through a dangerous political crisis. A year ago the nemesis of many decades of official corruption and of the spoils system seemed to be threatening the State. A series of Administrations had failed to do more than tinker with the repairs that were needed by every part of the State machine. An imitation of democracy, closer under some Prime Ministers than others, had failed entirely to produce administrative efficiency or to check the growth of a revolutionary movement modeled on German National-Socialism. At this critical point the King, who had watched these developments with increasing concern, intervened. He has met the totalitarian challenge by an experiment in authoritarian government. Most Rumanians are prepared to give a fair trial to the new regime.

The visit went according to the plan announced in *The Times* a week earlier:

When the King of Rumania and the Crown Prince Michael arrive in England on Tuesday (15 November), on a State visit to the King and Queen, the Duke of Kent will meet them at Dover. They will reach Dover harbour at 1.25 pm, and will travel by train to Victoria Station, where they will be met at 3.30 pm by the King and the Duke of Gloucester. The King will drive in state with his guests to Buckingham Palace, where he will entertain them at a State banquet in the evening. On Wednesday King Carol and the Crown Prince will go to Guildhall, where they will attend a civic luncheon. The Lord Mayor has asked those who have premises in the City on the route by which King Carol and his son will drive to display flags and other decorations. In the evening King Carol will entertain the King and Queen at dinner at the Rumanian Legation; and at 10.30 the King and Queen will give a reception at Buckingham Palace. This reception has been arranged in place of the usual Court Ball, because King Carol is still in half-mourning for his mother, Queen Marie of Rumania. On Thursday, November 17, King Carol will visit the RAF station at Odiham in the morning, and the Army in the Aldershot area in the afternoon. At night there will be an official dinner at the Foreign Office, at which the King, as well as King Carol and the Crown Prince, will be present. The next morning King Carol will leave for the Continent.

At the reception, Carol was invested with the Order of the Garter and his son and heir, Prince Michael, the Order of the Bath. The trinkets of diplomacy were never far away from the Romanian Court. In a meeting with Chamberlain, Carol had asked him whether Eastern Europe lay in the German sphere of economic influence. The Prime Minister replied, 'Natural forces seem to make it inevitable that Germany should enjoy a preponderant position in the economic field,' but that Britain was not 'disinterested' in 'political' trade deals. It was the English way of answering in the affirmative.

The economic importance of Romania during this period stemmed from its rich array of natural resources, above all oil. From the late nineteenth century, the extraction and refining of petroleum products had been one of the major drivers of the

Romanian economy. By 1910, six companies had emerged as the dominant players, most of them foreign owned or international joint ventures – the German-owned Steaua Română or Romanian Star (1896), Română Americana (1903), a JV with Standard Oil, Concordia (1904), Creditul Minier (1905), Unirea Aquila (1906), a French JV, and Astra Româno (1910), a Royal Dutch Shell company. In 1914, German capital controlled 35 per cent of the industry, followed by the British with 25 per cent, then the Dutch with 13 per cent, the French with 10 per cent and the Americans with 5.5 per cent. Romanian capital was a mere 5 per cent. After the First World War, when the Germans extracted over one million tons despite the temporary destruction of the fields by British engineers under the direction of Colonel Thomson, the assets were redistributed and the companies emerged with different owners: Astra Română remained with Shell; Steaua Română became Anglo-French-Romanian; Concordia Vega French-Belgian-Romanian (Petrofina); Unirea Anglo-Dutch; Creditul Minier Romanian; and Română Americana American (Standard Oil). The loss of production had been little short of catastrophic; it was to take until 1926 when the one million tons a year mark was overtaken for the first time since 1913.

In 1933, Germany imported a total of 370,000 tons of oil from the Dutch West Indies, the USA and Mexico – all sources that would dry up in wartime.[16] Hydrogenation from domestic coal provided another 100,000 tons and a further 100,000 tons were imported from Romania. Hitler knew that consumption would increase tenfold in the event of war and therefore security of Romanian oil supplies was critical to German economic planning, as was the capture of the Persian oilfields to German military planning. The risk of sabotage to the oilfields by the British, as had happened in the First World War,[17] was to be avoided at all costs. So he decided to embark on a sophisticated policy to undermine Romania's confidence in the Allied powers and ally Germany with sympathetic political movements within the country.[18] Thus, the interwar years were characterized by continuous German attempts to undermine Romania's relations with France and England, and to bring about a pro-German regime.

When Carol left London en route for Berlin, the clandestine leadership of the Guard started a violent campaign throughout

Romania, to coincide with Carol's visit to Hitler for talks on increased economic cooperation between Romania and Nazi Germany, in exchange for German guarantees against Hungarian territorial ambitions in regard to Transylvania. At the meeting in Berlin on 24 November, Hitler refused to give the King any assurances about Hungary; instead, he cautioned him against entering into any alliances with the Western powers, and demanded closer economic cooperation between Germany and Romania.

As he boarded the train to Bucharest, Carol was briefed on the latest excesses of the Guard in Transylvania, including the murder of the Rector of Cluj University, a close friend of Prime Minister Călinescu. He decided to act immediately and ordered the decapitation of the movement. On 30 November, it was announced that Codreanu and thirteen others had been shot after trying to escape from custody the previous night.[19] In fact, the fourteen legionnaires were probably executed by the Gendarmerie at Tincăbeşti near Bucharest, their bodies later dissolved in acid, and placed under 7 tons of concrete in the courtyard of Jilava prison. Hitler was livid – to the world at large, it looked as if he had colluded at the elimination of the Guardist leaders and his wrath manifested itself in a vicious media campaign against Carol and Romania.

On his return to Bucharest, the King made soothing noises about reinstating Germany to her 1914 pre-eminent trading position with Romania. The agreement was finally signed on 23 March 1939, when Romania pledged to develop its agricultural and mineral resources to meet Germany's economic needs, including a secret codicil to stimulate oil production and refinement in return for Germany providing her with weapons, planes and other military equipment. The Franco-Romanian Trade Agreement signed a week later was a pale imitation, hampered by the low price the French were prepared to pay for oil and the paltry amount of grain they required. The British-Romanian Trade Agreement signed in May was only a marginal improvement on the French one: the British tabled a £5,000,000 credit and offered to buy 200,000 tons of Romanian wheat at a favourable exchange rate. Chamberlain's words to Carol rang true. But Carol had much to celebrate. In eight years, he had broken the power of the two big political parties, isolating their leaders, Maniu and Constantin Brătianu. He had used the Iron Guard to terrorize Romanian democrats and when it captured the imagination of the masses, he turned on it and eradicated its leaders. He was now supreme. Yet, having destroyed all opposition in Romania, he could still be destroyed from outside and this is exactly what happened.

On 15 December 1938, the National Renaissance Front (FRN), led by the ageing Prime Minister Miron Cristea, Patriarch of the Romanian Orthodox Church, and presided over by the King, was founded, with its members required to wear light-blue uniforms and adopt the Roman salute as a mandatory greeting. A few political stalwarts like Maniu refused to don this absurd apparel. With the dismemberment of Czechoslovakia, a desperate Britain and France gave territorial guarantees to Romania in April 1939, but following the fall of France in June 1940, the increasing success of Germany effectively made them invalid. Carol therefore tried to ingratiate himself to Hitler. On 15 May 1940, he told the German Minister to Bucharest that 'Romania's future depends solely on Germany' and on 29 May signed an oil agreement with the Reich.[20] In June 1940, the National Renaissance Front became the Party of the Nation – all public officials were obliged to join. But the time for posturing was over. At 10.00 pm on 26 June, Molotov handed a note to Gheorghe Davidescu, chief of the Romanian diplomatic mission in Moscow, which demanded the 'return' of Bessarabia to the Soviet Union, as well as the 'transfer' of northern Bucovina to Soviet sovereignty. The Romanian government, still reeling from the news of the capitulation of France, sent its official response to Moscow on 28 June: 'In order to avoid the grave consequences that might follow the use of force and the opening of hostilities in this part of Europe, the Romanian Government is obliged to accept the conditions of evacuation indicated in the Soviet response.' More humiliation was to come. On 30 August, the Second Vienna Arbitral Award,[21] issued by Germany and Italy, ceded northern Transylvania to Hungary.[22] Combined with the loss of Bessarabia and Bucovina to the Russians – and the loss of southern Dobrudja[23] to Bulgaria in August – this Hungarian annexation spelt the end of the Royal Dictatorship and Carol was forced to abdicate on 6 September 1940. Romania had been stripped of nearly all her post-First World War gains with crippling economic consequences.

The legionnaires got wind of the King's plans to flee Romania and, keen to take their revenge on the man who had ordered the execution of their leaders, hastily organized an attack. Lieutenant Gheorghe Teodorescu, who was in charge of the guard that defended the train taking Carol out of the country, recalled:

> As we were coming into the Timişoara train station, soldiers stationed along the tracks were saluting us. The train slowed down as we approached the platform. I was keeping my eyes open to any movement on the platform, but there seemed to be no one there. The train almost came to a halt, when suddenly the doors of the railway station burst open and some 300 legionnaires wearing green shirts stormed the platform. The train immediately accelerated. I heard the order 'Legionnaires, fire!' being shouted from the platform. A few tried to climb on the train. I heard gunshots, and saw pieces of the station's wall damaged by bullets. Machine gun fire increased, and I threw myself on the floor to take cover. The train caught speed, and left the legionnaires behind. We made no more stops after that, in Jimbolia or at the border. Only after we were out of the country, we stopped and got off at Velika Kikinda, the first station we came across in Yugoslavia.[24]

Unknown to Theodorescu, a dramatic chase had been in progress, as the legionnaires stole a locomotive and went after the Royal train. Others still outside the railway station hijacked the county prefect's car and started following the train by road. After a wild pursuit over some 60 kilometres from Timişoara to Jimbolia, the chase finally ended when the King's bullet-marked train passed over the border into Yugoslavia.

He may have been down but Carol was by no means out. After an enforced seven-month sojourn in a small beach resort south of Barcelona, Carol 'escaped' to Lisbon where in May 1941, claiming his life was at risk, he asked the British if he could go to Canada.[25] The British responded with a suggestion that the West Indies would be more suitable; Carol parried with a request to go to Cuba. He duly set sail and after formal trips ashore in Bermuda and the British Virgin Islands, the Royal party reached Havana. By the end of June, the island's charms had withered and Carol decamped to Mexico where he quickly ensconced himself in high society.

Soon his confidence returned and he approached both Washington and London with the proposition that he should head a Free Romania movement. When given an official 'No thank you', Carol started up his own movement which never gained momentum. After a brief flirtation with the Russians, Carol was itching to return to Europe and left Mexico in June 1944 for Brazil, where he thought it would be easy to arrange a passage. He was wrong. The last person the Allies wanted to stir up the muddied waters of post-war Romania was the ex-King and he found himself marooned in Rio. He finally reached Portugal in September 1947, by which time he was a threat to no one. On Good Friday 1953, aged fifty-nine, ex-King Carol died from a heart attack.

The Germans had been busily planning for Carol's abdication and put their weight behind General Ion Antonescu, a doughty career soldier, who took over from King Carol. Goga had appointed this politically insignificant general, with whom the King was on bad terms, as his Minister of War. At first pro-French in outlook,[26] Antonescu had gradually adopted a different view under Goga's influence, one of preferred allegiance with the Deutsches Reich. After Goga's resignation, Antonescu had still remained in the King's cabinet and continued to maintain contacts with the Iron Guard. When he tried to form a government on 15 September, the democratic parties refused to participate, leaving the General with no option other than to offer seats to the Guard. Horia Sima, a provincial high-school teacher, had taken over as leader of the Legion after Codreanu's death. After the assassination of Prime Minister Calinescu, he had fled into exile but returned in 1940 as the Commander of the Legionary movement when the government began to free the remaining legionnares. He became a supporter of King Carol and on 4 July joined the Cabinet of Ion Gigurtu as Minister of Religion and Arts, alongside two other Iron Guard members, an appointment that lasted for four days. It was Sima whom Antonescu chose as his Deputy Prime Minister and as soon as he was in office, he called for Romania to be a totalitarian Legionary state, and for the abolition of all other political parties. Antonescu disagreed and took it upon himself to eliminate the Iron Guard at the first opportunity.

The marriage soon came unstuck when the Guard rebelled over

a three-day period in January 1941, giving Antonescu the mandate to stamp them out once and for all, this time with the wholehearted approval of the Führer, whose overwhelming wish was the political and economic stability of his major oil supplier. The General's efficiency mattered more to the Germans, who were preparing to invade Russia, than the preservation of the Guard's quasi-fascist ideology. Sima managed to escape and finally settled in Spain where, unmolested, he died in 1993.

On 20 September 1940, the German High Command sent a division to 'train' the Romanian Army but in effect to guard the oil installations. That November, Antonescu went to Berlin[27] to sign the Tripartite Pact with the Axis and announced that 'Romania on her own initiative has entered the political sphere of Germany and Italy.' On 4 December, a comprehensive economic treaty was signed between Germany and Romania. His goal, not dissimilar to the leaders of 1916 Romania, was to recover the lost territories of Bessarabia and Bucovina from Russia and northern Transylvania from Hungary; the difference was that it was Hitler who dangled the carrot this time, not the Allies. The Romanians share with the English the proverb, 'He who sups with the Devil, needs a long spoon.'

Antonescu was not the first Romanian leader to find himself caught between two opposing empires. For centuries the Princes of Wallachia, Moldavia and Transylvania had all walked the same tightrope over the seething conflux of three empires: Habsburg, Ottoman and Russian. The art of falling off was to be on the right side at the right time in the right place. For Antonescu in 1940, Russia was clearly his enemy, Germany his only friend.

SOE: early days in London

Before the outbreak of war, there was a small but influential Romanian émigré community in London. Initially it was organized around the former staff of the Romanian Legation, although from the beginning there were a number of divergent views, other than a shared hostility towards the Antonescu regime and its alliance with Germany. The figurehead was the former Minister Plenipotentiary,

Viorel Virgil Tilea; surrounding him were most of the Legation diplomats, such as Prince Matel Ghica and Dimitri Dimancescu. Whilst his stance was vigorously anti-Antonescu, Tilea's Carlist sympathies proved divisive and a second group, again anti-Antonescu but this time anti-Carlist as well, sprang up, headed by Victor Cornea, a Romanian writer and lecturer living in London. As a member of the National Peasants Party, he was the de facto representative of Iuliu Maniu in England.

In the summer of 1940, Major Eddie Boxshall and Colonel Ted Masterson, both SOE officers in London, established formal links with these Romanian émigrés and before long their efforts resulted in the creation of the Romanian National Committee (CNR) on 29 November 1940, with Tilea as President. The CNR was billed as the central organ of the Free Movement of Romania for Romanians in the Anglo-Saxon world of England, USA and Canada. At more or less the same time, at the end of 1940, the Free Romania Committee (CRL) was founded in the Middle East with the approval of Maniu, with the idea of establishing a unified representative body. Getting Romanians to agree is hard during the best of times and on this occasion the intense rivalry of the 'Tilea group' scuppered it.

Divisions between the Romanian émigrés worsened in the spring of 1941. The two groups, one Carlist, the other Manist, now formed separate organizations: the Romanian Democratic Committee (RDC), created on 1 May 1941, under the leadership of lawyer and university professor Victor Lefort, encompassed Tilea and his coterie; the other Romanian organization, the pro-Carol Free Romania Movement (FRM), was unveiled two days later. By now, the Foreign Office was ringing its hands in despair and was desperate to merge the two. They thus superimposed as a coordinator-cum-peacemaker, the well-respected soldier and anti-Carlist, Colonel George Mavrodi, who had close links to the democratic opposition in Romania as well as to SIS. Mavrodi arrived in London on 15 May 1941.

SOE: early days in Romania

After war had been declared between Britain and Germany in September 1939, the British government authorized sabotage operations in Romania to interfere with the transportation of Romanian oil to the Reich. D Section's Major W.R. Young visited Bucharest that month to interview potential recruits for SOE and by March 1940, a propaganda section with its own printing press started operating in the city. Concurrently, a collection of tugs, lighters and barges was assembled at Sulina by the British government sponsored Goeland Transport and Trading Company under the direction of William Harris-Burland based in Constanţa and Captain Max Despard, the Naval attaché in Belgrade. Crewed by seventy members of the Royal Navy and Royal Australian Navy who had arrived on SS *Mardinian*, this motley armada under the command of Commander A.P. Gibson RN sailed up the river until 3 April when it reached Giurgiu, a Danubian town which handled over 50 per cent of Romanian oil exports. Here things began to go wrong, for security was lacking and German counter-intelligence activity unexpectedly keen;[28] arms and explosives were seized by the Romanian authorities and a number of 'seamen' expelled. *The Times* reported on 9 April:

> The laying of minefields in Norwegian waters is coupled everywhere in the German Press with an alleged attempt by British agents to block the Danube for barge traffic, which is featured as another flagrant violation of neutrality, in this case Rumanian. The story is that a number of British barges and motor-boats while on their way up the Danube were found to be loaded with cargoes of explosives and arms; including guns, depth charges, machine-guns, and hand grenades. The barges are said to have been accompanied by 100 picked soldier-specialists under the command of five officers, who were all disguised as bargemen. The cargoes had been declared as goods in transit. The whole expedition is supposed to have been piloted by an agent of the British Secret Service camouflaged as a Vice-Consul. Its presumed aim, according to the German Press, was to block the channel of the Danube at the Iron Gates by sinking the barges in the river and blowing up part of the dykes. The arms and ammunition were to protect the party if they were surprised while at work. This story, be it noted, comes from Berlin, not from Bucharest. From the account given by the German News Agency one is led to

suppose that the 'plot' was discovered by German Secret Service agents, who informed the Rumanian Government. It is stated in Berlin to-day that the whole convoy is being detained in the harbour of Giurgiu, the Rumanian oil port on the Danube.

The British secret service agent referred to by the German News Agency was Merlin Minshall, who had sailed his barge *The Sperwer* down the entire length of the river in 1933, at one stage nearly dying from poison administered by a glamorous Nazi spy, Lisa Kaltenbrunner. According to his colourful memoir, *Guilt-Edged*, after being recruited by both SIS and NID, Minshall arrived in Bucharest as HM's Vice-Consul to implement his ambitious plan to block the Danube, which involved dynamiting the cliffs overhanging the Kazan Gorge and sinking a number of cement-filled barges as 'blockships'. After cobbling together a flotilla of half a dozen barges crewed by thirty naval ratings masquerading as 'art students', Minshall set off upriver from Braila in an Air Sea Rescue launch, which his colleague, Ian Fleming, had persuaded the Admiralty to part with. Alas, the Germans had got wind of the expedition and, having removed enough fuel from each ship to prevent them reaching the Iron Gates, they persuaded the Romanian Navy to intercept the convoy. Minshall's version of events is somewhat different to the official version and curiously selective in that he fails to mention Lieutenant Commander Michael Mason RNVR, his direct NID superior in the field.

The Giurgiu debacle was a major embarrassment for the FO, who noted that 'the unfortunate incident at Giurgiu . . . resulted in the seizing by the Romanians of a large quantity of war material belonging to us and the drastic reduction of <u>all</u> our activities on the river'. However, in parallel to these ill-fated activities, sabotage operations directed by SOE in Belgrade managed to sink four barges laden with cement, partially blocking the river for about four weeks in late April, early May.

Another arrow in the British sabotage quiver was a plan for the destruction of the actual oilfields around Ploieşti, which Romania had agreed that the British could carry out in the event of a German invasion. A $60 million bond would be issued by the British and French governments as compensation. In September 1939, Major

James Davidson-Houston, the assistant military attaché, together with Commander R.D. Watson RN, started preparations. The SS *Fouadieh* arrived at full speed in Galati under cover of darkness in order to preserve secrecy, which in the event was totally compromised by the flooding caused by her enormous wash. By October her cargo of explosives and Morris trucks had reached Râşnov where they were secreted in an artillery depot by British soldiers disguised as oilfield 'trainees', who had been in situ since September. The scope of the proposed sabotage operation was huge; over sixty-five oilfields needed to be knocked out, so training and reconnaissance continued throughout the winter. However, the 'German invasion' never took place and the oilfields escaped destruction. In July 1940, some fifty British subjects, all concerned with the oil industry, were expelled together with Major Davidson-Houston. A fallback plan to destroy Astra Română's high-pressure field at Țintea was thwarted when Romanian troops took over from the company's security guards.[29] A further plan to sink barges with limpet mines came to nothing as did a proposal put forward by the Jewish Agency.[30] The only maritime success story was that of NID's intrepid Lieutenant Commander Michael Mason RNVR, who sank a German HQ ship anchored on the Danube and put delayed-action bombs on a number of Russian tankers moored off Constanța.

Some sabotage was successfully carried on the 'tankcars' which were used to transport oil by rail to Germany. Major Young, working with a Canadian oilman called Treachy and a Scot called Anderson, oversaw the hobbling of at least 800 of these cars until he was expelled on 6 July 1940 after papers relating to Anglo-French plans to destroy Romania's oilfields were discovered by the Germans in France. In September, Treachy and Anderson were arrested and badly beaten up. Released in October, they reached Istanbul where they received medical treatment. No further attempts were made by SOE to sabotage the Romanian oil sector and by the end of the summer Germany, which had started the war owning just 0.5 per cent of the Romanian oil sector, had accumulated ownership of 47 per cent of the country's crude oil output.[31]

The idea of bombing the oilfields was raised at several Cabinet meetings. With Wellington bombers stationed in Greece, the Ploieşti fields were well within range. The problem was that the

Greeks felt that any raids launched from their territory would be seized on as provocative by the Germans and thus precipitate an invasion. So King George II of Greece told Britain that it was free to bomb Romania only after a German attack on Greece. This diplomatic impasse, combined with pessimistic RAF assessments of likely losses, effectively scotched the strategy, especially given the lack of Romanian support for the idea.

In Olivia Manning's novel, *The Spoilt City* (from her *Balkan Trilogy*), Commander Sheppey, portrayed as an absurd naval officer with one arm and an eye-patch braying like an ass about his sabotage plans, tries to recruit members of the legation to assist him with his plans to blow up the Iron Gates. Sheppey is in fact a cruel caricature of a real wounded war hero, General Carton de Wiart, who had lived for years in Poland and had appeared briefly in Bucharest in charge of the fugitive British Military Mission from Poland after the German invasion of that country at the beginning of September 1939. Having arranged for the evacuation of the mission, de Wiart vanished, re-emerging with the British assault troops in the attack on the Norwegian port of Narvik in 1940.

In January 1941, George Taylor, D Section's tame Australian businessman, was briefed over dinner at Claridges by Dr Hugh Dalton and his executive director, Sir Frank Nelson, to bring SOE preparations in the Balkans to a peak of readiness. It was a tall order. First he was charged with dissuading Prince Paul of Yugoslavia from signing the Tripartite Pact, and, in the event of failure, to orchestrate a coup to replace him; secondly, in the event of a German invasion of Yugoslavia, he was to arrange sabotage of the Romanian oilfields and other deposits of strategic natural resources in the Balkans; lastly, he was to make preparations for guerrilla organizations who would be prepared to fight the Germans - since no Balkan country had yet been invaded, this was tantamount to preaching defeatism. Taylor set off on a whirlwind tour of Ankara, Sofia, Athens, Belgrade and Budapest but it was too late.[32] When the British Mission in Bucharest pulled out in February 1941, a lone wireless set was left behind with Prince Stirbey, the father-in-law of Eddie Boxshall who ran the SOE Romanian desk in London. A hugely wealthy and enlightened aristocrat, Stirbey had been the confidante of Queen Marie in the

First World War and instrumental in bringing Romanian into the war on the Allied side. Detested by King Carol – he had once survived an assassination attempt by the King's agents on a train – Stirbey had managed to retain his status as an independent Romanian 'patriot'. However, he had no popular mandate and the real leader of the democratic opposition was Iuliu Maniu.

Born into an ethnic Romanian family in Badacin, Maniu had joined the Romanian National Party of Transylvania and Banat (PNR) and became a member of its collective leadership body in 1897, representing it in the Budapest Parliament on several occasions. After serving as an advisor to Archduke Franz Ferdinand on a project to redefine the Habsburg Empire along the lines of a United States of Greater Austria, when the Archduke was assassinated at Sarajevo in 1914, Maniu changed to supporting a union with the United Provinces, a campaign which culminated in the Alba Julia gathering on 1 December 1918 when Transylvania demanded separation from Hungary. Within twenty-four hours, he had been appointed head of Transylvania's Directory Council.

After the creation of Greater Romania in 1919, Maniu found himself at odds with the national leadership, especially after Prime Minister Averescu dissolved the Transylvanian Council in April 1920. Consequently, Maniu refused to attend Ferdinand's coronation as King of Greater Romania at Alba Julia in 1922, seeing it as an attempt to impose Orthodoxy on the cherished multi-faith tradition of Transylvania.[33] Maniu himself was a Uniat, a Catholic following the Orthodox rite, an idea that had been introduced in 1700 by the Habsburg Emperor Leopold I as a way of converting members of the Orthodox faith in Transylvania.[34] Fearing that the Liberal Party had a stranglehold over Romanian politics, the PNR and the Peasants Party united in 1926, and Maniu was elected leader of the new group, the National Peasants Party (PNȚ), which finally came to power in November 1928, after both Ferdinand and Brătianu had died.

Two years later, Maniu orchestrated Carol's return and the consequent unwinding of the Regency, in hindsight a mistake since Carol did not respect the terms of his agreement with Maniu, refusing to resume his marriage to Queen Helen. Soon Maniu's government was in open conflict with the King's inner circle, the *camarilla*, presided over by Lupescu, as it tried to deal with the major problems caused by the Great Depression and ensuing strike actions. His position untenable, Maniu resigned and the country slid towards authoritarian rule.

SOE London decided that Maniu was the only man to support in Romania once the British diplomatic mission had left on 12 February 1941. He headed a powerful and well-organized opposition in Transylvania, and in the summer of 1940 had been approached by representatives of SOE in Istanbul, Colonel Bill Bailey and Alfred Gardyne de Chastelain.[35] They were convinced that Maniu could bring Romania into the war on the Allies' side. Not all observers agreed. Claire Hollingsworth, the veteran foreign correspondent, opined that Maniu was 'the last conceivable person to ride the wind and direct the storm'. Hugh Seton Watson, writing as in an internal SOE report when he was an SOE officer in 1943, was equally unconvinced: 'He [Maniu] had received his training in an age and an atmosphere in which moral protest counted for something. He was an anachronism in times when only resolute resistance could save the liberties in which he so firmly believed.'

'Chas' de Chastelain was to become the one of the leading lights of SOE's Balkan operations. Born in London in February 1906, of Anglo-Scots parents and of Huguenot background, he was educated at Dollar Academy in Scotland and the Battersea Polytechnic in London, where he received a degree in Petroleum Engineering. On graduating, he moved straight to Romania and worked for Unirea in Bucharest, rising to a managerial position towards the end of the 1930s. In 1933 he married Marion Walsh, the daughter of Jack Walsh, an American accountant with Standard Oil of New Jersey in Romania. She had recently been forced by her domineering mother to marry a Romanian nobleman but the marriage was over the day it began and was soon annulled. The de Chastelain's first child, Jacquie, was born in 1936 followed in 1937 by John. Marion returned to the USA with the children when war broke out and worked for Sir William Stephenson, the Canadian businessman who was running the British Security Co-ordination operation in New York.

Under Major Young, de Chastelain had set up a network around the key figures of Rica Georgescu (codenamed Jockey), a friend of his who ran the US Română Americana Oil Company and who was devoted to Maniu, and Popovici, de Chastelain's former assistant at Unirea and a formidable 'fixer'. Prince Matei Ghica, a pilot who owned his own aircraft, was also recruited in case there was a need to fly Maniu out of the country. De Chastelain had taken over all[36] SOE's Romanian activities from Young in July 1940 until he had to leave himself at the end of September, when he handed over to H.G. Watts, who in turn handed over to R. Hazell. On 15 January 1941, de Chastelain was allowed to return to Romania as a diplomatic courier.

SOE was mightily exercised by the unrestricted access Germany had to Romania's oilfields – at this stage she was still a neutral nation. Control of the industry at this stage was similar to the post-First World War reshuffle but there had been some key changes:

- Astra Română, the largest, was 60–75 per cent owned by Royal Dutch Shell (in turn 60 per cent Dutch and 40 per cent British), the remainder by French and Romanian shareholders. Astra was run out of London.
- Steaua Română was over 50 per cent owned by Romanians (State 19 per cent, banks 19.8 per cent and others 12.4 per cent), the rest by French and British interests, mainly Anglo-Iranian (BP) and Royal Dutch Shell through Steaua British, and OMNIUM-Paribas. In reality, it was run by the British and the French.
- Concordia was 60 per cent Romanian owned (mainly Banca Commerciala Romana) and the rest by Petrofina, itself owned by Société Generale de Belgique and Banque de l'Union Parisienne. Again run by Petrofina.
- Unirea, owned by Phoenix Oil and Transport London.[37]
- Colombia, entirely French owned (L'Omnium Français des Petroles and Group Desmarais).
- Creditul Minier, purely Romania.
- Română Americana, a subsidiary of Standard Oil.

The Germans who, under the terms of the Treaty of San Remo in 1920, had been dispossessed of all their holdings in the Romanian oil industry, had made slow progress in re-establishing themselves and by 1937 controlled Mirafor, Consortuil Petrolului and Buna Speranţă, which together accounted for a paltry 0.22 per cent of production compared to the 67 per cent of Britain, France, Belgium and Holland.

In 1939, after a hesitant start when the British Treasury was reluctant to make good the commercial agreement[38] signed that May between Britain and Romania, which pledged to stimulate the production and export of oil to Britain, Britain had subsequently successfully defended its strategic and commercial interests in Romania by some quick-footed economic warfare against Germany. On 6 September, the British Ambassador to Bucharest, Sir Reginald Hoare, called a meeting of Astra, Steaua and Unirea, the three oil companies controlled by the British. They agreed to purchase the greatest possible amount of petrol produced by their Romanian subsidiaries, thereby cornering the market and at the same time to stop sales to Germany. By 16 September, Steaua and Unirea had ceased trading with Germany; Astra followed in February 1940. Their market intervention had the effect of more than doubling the price of petrol in *lei*, leaving Germany in a very weak position. The OKW liaison officer with the Ministry of Economy calculated that Germany would have a 200 million short-fall in RM (Romanian money) as counterparty for her planned purchases of Romanian petroleum products between January and September 1940. Success was to be short-lived: King Carol flew to Berlin and signed an agreement which in effect reduced exports to Britain and introduced a quota system for foreign countries, including guaranteeing Germany a fixed amount. British policy was left in disarray.

The British government therefore abandoned its preventative purchasing strategy and looked to the private sector to come up with a new ploy to thwart German control, while the Ministry of Economic Warfare looked at more military options such as sabotaging the Romanian oilfields and refineries, and blocking the Danube. Rica persuaded Stoicescu, the Chairman of Creditul Minier, the only purely Romanian oil company, that Romania should buy rather than appropriate Allied property. That way Creditul Minier could obtain the British company Unirea's two refineries and marketing network for a song – and one of the country's biggest oil conglomerates would be Romanian, not German. Antonescu endorsed this idea. Gheorghiu, the managing director of Creditul Minier, returned to see Rica who suggested that he should get in touch with de Chastelain, a former marketing manager of Unirea, to put the proposal to the British company. He also asked him whether he would be prepared to act as Maniu's courier to the Allies.

Gheorghiu had two meetings with SOE in Istanbul when he outlined Maniu's plans. Since Romania was allied to Germany rather than occupied, there was some room for manoeuvre. A carefully planned coup – with the Army behind it – could do real harm to the Deutsches Reich. Timing would be critical – it must take place when German troop levels were at a minimum and all the key posts occupied by pro Maniu people. If it failed, Germany would occupy Romania.

Events meanwhile had moved on. On 6 June 1941, Antonescu had a meeting with Hitler, who confided in him the plans for Operation BARBAROSSA, the invasion of Russia. This was music to the General's ears and he offered the support of the Romanian Army, expressing his desire to retake Bessarabia and northern Bucovina. It was therefore decided to create the General Antonescu Army Group in Moldavia, made up of the Third and Fourth Romanian Armies and the Eleventh German Army. The Group was to be disbanded once its troops had reached the River Dnestr. These decisions were taken unilaterally and King Michael only found out about it on 22 June, a day after the invasion began. However, Antonescu had the support of public opinion and of the majority of the former political parties, and by 26 July the Army Group had recovered all the Romanian lands to the east of the Prut and in northern Bucovina. Now a marshal with the Knight's Cross of the Iron Cross, Antonescu propounded that the Romanian war effort had to continue beyond the 1940 borders, his justification being that the war must be prosecuted until the enemy, Russia, was defeated.

Romania's entry into the war against Russia caused SOE to expand its propaganda activates. On 27 July 1941, the SOE-managed National Liberation Station, a new radio station on the 42-metre waveband, launched its first anti-Axis campaign, compered by George Beza and Petru Vulpescu, two high-profile Romanian exiles.

In August 1941, Rica and the whole of the fifteen-strong

Popovici network were arrested. Security had always been a problem – the network's W/T operator had a fondness for getting drunk in Bucharest restaurants and having gypsy musicians play 'God Save the King' when the place was packed with Germans. SOE quickly despatched a courier with $40,000 to grease the wheels of justice. It was money well spent and the magistrate, Colonel Bărbuvescu, stopped proceedings. Moreover, Maniu told Antonescu that he intended to be the first witness for the defence. Maniu's name was therefore left out of the draft indictment and General Antonescu suspended the death sentence on Rica *sine die*.

After this disaster, SOE was desperate to re-establish contact with Maniu. In a situation report of 1942, SOE had estimated Romanian losses in Russia as at September 1941 as 200,000–250,000 killed, wounded, missing and desertions, including 3,000 officers.[39] Hardly a single family had escaped without some loss. 'The regime becomes more and more hated, and the only argument which enabled it to carry on is the Russian danger and the threat of the loss of Bessarabia and Bucovina'. This view underestimated the surge in popularity of Antonescu – he had recaptured Bessarabia and Bucovina from the Soviets in July,[40] and had been promoted Marshal by the young King Michael in August 1941.

Following the arrest of Georgescu, SOE managed to infiltrate another W/T set with the help of a 'rich, alert and ingenious' Turk called Tozan who was the Finnish Consul in Istanbul. Having successfully arranged its delivery by courier, on 14 March 1942 Tozan left for Sofia by road, his car stashed with precious stones, foreign currency, cigarettes, ciphers and signal plans. The journey to Bucharest was uneventful and after passing over his cargo, Tozan headed for Budapest where he was arrested and sentenced to twelve years by a Hungarian court for espionage. Ever resourceful, he managed to get released after two years and returned to Romania where he resumed his contacts with Maniu until he reached Istanbul in July 1944 in a small sailing boat.

Maniu had wanted a guarantee from Britain and America that they would honour the terms of the Atlantic Charter,[41] which had been concluded by Churchill and Roosevelt on 12 August 1941. The problem was that Russia was not a signatory and as early as February 1942, the FO had minuted that 'HMG cannot be responsible for whether Russia would implement any agreement which she might give nor can HMG negotiate with them in order to discover if there is any formulae which might be acceptable to them and to Romania.'[42] Sir Orme Sargent, the Permanent Under Secreaty at the FO, mused that 'this would open up the whole question of Russia's position in Europe, which the American government were not prepared even to discuss now.'

The American position to put it bluntly was contemptuous of Romania's performance to date. An American representative said to Maniu:

> It was a pity that Romania's sympathy for the Allies could not be generally made well known in the US, since public opinion there, as a result of Romania giving up everything to the Germans without a struggle, was putting Romania in the same category as Hungary, and it was already being hinted at in the US press that after the war Romania with those other two countries would not be represented at the peace conference table.[43]

The Germans were well aware of this line of Romanian thinking. In an address to a group of high-ranking Romanian officers in 1942,[44] Field Marshal List wryly observed: 'We are perfectly well informed in Berlin about what the Romanian people think of their German allies. We know that the Romanians wish the Germans to crush the Russians, and the British and Americans to crush the Germans.'

For Britain, it was one thing for Antonescu to join the German invasion of the USSR with the limited aim of recovering Bessarabia and Bucovina, but it was another to lead the offensive in the Ukraine against Britain's Russian ally. Churchill, under considerable pressure from Stalin, finally declared war on Romania on 7 December 1941. On 12 December, the day after Germany and Italy declared war on the US, Antonescu was advised by Berlin that as a signatory of the Tripartite Pact, Romania was also at war with the US. Four days later, Britain agreed with Stalin that the post-war borders between Russia and Romania would incorporate Bessarabia and Bucovina into the USSR. The Marshal had well and truly cooked his goose.

With little happening on the ground in Romania, SOE formed the VLAICU Mişcarea Luptătoare ('fighting movement') in June 1942. The idea was to create a fictional Tito-like figure, a heroic partisan resistance fighter, to whom potential resistance could rally round. The Vlaicu legend, the name of two previous Romanian folk heroes, gathered momentum and with regular broadcasts from Palestine (purportedly in Romania), supported by printed materials either dropped by air or smuggled in, it soon began to have an effect on the Romanian authorities, even if of a nuisance value only.

From late 1942, SOE set up Romanian sections in Switzerland, Portugal and Sweden to support its main intelligence-gathering effort based in Istanbul. Of these, Lisbon was the 'hot bed par excellence of Romanian intrigue'. The cast of characters included: Victor Cădere, the Romanian Minister to Portugal; Jean Pangal, the Romanian Red Cross delegate to Portugal and former head of Carol's Personal Secret Service; the Polish Colonel Kowalevsky, former Polish military attaché in Bucharest; Nic Dianu, former Minister at the Hague; and Sergiu Lecca, press attaché and secret service agent. Of these, Pangal was the most vulnerable link because he was in touch with the Germans as well as being on the Polish payroll. His pro-Carlist sympathies endeared him to Viorel Tilea in London and resulted in information reaching the Germans via Cădere and Antonescu.

Intelligence gathering was one thing but soliciting Russian support was another. In a letter written to SOE on 13 March, Sir Orme Sargent explained that he had heard back from Sir Archibald Clark Kerr, the Ambassador in Moscow, about whether the Soviet government would be interested in establishing contact with Maniu:

> It looks as though the Soviet Government do not intend to commit themselves in any way regarding Roumania. That being the case I fear there is nothing more we can do for the present, since our own policy in regard to Roumania must be determined by that of the Soviet Government. I am afraid, therefore, that we are not in a position to pursue our negotiations with Maniu until and unless the Russians show more interest in the matter.

In April 1943, Romania opened negotiations with the Vatican on possible peace moves and that May, a Romanian consular official, Catalin Vladescu-Olt, showed the 'Colonel Black scheme' – General Sănătescu's blueprint for a *coup d'état* against Antonescu – to SOE in Istanbul. Sir Alexander Cadogan noted in his diary on 11 August: 'Reumanians also nibbling, but I don't care what happens to them.' But little was actually happening, prompting the Foreign Office to note on 7 November that 'nothing will save the Romanians except the overthrow of the Antonescu Government and its replacement by men willing to swallow the bitter pill [of unconditional surrender]'. After the capitulation of Italy in September 1943, peace feelers came in fast and furiously from all sides; the Foreign Office stated that it could not consider individual approaches from the Romanian government or private persons and communicated this position to its embassies in Madrid, Stockholm, Ankara and Lisbon. The latter capital was, as usual, a hive of activity. On 16 November, Colonel Popescu arrived from Bucharest and confirmed that peace feelers had been extended to the three allies, with the proviso that there was a three months breathing space for Romania to extricate itself from the Axis camp. At the end of December, Pangal, acting for Foreign Minister Mihai Antonescu was in contact with the British Minister in Lisbon with the line that in the event of Allied troops entering the Balkans, Romania would join them. The Minister replied that Romania must sign an unconditional surrender to all three allies.

The Allied air offensive

The declaration of war had opened another line of attack against German dependence on Romanian oil, this time military. The city of Ploieşti was the centre of the Romanian oil industry, situated on the plains below the Transylvanian Alps, about an hour's drive north of Bucharest. Commercial refinement of oil had begun there in 1857 and by 1942 the refineries at Ploieşti were producing nearly a million tons of oil a month, accounting for 40 per cent of Romania's total exports. Most of that oil, including the highest-quality 90-octane aviation fuel in Europe, went to the Axis war effort, providing nearly a third of the petrol that fuelled Hitler's war machine. In return, Germany protected Romania's natural resources; specifically, German gunners and fighter aircraft guarded the multiple refining and storage plants that ringed Ploieşti.

The first bombing mission over Ploieşti was carried out by thirteen American B-24s which took off from an RAF airstrip at Fayid, Egypt, on the night of 11 June 1942. One of the bombers was forced to turn back to Egypt when frozen fuel transfer lines cut power to three engines. The remaining twelve continued on towards Ploieşti where they dropped their bombs on what was believed to be the Astra Română refinery. While this first raid on Ploieşti was unremarkable and inflicted only minimal damage to the refineries and hence German oil supply, the mission represented a significant step for American air power, for not only were these the first bombs dropped over Europe by Americans, but it was also a demonstration of the great range the B-24 afforded Allied operations. Of the twelve Liberators that reached Ploieşti, six landed safely in Iraq (the designated recovery point for the mission) and two landed in Syria. Four bombers were forced to land in Turkey where the aircraft were seized and the crews interned.

Immediately after this raid, the United States began to plan Operation TIDAL WAVE, a sequel mission scheduled for August 1943. The concept of this mission was further developed in January 1943 at the Casablanca Conference when TIDAL WAVE was discussed on the basis that a successful bombing raid against Ploieşti could deny Hitler a third of his fuel production and thereby shorten the war by six months. Immediately after the conference, US Colonel Jacob Smart flew to England to begin detailed planning, including the recommendation that the raid be carried out at low level. He enlisted the advice of Lieutenant Colonel W. Lesley Forster who had managed the large Astra Română refinery at Ploieşti for eight years prior to the war, and had first-hand knowledge of the target.

When the first of 178 Liberators took off at 5.00 am on the morning of Sunday, 1 August 1943, it marked the culmination of months of planning and practice. Yet the Germans as they tracked the waves of bombers over the Mediterranean were well aware that a major bombing raid was underway and when the formation reached Corfu, German air defences throughout the region went on alert. As many as 200 Axis fighters were in the vicinity of Ploieşti, including four wings (fifty-two planes) of ME-109s at Mizil, 20 miles east of the city. More than 200 large anti-aircraft guns ringed the city limits to protect the refineries, including 88-mm flak guns and 37-mm and 20-mm rapid-fire cannon. Across the city barrage balloons were raised on their explosive laden steel cables.

The battle that subsequently raged was one of the fiercest air battles of the whole war. Flying at low level, the aircrews pressed home their attacks with unbelievable courage through a wall of exploding bullets, shrapnel and flechettes. In all, of the 163 bombers from the five bomb groups that reached their target, only eighty-nine made it back to Benghazi. The following day only thirty-three of these were pronounced 'fit to fly.' Casualties for the 1,726-man force that had flown into the maelstrom over Ploieşti were appalling. Nearly a third of the crews failed to return with more than 300 known dead and 140 captured. Of those who did make it home, more than 440 were wounded.

Allied assessment of the attack estimated an immediate loss of 66 per cent of cracking abilities at the Ploieşti refineries. Although damage at a number of the primary targets was severe, others escaped largely untouched. The Germans had also made contingency plans to repair the refineries, many of which had to date been operating at well below maximum capacity. Within weeks, most of the damage was made good, and with the exception of the severly damaged Steaua Română refinery at Câmpina, all the others quickly resumed pre-raid production levels. In 1944, production would again be severely disrupted, but not entirely destroyed, after multiple raids by the Fifteenth Air Force, which dropped 10,000-lb bombs on the refineries, this time utilizing traditional high-altitude techniques.

Romania's fall from grace

The April 1943 meeting between Hitler and Antonescu had not been a success. The Führer had castigated the Marshal for poor performance in meeting food contracts and for allowing anti-German propaganda to be freely distributed around Romania.

Furthermore, von Ribbentrop harangued the Marshal for tolerating Maniu's critical letters to him: 'In Germany a man such as Maniu would have been hanged long ago.'[45] Antonescu held his ground, defending Maniu as a national icon, but a chink had opened up in the once seamless armour of the German-Romanian military love affair.

The Marshal had indeed begun to waver. Despite winning a refendum in 1942 after the 73-day siege of Odessa had been brough to a successful conclusion, the disastrous defeat of the German and Romanian Armies at Stalingrad in February 1943 forced Antonescu to reappraise his alliance with the Deutches Reich; the Romanian Third and Fourth Armies had lost 158,854 men (dead, wounded and missing) between 19 November 1942 and 7 January 1943. Such losses were militarily and politically unsustainable, so Antonescu began to think about extricating Romania from the war and allowed his Foreign Minister, Mihai Antonescu, to float the concept of the withdrawal from conflict of the Nazi allies – Romania, Hungary, Italy and Finland.

Mihai Antonescu believed Benito Mussolini was powerful enough to stand up to Hitler, and that Italy could successfully negotiate an armistice with the Western Allies. Under Antonescu's plan, the four states and other European nations would turn against Hitler and join the Allies against Germany. In his capacity as Foreign Minister, Antonescu paid a visit to Mussolini in June 1943, when he learnt that Mussolini agreed with certain aspects of his plan, but was less than enthusiastic in regard to actually implementing it. Antonescu subsequently increased his efforts to improve Romania's relations with the United States and Great Britain, and established contacts with Allied representatives in Bern,[46] Istanbul, Madrid and, finally, in Stockholm. As such, he stopped the deportations of Romania's Jews, allowed Jewish emigration to non-Axis nations and repatriated those who had survived Transnistria. The meetings and memoranda were directed mainly at the British and American representatives, who responded that Romania should deal primarily with the Soviet Union. Talks therefore started in April 1944 in Stockholm with the Russian representative, but no progress proved possible since Marshal Antonescu refused to budge on the subject of the Romanian claim to northern Bucovina and Bessarabia.

With renewed impetus, it was essential that a SOE team of an officer and wireless operator was sent into the country to open up W/T communications with the opposition. SOE chose Captain David Russell to lead the mission, code-named RANJI.

A maverick picked to command the RANJI Mission

David Russell was born on 28 August 1915 to Captain and Mrs E. Russell at Bridgefoot House, South Mimms, Hertfordshire. Educated at Eton where he was a member of the OTC, rising to the rank of corporal, Russell went up to Trinity College Cambridge where he read Agriculture and Estate Management, and also converted to Roman Catholicism under the aegis of Father Alfred Gilbey, the charmimg and urbane RC Chaplain to the under-graduates. He continued his studies at the Royal Agricultural College, Cirencester and then started a career in farming based at Broke Hall at Nacton near Ipswich.

At some stage in his early life, Russell had spent time in Germany, for in his Scots Guards personnel file there is an entry: 'Germany – lived there for 3 years', as well as references to travels in Austria, Italy, Holland, Sweden, Norway and Poland.[47] In a later SOE personnel file, he stated he was familiar with Koln-Bonn, Westphalia, Oberbayern and Oels Oberschlesien. These journeys may have something to do with his interests – 'twenty hours flying time, two seasons motorcycle racing on the continent and skiing & climbing'. Family sources tell of an ill-starred love affair with a married German baroness and of a brief engagement in 1941 with the great-great-granddaughter of Tsar Nicholas I, the Georgian Princess, Nataliya Konstantinovna Bagration-Moukhranskya.[48] One outcome of these exotic travels and liaisons was that he was fluent in German, proficient in French and familiar with Norwegian.

On the outbreak of war, Russell was introduced to the Scots Guards by Lieutenant General Sir William Pulteney, who wrote[49] to the Lieutenant Colonel that 'he is a very good boy but a little nervous with strangers.' His father also wrote in, pointing to his son's fluency in German and hoping it might come in use. Commissioned from Sandhurst on 25 May 1940, Russell reported to Pirbright on 13 July (he had had to stay on at RMAS for extra training) and joined the Scots Guards Training Battalion on 5 October.

Wartime soldiering in England did not suit him and he had applied to join the RAF as early as August 1940; his application had been accepted. Then something untoward happened for there is a note in Russell's personnel file, as follows: 'This officer behaved in a very foolish manner recently and in consequence the Lieutenant Colonel told him he was not prepared to recommend his employment with the RAF.'[50] However, the Lieutenant Colonel had exceeded his authority and was not empowered to do this; on 19 November, Russell, on guard duty at HM Tower of London, wrote to the Commanding Officer of the Scots Guards Holding Battalion, asking for his transfer to be validated, and again on 22 January 1941. On 21 April 1941, Russell was posted to C Company, 1st Battalion the Scots Guards at Petts Wood in Kent, where he continued to push for his transfer. On 3 September, he attended a RAF board and was selected as an observer. Following eye training, he was subsequently passed fit for training as a pilot. Finally his plans to fly were coming to fruition.

Russell was aghast when he was posted to 2nd Battalion Scots Guards in the Middle East, and immediately rang the Lieutenant Colonel to ask not to go due to his imminent transfer to the RAF. The answer came back that there was no other officer available to send, and in any case he could move across to the RAF once he had arrived in theatre. Russell embarked at Liverpool on 14 February 1942 and arrived in Egypt on 10 April. The highlight of the voyage had been a stopover at Cape Town where Russell, together with a fellow officer, had hired a Portuguese taxi for the week and driven up the coast. His companion remembered visiting the Boer Club and the bars and brothels of the mixed-race District 6, 'an experience which I still remember and treasure'.

On arrival at Fayid LOB in Suez, where officers had to 'sit until needed', Russell, without telling anyone or asking permission, hired a taxi and drove straight to Shepherds Hotel in Cairo. A contemporary recalls:[51] 'David did not do what he was told. He did what he enjoyed and what was useful.' Here he met Randolph Churchill and Evelyn Waugh. Checking out after ten days, Russell stopped an Army ambulance returning to Fayid on the steps of

Shepherds Hotel and told it to drive to the LOB. He lay down on the stretcher bunk and promptly fell asleep. By 25 May, he is shown attached to ME Commando (but on the strength of 2nd Bn Scots Guards X list) – his unauthorized visit to Cairo had paid off paid off but there is no record of his benefactor. In all likelihood, it was David Stirling himself.

On 30 June, Russell joined L Detachment of David Stirling's SAS Brigade. At six foot two, he was described by Carol Mather as 'a wild and independent character with a zest for life but better at giving orders than taking them!'⁵² Three weeks later he took part in the attack on LG 21 airfield at Fuka as patrol commander of two jeeps and then, along with three others – Mather, Jordan, and Bailey – was tasked by Stirling to attack soft-skinned vehicles in the Axis build-up area behind the Alamein line. Russell excelled on this mission. Speaking fluent German, he would contrive to hail down individual Afrika Corps trucks as they approached. When the driver stopped, he asked him whether he could borrow a pump. With the driver rummaging around for one, Russell would nonchalantly slip a delayed action bomb into the back of the vehicle; he managed to do this eight times.⁵³ Putty Pulteney's boy who was 'nervous with strangers' had long vanished.

It was during this operation that Headquarters ME ordered Stirling back to Cairo to assist in planning Operation AGREE-MENT, a daring raid on the main Afrika Corps supply base at Tobruk with a diversionary attack by the SAS on Benghazi.⁵⁴ The plan was the brainchild of SOE's Colonel Jock Haselden, an extraordinary character born in Egypt of a Greek mother and English father, who had run the family cotton mills before the war. A fluent Arabist, Haselden could pass himself off as a desert Arab and had worked with the LRDG since their inception, spending weeks behind enemy lines. It was Haselden who had guided into shore the commandos in their attempt to kill Rommel in November 1941 at Beda Littoria.

The plan was ambitious. Commando Force B under the command of Haselden, having been guided by the LRDG to the perimeter of Tobruk, was to assault the coastal guns at Mersa Umm es Sciausc. If successful, a sea landing was then to be effected by Force C consisting of a company of Argyll & Sutherland Highlanders, with a machine platoon from the Royal

Northumberland Fusiliers. When a perimeter had been secured, Force A, consisting of two destroyers – HMS *Sikh* and HMS *Zulu* – with 382 marines on board was to sail into the harbour. Demolition squads would then destroy pier and dock installations, sink all shipping, take out the tank repair workshop and, finally, blow up Rommel's bomb-proof oil storage tanks. With Tobruk rendered useless, Rommel's supply lines would be extended by 200 miles to Benghazi, thus handicapping his advance.

Force B consisted of a detachment of eighty-six commandos under the command of Major Colin Campbell, and six Special Service officers; also attached were six other officers including Lieutenant Tom ('Tubby') Langton, an Irish Guards officer now in the SBS. A former rowing blue, he had recently completed trials of hanging onto the back of a MTB and sticking limpet mines on enemy barges. He concluded that most of the mines ended up stuck to him! A veteran of the Keyes raid against Rommel, Langton was made unofficial adjutant by Haselden.

The method of inserting Force B was audacious. Haselden explained:[55] 'We are going to drive openly into Tobruk one evening just at dusk. We will enter as prisoners-of-war captured at the Alamein front, under the guard of German soldiers [and in German-designated captured Allied trucks).[56] We are going to capture a bridgehead just outside Tobruk harbour itself, under cover of the biggest air raid this coast has ever seen.'

The 'guard of German soldiers' was to be provided by SIG (Special Interrogation Group), a sub-unit of D Squadron, 1 SAS commanded by Captain Herbert Cecil Buck MC.[57] A brilliant German scholar at St Peter's Hall Oxford, a university fencer as well as a good musician and poet, Buck had been commissioned into the Punjabis and then transferred in 1939 to the 1st Battalion Worcestershire Regiment. Wounded in action and captured by the Germans at Gazala, he had escaped wearing a stolen Afrika Korps uniform. Surprised by how easy it was – speaking German – to pass unmolested through Axis lines, he had the idea of creating a sabotage unit composed of anti-Nazi Germans.

In March 1942, Colonel Terence Airey of G(R) Branch directed that part of the recently disbanded No. 51 ME (Jewish) Commando, consisting mainly of German-speaking Palestinian Jews, was to be formed into 'a Special German Group as a sub-unit of ME Commando . . . with the cover name "Special Interrogation Group"', to be used for infiltration behind the German lines in the Western Desert, under command of Eighth Army. That June, the SIG were given their first major task to assist David Stirling and his SAS group to blow up German airfields at Derna and Martuba on the coast 100 miles west of Tobruk, which were threatening the Malta supply convoys.

Buck's second-in-command was none other than David Russell. By now known as the Flying Scotsman for his love of fast driving, Russell had been able to use his mastery of the German language and its many dialects to good effect, operating behind enemy lines dressed in German uniform for several months.

When the small SIG team reached Kufra in RAF Bombay Transports, they met up with the LRDG and other commandos. Here they continued drilling in German uniform and using German commands as their British comrades looked on in amazement. However, there was little fraternization because as one LRDG veteran, Jock Fraser, told Peter Smith, the author of *Massacre at Tobruk*, 'we all distrusted these guys though some were very brave men.'

On 6 September, Force B left Cairo and after being guided to the perimeter of Tobruk by Captain David Lloyd-Owen's LRDG Y Patrol, the raiders joined the stream of German traffic – Buck was in the lead truck dressed as a German officer. Apart from a tense moment when there was a minor accident with a German staff car, the four truckloads of commandos remained undetected and reached their dropping off point just as the diversionary RAF air raid began at 2230 hours. Haselden with Buck and Russell, plus some other members of SIG, attacked an Italian platoon and soon a general firefight started. Force B's objective was taken, allowing Langton to signal Force C to land at 0230 hours. However, in the darkness and heavy gunfire, only two of the sixteen MTBs were able to land their detachments and it proved impossible to secure any meaningful perimeter. At 0348 hours the marines were released for their shore run from the two destroyers but it soon became clear that the landing had been aborted and the marines returned to their mother ships.

At about 0505 hours on what was later to be called Black Monday, HMS *Sikh*[58] was hit by the shore batteries (she later sank and her crew were taken prisoner) and all three raiding forces now focussed on extricating themselves. There was now no question of Force B following the original plan of holding out for twelve hours until taken off by the destroyers. At this stage Russell and Buck, who had been missing from the defensive perimeter established by Haselden, reappeared. Where had they been? To release British POWs? To capture a German general in the YMCA building? Or to break into the garrison strong room and remove the cash? There was no time for speculation. Haselden gave the order to withdraw down a wadi in the remaining two trucks. Russell collected one of them and drove it to the road to pick up the surviving commandos, including the wounded. At this stage, Haselden then decided to fight a rearguard action to allow the commandos to escape. With Russell and others, he managed to hold off the attacking Italians until killed by a grenade.

Russell made his way to a beached MTB and opened up with its twin Brownings to give covering fire whilst the rest of the force extricated themselves from the wadi. Russell, Buck and three members of the SIG then headed across country for the Allied lines. After terrible hardships and many close calls, including walking through the lines of two Italian infantry battalions, on 18 November,[59] a British armoured car crew[60] saw a wasted skeleton of a man walking out of the desert. He was bearded, long-haired, starving and in rags, but he seemed quite composed, almost unemotional at meeting them. They heard him say, 'I'm Lieutenant David Russell.' Tubby Langton had also managed to escape, arriving a few days earlier on 13 November after a 78-day march. In all, only six members of Force B made it back.

On 8 January 1943, Russell's MC was gazetted. The citation read that he 'exhibited great bravery and complete disregard for his personal safety throughout the operation . . . In circumstances of extreme danger and difficulty, this officer displayed the highest courage, endurance and devotion to duty.' Although offered command of the Guards Patrol of the LRDG and also 'asked for' by George Jellicoe of the SBS,[61] Russell was determined to have his own show and in April 1943 he was posted to SOE Cairo – Force 133 – reporting to Colonel Ted Masterton,[62] head of the Romanian section. From now on, he was to be known as DH/561. Curiously, Russell did not speak Romanian.

RANJI sets off

Code-named Operation RANJI, on the night of 15/16 June 1943, David Russell (alias Albert Thomas) and his wireless operator, Nicolae Țurcanu (alias Antonio Vella), Callsign Reginald, were dropped into a reception area run by Major Jasper Rootham in the Homolje region in Yugoslavia.[63] In his wartime memoir, *Miss Fire*, Rootham recalled: 'David Russell, tall, fair-haired and blue-eyed, with an infectious smile, instantly won all hearts, not least because he was the Serbs' idea of what an Englishman should look like.' RANJI initially remained with Rootham's mission east of the Krsh and, at the end of the month, Russell conducted a recce in the Golubac area to find a secure Danube crossing point. Rootham wrote that on 23 July:

> David Russell took leave of us. I had been worried about his enterprise, which in its present form seemed a madcap one, and I could not forget Velja's warning [Velja was the local chetnik commander who had offered Russell a bodyguard of thirty armed men to secure a base in a Serbian-inhabited village in Romania, otherwise 'he   would not give much for Russell's chances': Cairo ruled the bodyguard out of court]. I spoke seriously to Russell and said that, in Erik's [Greenwood] absence, as the person who was nominally the senior officer I was quite prepared to forbid him to go, and to tell Headquarters so. He thanked me, but said he wished to go. He had undertaken to see the thing through, and he would do so.

Linking up with Captain Vuchkevich near the Danube, Russell selected a Serb *chetnik*, who appears to have used the name Petre Mihai (code name Pera). Impressed by this former sergeant major in the Gendarmerie who spoke good German and Romanian, Russell persuaded Vuchkevich to second him to the Mission as a guide.

They crossed the heavily patrolled Danube River on 2 August at a point somewhere between Upper and Lower Lipova and moved 50 miles across enemy territory. From their first LUP at the Vintza commune, they made their way to Mehadia where the former mayor, Madgearu, was a well-known supporter of Maniu. After staying the night with him, he suggested that they would be safer staying in one of his two vineyards – his constant drinking of *tuica*[64] revealed how nervous he was. But before they left, he insisted that they left their weapons and uniforms with him so that he could hide them in his other vineyard.

As an afterthought, Russell asked him to stash the propaganda leaflets they had brought with them and to distribute them in the village two to three weeks later. Leaving them alone for the night, Madgearu disappeared and returned the next morning, completely drunk. When he had sobered up, he told them he had distributed the leaflets throughout the town. Not surprisingly a house-to-house search conducted by the Gendarmerie, police and Gestapo was in full swing.

'Why did you distribute the leaflets?' asked the team in one voice.

'Why not? Did you want me to make soup with them?'

By now Madgearu was such a liability that Russell and Ţurcanu persuaded him to go off and find a car to take them to Timişoara 'where they had important business'.[65] As soon as he had gone, they promptly made their way to the station, caught the train to Turnu Severin and then backtracked to the village of Vârciorova. Here they made contact with the Pitulescu brothers, the eldest of whom had been the Postmaster General of Romania and was now the leader of the local National Peasants Party. The problem was that the team did not have a password from Maniu and therefore Pitulescu would need to get his approval before he could engage with them. He set off for Bucharest only to find that Maniu was in a hospital in Braşov to the north and therefore had to wait.

For three weeks, the three-man SOE team remained in the woods close to the village. Towards the end of August, due to increased enemy patrolling, they moved to the far end of a heavily wooded valley called Fundul Vâdiţei, about 4 to 6 kilometres fromr the village, where they occupied an abandoned fishermen's hutdug into the ground and covered with branches.[66] Here they encountered a local woodsman called Dumitru Burcu but he appeared to be friendly and gave no cause for concern. Every day, Ţurcanu went down to the Pitulescu house to send messages (composed by Russell) while Russell and Petre Mihai remained at the LUP.[67]

Murder most foul

It was on one of these occasions – on Saturday, 4 September 1943 – that Russell was killed in mysterious circumstances, found shot in the head from behind, less than a week after his twenty-eighth birthday. An investigation immediately started, both on the ground and back at SOE HQ in Cairo. Who had shot Russell and why?

Ivor Porter, who was a member of the next SOE Mission into Romania, writes in his book, *Operation Autonomous*, that it was generally thought that Russell was murdered by his Serb *chetnik* guide for the gold sovereigns he carried. However, an examination of the Reginald files at SOE leads to a somewhat different if inconclusive verdict.

According to Țurcanu, who had been detained at the Pitulescu house until the early hours of the morning of 5 September due to poor radio transmission conditions, he had returned to the hut and found Russell dead, shot in the head. Everything in the hut had been turned upside down. Both Russell's watches[68] were missing and Petre Mihai was nowhere to be found. Ironically, Pitulescu arrived back from Bucharest that same day with authority from Maniu to engage with Russell's SOE mission.

Before his untimely death, Russell had followed SOPs and cached the bulk of the Mission's money and sensitive paperwork in a tree about 50 metres away from the hide. After recovering the cached stores, Țurcanu made his way to Bucharest with the radio and money (100 gold sovereigns) where, after making contact with the Manists, he was installed in a flat and able to continue his transmissions. To his surprise, Petre Mihai arrived shortly afterwards, together with Alecu Pitulescu, and Țurcanu completely exonerated him from any suspicion after hearing his story.

> We [Petre Mihai and Russell] bathed in the stream, drank a brandy and then went into the hut where we continued talking until we fell asleep. At about 9.30 or 10.30 pm, I awoke to the noise of crackling leaves (Russell was awake as well) . . . steps became louder and louder . . . I then burrowed my way out of the back of the hut. I see suddenly a flash of light, exactly like the light of a torch . . . and at the same time, I hear

the shout 'Hands up or I shoot'[69] and I could hear a number of shots being fired as if from an automatic rifle.

As far as the Pitulescu family in Vârciorova was concerned, the finger pointed at Dumitru Burcu, the woodsman, who was spending money 'freely on his young women' shortly after the incident. Mrs Pitulescu also had in her possession a long written statement by Petre Mihai, who had presented himself to the family the day after the murder, but she could not decipher it since it was in Serbian.[70]

Suspicion remained on Petre Mihai, although there was considerable evidence of police and military patrols in the area and several bands of cut-throat thieves including Serbian guerrillas. In an OSS report dated 3 November 1944, a source claimed that between 29 August and 19 September 1943, Romanian officials knew about a three-man W/T party. The information was highly accurate: Vella Nicolo Antonio, 'a soldier of fortune'; Albert Thomas, 'a British or American'; Petre Mihai, 'a Serb *chetnik*'. A forest ranger had reported them, noting that Thomas was in British Army battledress and Petre Mihai in Romanian peasant costume. Curiously, there was even a record of the languages they spoke.

If motive was difficult to pin on any of the suspects, then the murder weapon was equally hard to come by. According to SOE files, police reports state that the body was recovered after some days and that the bullet was a 12 mm or .455. Such forensic evidence is surprising, given that Russell had been dead for some days and that the capabilities of the police in this department were rather limited. But whose gun? When the Mission had stayed with Madgearu, they had allowed him to cache two out of their three .455 revolvers. This is made clear by Russell when he signalled Cairo on 24 August: 'Only weapon is one pistol. Please send colt automatic and magazines.'[71] Suicide was ruled out.

Țurcanu managed to send a signal to SOE on 20 September:

To TED from MALTA. The difficulties and perils have passed a little. After three days will be in contact continuously. I have found a serious contact with a solid pro-English organisation. THOMAS shot dead on 4 Sept in Forest Vârciorova by unknown persons and in the night they stole our things but the money and the secret papers were hidden and they are complete. For the present the money is hidden with Pitulescu. I am in Bucharest/give urgent instructions/all will be executed/(DICK) and his people up till now have done nothing for us. Frightened for their safety. Regards MALTA (and from) Protopopescu, Head of Pro-English organisation.

In weekly Progress Report No. 61 for the week ending 23 September 1943, the SOE desk officer wrote:

News of the death of Captain T.C.D. Russell, M.C., Scots Guards, on 4th September, has reached us in a W/T message from his wireless operator.

The loss of this very gallant officer, if this proves to be true, is a big blow to our work in Romania. As leader of the first mission he did a very excellent job in crossing the Danube from Yugoslavia to Romania at a time when this river was being actively patrolled by the enemy on account of acts of sabotage which had taken place. He also moved through very difficult country a distance of some fifty miles in order to reach Vârciorova. On the way he must have been hunted because upon arrival at Vârciorova he reported the loss of almost all his kit.

Without having indications from us he made a most valuable contact in Vârciorova. With the help of this contact he was able to shelter in the Vârciorova forest for a period of about three weeks. During this time a number of members of Serbian guerrilla bands were caught by the Romanian military authorities in their attempt to cross the Danube. The result of this was that the whole area was searched for members of these bands who had escaped, and it was probably due to this that Russell's hiding place was discovered.

The contact Russell made in Vârciorova was the leader of the local Peasant Party. He would not agree to active cooperation with Russell until he had received instructions to do so from the chief of the party. In order to obtain this he went to Bucharest, and it was most unfortunate that just at this time the leader of the political party was in hospital in Braşov. This additional delay in seeing the chief has probably cost Russell his life. We have received a message from Bucharest in which we were advised that the leader of the party had given Russell's contact the necessary authority. It was probably before the latter's return to the Vârciorova area that Russell's whereabouts was discovered.

The wireless operator, that is the second member of the mission, has arrived in Bucharest, and is in safe hiding there. It is not clear yet whether he got there with the help of Russell's contact and other members of this political party, or whether he made his own arrangements.

Until more proof of Russell's death is received we think he should be considered as 'missing, believed killed', because we only have the W/T operator's word for his death up to the present, and he himself may have had to make a hurried getaway when the shooting incident occurred, and having seen Russell fall, assumed that he was killed without being able to confirm it.

In conclusion, it is pointed out that Russell probably undertook one of the most difficult of missions, bearing in mind that Romania is enemy country, and no reception arrangements could be made for him. The result of the mission is that we are in W/T communication with Romania, which we have been trying to establish for the past two years.

On 26 September, Ţurcanu managed to get another message to SOE in Cairo:

Thomas was killed in the middle of the forest on the river Vodita six kilometres from Vârciorova. Four weeks exactly we remained in this region moving from place to place. The W/T contact was made at night from Vârciorova in the loft of the engineer Pitulescu's house. I was obliged to remain there until morning on account of the difficult terrain. On the day of the crime Saturday 4 September I went for my W/T contact at 1530 GMT but not being able to make good contact, I remained there for the contact at two o'clock in the night. Returning with food to the hiding place accompanied as usual by Lazar Radoi the father in law of engineer Pitulescu and upon arrival there discovered the dreadful crime. Thomas was shot and robbed of his clothes and Romanian money which he had upon him. The Serb was not there. We suspect that the crime was committed by thieves or by others whom we think we know, more especially a man from Mehadia who took all our arms and equipment. This individual threatened us from the first day and by a miracle we escaped by running away, succeeding in taking with us the wireless and money, and afterwards we arrived at Pitulescu. One wireless set we left with Major Rootham. The Serb presented himself the second day to engineer Pitulescu, reporting what had occurred and at the same time giving a written declaration. Afterwards with engineer Pitulescu he arrived in Bucharest, being together in safety. I await with impatience your instructions. The Serb is a Sergeant-Major in the gendarmes, taken by Thomas from Mihailović as a help for the journey, knowing Romania well. I arrived in Bucharest on my own with papers prepared by me. The Serb arrived in Bucharest with Pitulescu with papers also prepared by me. Through Pitulescu, Alecu knows of me. Being alone and without support I presented myself to Capt. Protopopescu, my sole contact at the present time. I work in his house and I work as a clerk in his firm. Ask references about him from Burland. Confirm that the name NELU is for him.

Captain Charles Maydwell, formerly of the Rifle Brigade and Russell's senior officer, informed the family. Writing after the war, Jasper Rootham remembered:

David Russell was a man whom I had not known before, but although we were together for such a short time, it was in circumstances which led us to a quick knowledge of one another. I think he was an adventurer in the best sense of that word. Motor-cycle races and climbing in and out of Cambridge Colleges were things which he had in the past perhaps spent a disproportionate amount of time, but in war he found an outlet for the unease which had evidently beset him in time of peace . . . He often spoke with some apprehension of what would happen to him after the war, and I remember that he said that the best thing he could think of was to offer his sword to Chiang Kai Shek. Apart from his courage, which was obviously great, the thing which I noticed most about him was his consideration for others in small matters.[72] This is a quality which bulks much larger under guerrilla conditions than it would in ordinary life, and its presence or absence is a good test of what a man is really like.

Operation AUTONOMOUS: jaw jaw, not war war

After Russell's death, Țurcanu was run by Alecu Ionescu, Rica's assistant, and it was now that SOE mounted Operation AUTONOMOUS, the objective of which was no less than Romania's unconditional surrender and, that achieved, to organize as effective resistance to the Axis war effort as possible.

It is unclear how much SOE knew about Romania's own plans to extricate itself from the Axis camp. On 19 January 1943, a few days after his return from Hitler's headquarters at the Wolfschanze, Foreign Minister Mihai Antonescu informed the Italian Minister in Bucharest, with whom he was on good terms, that the atmosphere within the German leadership was depressing and that the German leaders had been forced by the battlefield reverses in Russia to fall back on a Fortress Europe defensive strategy. In his view, such a strategy was doomed to failure. Antonescu suggested that Italy and Romania should sound out the Western Allies in regard to a peace treaty, and in the case of Romania one that protected it from the Russians.

Having learnt about Mihai Antonescu's scheming, Hitler, at his 12 April 1943 meeting with Marshal Antonescu at Klessheim, demanded his replacement. Nevertheless, after a brief punitive 'leave of absence', Mihai Antonescu was reinstated and succeeded in presenting a new plan to Mussolini directly. During a five-hour conversation with the Italian dictator on 1 July 1943 at Rocca delle Camminate, Mihai Antonescu proposed the foundation of a bloc of small states of the Danube Basin or the Balkans in order to impede the Soviet advance. Surely Germany, which was withdrawing from the Eastern Front, would welcome such a proposal. Mussolini was suitably impressed by the Romanian Foreign Minister's plea and promised to talk to Hitler in two months' time. However the Allied landing in Sicily on 9/10 July rendered this promise obsolete.

Mihai Antonescu now turned his attention to the Western Allies, who, he felt, would not be keen to see Russia extend its sphere of influence to the Danube Valley and the Balkans. But his project of setting up a bloc of small states had no chance so long as none of the big powers supported it. There was initial interest in British circles and on 1 December 1943, during the Teheran Conference, Churchill asked Stalin what he thought about the idea of a Danubian Federation. Stalin replied that such a federation would not be viable, that the Germans would take advantage of this 'by putting flesh on something that is only skeleton, thus creating a great new state'. The Soviet leader also wanted to know whether Romania and Hungary, who were both engaged in fighting Russia, would be members of such a federation. Their conversation moved on to other topics.

Likewise, in early 1943, former Prime Minister Mironescu was given a mandate to approach the leadership of Miklós Horthy's government in Hungary, in an attempt by Marshal Antonescu to have both countries achieve a new territorial settlement and a common withdrawal from the Axis Powers. He began talks with Count Miklós Banffy's delegation in Bucharest on 9 June, but these negotiations ended when the two sides could not agree on a future status for northern Transylvania, a region held by Hungary at the time as a result of the Second Vienna Arbitral Award.

Meanwhile, the SOE plan to send AUTONOMOUS to Romania was well advanced. Their mission was to inform Maniu that he was to send an emissary to the Allies to discuss operational details of the overthrow of the Antonescu regime. A reception area had been arranged on an estate belonging to the Racotta family. Rica had asked Sandu Racotta to help with AUTONOMOUS and he had volunteered his estate at Storobaneasa to the south-east of Alexandria, a town about 20 miles north of the Danube. Sandu, code name Stefan, and Ţurcanu were to man the DZ with a group of six, five of them holding electric torches in a V-formation to mark it when they heard the aircraft overhead. But bad weather conditions caused unpreventable delays and the flight on 21

November was postponed. On 22 November, AUTONOMOUS, consisting of de Chastelain and Ivor Porter, managed to get airborne with a flight of three Halifax bombers. Although they were overhead of the pinpoint at 2324 hours, thick cloud obscured the DZ and after two hours circling around, the aircraft returned via Sofia and Tirana. A navigational error resulted in the aircraft drifting 30 miles off course, thereby missing its base and running out of fuel. The crew and passengers bailed out over southern Italy and were all safely recovered, although the SOE contingent was decidedly ill-tempered. Sandu's party had in fact been there on 21 November but on the following night bad weather and a broken-down car had prevented them reaching the DZ.

On 5 December, a third attempt was made but once again the DZ was not marked, and de Chastelain and Porter returned to base. A break in the weather on 21 December saw the mission once more leave for Romania, though this time Maydwell, a former oil man, had been replaced by Captain Silviu Meţianu, a Romanian sabotage expert, on the orders of SOE in London without any consultation with de Chastelain. At the time, it struck Porter as a strange decision since this was essentially a political mission to brief Maniu on what to tell his emissary for the Three Power talks in Nicosia. Before emplaning, de Chastelain handed in his pistol, saying, 'We are going to be with friends, so we won't need firearms.' Porter followed suit but Meţianu conspicuously retained his sidearm.

The orders to the pilot, who had been specially requested by de Chastelain, were clear: if the pinpoint was obscured by bad weather and there was no sign of the agreed signal, then the aircraft was to proceed to Bucharest to drop propaganda leaflets and then return on the same course to see if conditions had improved. The Mission jumped on the first run but there was no reception committee. De Chastelain later recalled: 'There was no moon, the earth was ploughed and black, while the ground mist was so thick one couldn't see one's feet.' He found Porter[73] nearby but it was much later when they located Meţianu swinging in his parachute harness from a tree. When dawn broke, they lay up in a wood and worked out that they were about 5 kilometres south of Plosca, a good 15 kilometres from the DZ. Within twenty-four hours they had been arrested by the local Gendarmerie and handed over to the Romanian military authorities. The incorrect drop zone was to rankle SOE for years to come and there is a note in the mission file that challenges the pilot's report that he 'saw momentary glimpse of signal fire through cloud': surely the crew knew that only electric torches in a V-formation were deployed as markers.[74]

The three members of AUTONOMOUS were taken to Bucharest where they were held in Gendarmerie Headquarters and interrogated, first by the Romanians and secondly by the Germans. It was at this stage that both the Marshal and Mihai Antonescu realized that the British prisoners provided a valuable lifeline to them in their efforts to find a way out of the war. Thus, to the infuriation of the Germans, they refused to accede to Nazi demands to send de Chastelain to Germany, reminding their allies that he was a POW under the Geneva Convention. At one stage, even Hitler raised the subject of de Chastelain with Antonescu, who refused to budge. His stubbornness may well have resulted from a message sent to him by Churchill, prompted by Sir William Stephenson.

A First World War Canadian flying ace, Stephenson had settled in England where he became a successful industrialist. As a result of his network of business contacts, he was able to provide Churchill with information about how the Nazi government was building up its armed forces and hiding massive military expenditures in violation of the terms of the Treaty of Versailles. This was the beginning of a close relationship between the two men and on the outbreak of war, Churchill sent him to the United States to establish and run the British Security Coordination (BSC) in New York. Headquartered in Room 3603 in the Rockefeller Center, BSC became the umbrella organization that by the end of the war represented all the British intelligence agencies – MI5, SIS, SOE and PWE – throughout North America, South America and the Caribbean.

In his dual role as the senior representative of British Intelligence in the Americas, and as Churchill's personal representative to President Roosevelt, Stephenson was one of the few people authorized to view the Ultra transcripts of German signals traffic provided by the Bletchley Park codebreakers. He was entrusted by Churchill to decide what Ultra information to pass to various branches of the US and Canadian governments.

In 1940, Marion de Chastelain had returned to England from

Romania and took their children by sea to live with her parents in New York. There she was recruited to work for Stephenson, travelling regularly to Washington DC to debrief agents working on behalf of the Allies. As a fluent French speaker, she was the controller of an American agent, code-named Cynthia, who was sleeping with the Vichy French embassy's press attaché in Washington; documents obtained by Cynthia are thought to have played a part in breaking the Vichy naval code before the TORCH invasion of North Africa in 1942. By 1943, two years after the entry of the USA into the war following Pearl Harbor, and the consequent closure of Axis embassies in Washington, her work for Stephenson came to an end and arrangements were made for her to take up a position with SIS in England. Accordingly she sailed from Halifax, Nova Scotia with her children to Liverpool, and then by rail to London, where she learnt that her husband had been captured in Romania.

Marion was appalled because, unbeknown to the British authorities, she had told her husband about Ultra. If the Romanians handed Chas over to the Gestapo, he could break under interrogation and reveal to the Germans that their Enigma code had been cracked. There was no question about the correct course of action and she immediately reported her indiscretion to her superiors in the British Intelligence community. So seriously was this breach of security viewed that Churchill sent a telegram to Marshal Antonescu in which he made it clear that he held him personally responsible for the safety of the British Mission. It had its desired effect and very soon de Chastelain and Porter were reinstated to their role of providing a radio link between Britain and Romania; traffic began to flow between Maniu, the Antonescus and the Western Allies. On 2 April, a meeting was arranged with Maniu, who promised to stage a coup, once the offer of Allied military assistance was in place. There was however no such offer and Maniu's innate and long-held suspicion of Russian intentions prevailed.

Peace negotiations begin – but not in earnest

Peace negotiations started in Cairo on 17 March 1944. Romania was represented by Prince Barbu Stirbey, later joined by

Constantin Visoianu; the Allies were represented by Lord Moyne (UK), Ambassador MacVeagh(US)[75] and Ambassador V.M. Novikov (USSR). Stirbey had gone to Cairo with the full approval of Marshal Antonescu, having actually had an interview with him before leaving the country, for the purpose of discussing the position he was going to adopt during the negotiations. Although he was technically a messenger of the opposition, Stirbey considered that the best solution was the agreement of the terms of any truce by Antonescu himself. His instructions were straightforward: to obtain military help against the Germans and to secure the best possible terms regarding any post-war territorial settlement for Romania, while at the same time looking for any support that the Western Allies could provide in countering impending Russian domination.

There was in reality little to discuss for the main purpose of the talks from the British and American perspective was to create the most favourable conditions for the D-Day landings in Europe. Any misinformation or deception which induced the Germans to withdraw troops from France to shore up other vulnerable parts of Fortress Europe was to be encouraged. So although initially the Allies agreed that the negotiations at Cairo were to be kept secret, Stirbey's arrival was deliberately leaked to the press on 14 March; indeed, some Allied newspapers presented him as an official representative of the Romanian government. The hope in Washington and London was that, worried about the possibility of losing Romania with its crucial oilfields, Hitler would increase the number of troops there, perhaps even deciding on a complete military occupation.

Possibly unknown to the Allies, Hitler and Marshal Antonescu had covered the same ground at their talks at Schloss Klessheim on 26 and 27 February, and as a gesture of confidence the Führer ordered preparations for '*Margarete II*', the secret plan for the military occupation of Romania by Wehrmacht troops, to be shelved. Later, on 23 March, in order to convince the Marshal to remain in the German camp – no easy task after the German occupation of Hungary four days earlier – Hitler told him that Germany no longer considered itself a signatory to the Vienna Diktat of 30 August 1940. Although he couldn't go public with this statement, Marshal Antonescu was convinced that he had finally regained the hallowed territory of Transylvania annexed by Hungary.

To help Antonescu make up his mind to leave the Axis camp, Anglo-American bombers attacked Bucharest on 4 April 1944, aiming mainly to interrupt military transports from Romania to the Eastern Front. Lasting for two hours, the operation destroyed hundreds of buildings and killed or injured over 6,000 people according to unofficial statistics. On 15 April, a massive bombing mission by the RAF, carried out by P-61 Black Widows, dropped cluster and incendiary bombs on the city, leading to widespread panic and damaging buildings such as the University of Bucharest. The raids, however, failed to accelerate the peace process and furthermore, the SOE W/T went off the air for ten days.

Throughout April, various armistice teams went back and forth between the Allies and Bucharest. Both Maniu and Antonescu continued to treat the armistice terms as open to negotiation: the former procrastinated over the timing of any coup without some form of military assistance from the Allies; the latter was fixated by the lack of territorial guarantees for Transylvania. On the last day of April, Churchill received an outraged telegram from Molotov, complaining that the British, through AUTONOMOUS, were negotiating with the Romanians behind Russia's back. The timing of this outburst coincided with a serious setback for the Soviet Army. In early April, Stavka had ordered the Soviet 2nd Ukrainian Front and 3rd Ukrainian Front to commence a coordinated invasion of Romania, directed towards the capture of Iaşi with a secondary objective of establishing bridgeheads across the Prut River. Despite initial Soviet success, a series of skillful German and Romanian counter-attacks managed to bring the Soviet offensive to a grinding halt, reducing Soviet tank strength to a point where a continued attack into Romania was not possible. In three days of fighting, the Wehrmacht LVII Panzer Corps (mainly the Grossdeutschland and 24th Panzer Divisions) and L Army Corps claimed the destruction of over 350 Soviet tanks.

In a minute of 7 May, Churchill asked Eden:

Why were these two important oil men picked? It does seem to me that SOE barges in an ignorant manner into all sorts of delicate situations. They were originally responsible for building up the nest of cockatrices for EAM in Greece . . . It is a very thing that the relations of two mighty forces like the British Empire and the USSR should be disturbed by these little pin-pricks interchanged by obscure persons playing the fool far below the surface. A great deal of small talk should be cut down. I am willing to discuss with you the whole position of SOE and whether it should not be divided up between the Military and the Foreign Office . . . Why should we be confronted with the descent of two oil men in Romania, in November, with vague powers who immediately tumble clumsily into the hands of the enemy? What reliance can be put upon Col de Chastelain's cypher when it is in the hands of the enemy and can be used by Maniu whether he is a free agent or not?

Such was the Prime Minister's fury that Eden suspended all SOE operations in the Balkans and cancelled all clandestine operations planned for Romania. However, Lieutenant Colonel Simonds of N Section had been busy inserting MI9 teams from his pool of Palestinian Jewish parachutists and Eden had partially to lift the ban because Operation ANTICLIMAX-GOULASH, a two-man MI9 team had been dropped near Craiova in Romania on 2/3 May to rescue 300 British and American airmen, and to render assistance to Jews. They were captured the following day, so two further teams were dropped in the Arad area in Operation ANTICLIMAX-SCHNITZEL on 3/4 June and Operation ANTICLIMAX-RAVIOLI on 30/31 July. Both reached Bucharest. Operation ANTICLIMAX-DOINER was dropped later that summer. Mihai Antonescu indirectly supported their activities for in June 1944 he had been in contact with the Zionist leader, A.L. Zissu,[76] and allowed the Palestine Office to openly operate in Bucharest, supplying identity papers to Jewish refugees from Hungary, Poland and Slovakia en route to Palestine.

A conciliatory telegram from Churchill to Molotov was nullified when Sir Archibald Clark-Kerr dissembled to Molotov a few days later that 'the fact that the Germans allowed the Romanians to keep captured British officers who were using a W/T set and ciphers for communication to the outside world seemed strange to him and that relations between Marshal Antonescu and Maniu were a mystery to him.' On 12 May, the Foreign Office signalled Cairo: 'In view of Soviet suspicions please see that de Chastelain is at once instructed to make no further use of his cipher and to send out no more messages.' Lord Selborne, the minister responsible for SOE, was unrepentant and felt that Molotov's annoyance was 'unreasonable'. This view was not shared by General Ismay, however, who noted: 'It was a blunder to send in de Chastelain without telling the Russians. Lord S should be apologetic for his share in this, not saucy. PM now daily weighs against SOE and I have to defend this "chip off the old blockhead" and his disordered following.' In the end, wise heads prevailed and Molotov's complaint was seen for what it was – an attempt to send a Soviet Mission to Greece as a quid pro quo. However, the Foreign Office had had enough of SOE's incursions into the arena of foreign policy and when Alexander Crețianu, Prince Stirbey's nephew, arrived as the new Romanian Minister in Ankara, and tried to meet with Colonel Bill Bailey whom he knew well, the FO ruled that neither the Ambassador nor SOE could contact him.

In early May, Madame Arion, a Dutch woman married to a Romanian, told the Dutch Minister in Istanbul that Prince Sturdza, the Marshal of Court, had suggested that after the Russian capture of Iași, King Michael should go there and surrender the Romanian Army to the Russians. When word of this reached the Foreign Office, the reaction was that this was a matter for the Romanians to decide on and not the Allies. Frustration with Romania's inability to disengage from the war was beginning to boil over.

After the Normandy landings on 6 June, the Cairo negotiations were no longer of any interest to the British and Americans. They considered Maniu an old, weak-willed politician, and they were not prepared to give him any undertakings that could have created future difficulties in their relations with the Soviet Union. Furthermore, by the end of June they had already agreed that Romania was to be included in the USSR's sphere of influence. The negotiations therefore closed down in the summer of 1944 and Maniu's W/T messages went unanswered. The fact that they were inconclusive, the German Foreign Minister von Ribbentrop perspicaciously remarked to Mihai Antonescu during his visit to Germany, was because 'British relations with Russia had gone so far beyond the point of no return that nothing could come of the Stirbey mission. Britain's Romanian policy had indeed been subsumed into her Soviet policy. She had no longer anything to offer Romania.'[77]

Ribbentrop was indeed correct. Going at least as far back as the spring of 1943, Great Britain considered that Romania fell predominantly within the Soviet sphere. Eden's briefing on Romania before his March 1943 visit to Washington stated: 'Our policy toward Romania is subordinated to our relations with the Soviet Union and we are unwilling to accept any commitments or take any action except with the full cognizance and consent of the Soviet government.' In a note to Sir Archibald Clark-Kerr in Moscow, he reiterated the British position to pass on to the Russians: 'As we have often emphasised, we considered that the Soviet government should take the lead in our joint efforts to get Romanian out of the war and we should give them all the support in our power.' During Eden's visit to Washington, Roosevelt also agreed to the Soviet claim to Bessarabia on the ground that the Soviets would be entitled to regain this province 'as it had been Russian throughout most of its history', an assertion that is, of course, historically incorrect.

On 5 May 1944 Eden, had suggested to the Soviet Ambassador in London a demarcation of the relevant zones of activity in the Balkans, according to a line which left Romania and Bulgaria within the sphere of Soviet interest, while Greece and Yugoslavia remained in the British. By 18 May, the Ambassador reported to Eden that the Soviet Union had tentatively accepted this division of the Balkans, and on 31 May Churchill asked Roosevelt for his 'blessing' to a plan to assign wartime responsibility for Romania to the USSR and for Greece to Britain. Even before the October 1944 conference, when the Churchill-Stalin agreement was penned, giving the USSR 90 per cent of influence in Romanian affairs, Moscow had made unilateral decisions on the fate of Romania.

While the Western Allies were talking to Maniu, separate yet parallel negotiations were taking place in Stockholm, where the official representative of Romania, Minister Frederic Nanu, was engaged in talks with the USSR's Ambassador, Mrs Alexandra Kollantay. These negotiations were carried on in secret by the Soviets, without the knowledge of their allies.

Antonescu's request for a fifteen-day term for a settlement with

Germany, the establishment of an unoccupied area in Romania where the Romanian government could move to, and goodwill in respect of the economic difficulties of Romania as and when war damage compensation was calculated, was surprisingly well received by Moscow. Since his main concern was to assure the fastest possible advance of the Red Army, Stalin had correctly calculated that the opposition, and Maniu in particular, was unlikely to overthrow the Marshal and therefore he was better off unilaterally negotiating with Antonescu, the only man who could deliver the crucial logistics base for his advancing armies. The Soviet Ambassador in Stockholm promised that her government would give an answer to these requests, but Romania had left it too late.

The Changing of the Guard

From the spring of 1944, when the front reached and even crossed the Romanian borders, Marshal Antonescu had become actively involved in directing military operations. After failing to convince Hitler to withdraw the Seventeenth Army (which contained seven battle-hardened Romanian divisions) from Crimea, while there was still time to pull it out in an organized fashion without unnecessary losses, he had to go to the front and assume direct command over all Romanian troops after the Soviet Iaşi-Chişinău offensive started on 20 August 1944. Ordering their withdrawal to the Adjud-Focsani-Namoloasa-Galati fortified line, he returned to Bucharest and on the afternoon of 23 August was summoned to the Royal Palace, where King Michael asked him to sign an armistice with the Allies immediately.

Following his refusal, the King ordered his arrest, and that of Mihai Antonescu and his other close associates. After a short detention in the Palace's strong room, General Constantin Sănătescu, the new Prime Minister, handed him over to the Romanian Communist Party, who locked him up in a house in the Vatra Luminoasa neighbourhood of Bucharest. He was later passed on to the Soviets on 1 September, and transported to somewhere in the vicinity of Moscow, before returning to be tried by the so-called People's Court. Following a mock trial, on 17 May

1946 he was convicted to six death penalties, two life in prison sentences, eighty years in jail and 140 years of civic degradation. The execution took place on 1 June 1946.

Immediately after broadcasting to the nation, King Michael summoned de Chastelain and Porter to the Royal Palace. Radio communications with Istanbul had broken down and it was imperative to keep the Allies fully in the loop during the first days of the coup. While not relying on the arrival of Anglo-American troops, the King was counting on supplies of arms and material. De Chastelain suggested that he should fly post haste to Istanbul with news of the coup and instructions for Stirbey in Cairo, and was soon heading east in a decrepit Lockheed, flying at low level to avoid German ack-ack. He said he would be gone for four days; in reality, he never returned,[78] for sadly the harsh truth was that Romania was now given over to the Russians.

King Michael named General Sănătescu to head the new government, which was dominated by Maniu's National Peasants Party and Brătianu's National Liberal Party. Sănătescu appointed Lucretiu Pătrăscanu, a Communist Party Central Committee member, as Minister of Justice. Pătrăscanu thus became the first Romanian communist to hold high government office. The coup certainly helped to shorten the war, yet such is its proximity to the Russian Iaşi-Chişinău offensive that it is difficult to gauge by how much. For certain, no oil was exported to Germany after August 1944, compared to a figure of 50,000 tons of benzine in June.

Around this time, the OSS was busy rescuing aircrews. Under the direction of Frank Wisner, a former Wall Street lawyer, who headed the Office's operations in south-east Europe, some 1,350 American air crew POWs held prisoner in Romania were rescued by a US Air Crew Rescue Unit, with Soviet troops only days away from Bucharest. Despite continuing fighting between Romanian and Red Army forces, and the presence of the Wehrmacht and Luftwaffe in the immediate area, the rescue team used the Popeşti-Leordeni Airfield where twelve B-17 Flying Fortresses flew the prisoners out in hourly shifts.

In a further operation, again under the eye of Wisner, the Romanians rounded up more than 750 American air crew POWs in the Balkans and, having put them on an improvised freight train, transported then through the Balkans and Turkey to Syria. US Air Transport Command in Cairo was ordered to assemble enough transport aircraft to pick all of them up from a landing ground north of Aleppo and take them to Cairo.

But little was as it seemed with the OSS. It was later learnt that the OSS had infiltrated more than 150 German and Romanian Nazi intelligence agents who were specialists on the East European and western USSR region into this group of POWs and slipped them into Cairo, from where they went on to form a nucleus of 'experts' to work with their American counterparts against the Soviets after the war.

Wisner later went on to attract rather more attention than was becoming of a clandestine operative. He had set himself up in the thirty-room mansion of Mita Bragadiru, owner of Romania's largest brewery, and befriended the brewer's wife, Princess Tanda Caradja, in order to break into Romanian society. Soon he was a confidant of King Michael and the Queen Mother, moving effortlessly from one high-society party to another. This all came to an abrupt halt on 6 January 1945 when the Red Army rounded up all men between seventeen and forty-five, and all women between eighteen and thirty, of 'German ethnic origin, regardless of citizenship' and deported them to Russia. Wisner, as he watched this tragedy unfold, realized that the USA was powerless to prevent it and returned soon after to Washington.

The Red Army occupied Bucharest on 31 August 1944. In Moscow on 12 September, Romania and the Soviet Union signed an armistice on terms dictated by Moscow. Romania agreed to pay reparations,[79] repeal anti-Jewish laws, ban fascist groups, and hand back Bessarabia and northern Bucovina to the Soviet Union. Representatives of the Soviet Union, the United States and Britain established an Allied Control Commission in Bucharest, but the Soviet military command had the upper hand. Ivor Porter, who had stayed on as the SOE member of the BMM, now found time to enjoy himself, including having dinner with the girlfriend of one of his former German gaolers, who was now himself incarcerated. His Russian interpreter, the beautiful Princess Nadia Cantacuzino, added a touch of glamour to routine office work;[80] her husband, Prince Constantin, was the highest-ranking Romanian fighter ace with fifty-seven confirmed 'kills' and thirteen probables. He is probably one of the few pilots, if not the only one, to shoot down Soviet, US and German aircraft, and in the process flew British Hurricanes, German Messerschmitts and American Mustangs!

By the time hostilities between Romania and the Soviet Union ended, Romania's military losses had totalled about 110,000 killed and 180,000 missing or captured; the Red Army also transported about 130,000 Romanian soldiers to the Soviet Union, where many perished in prison camps. After its surrender, Romania committed about fifteen divisions to the Allied cause under Soviet command. Before the end of hostilities against Germany, a further 120,000 Romanian troops perished helping the Red Army liberate Czechoslovakia and Hungary.

On 2 December, King Michael replaced Sănătescu with General Rădescu. Somewhat to his chagrin, the following February the General embraced the words of the Yalta Conference to allow the European peoples 'to create democratic institutions of their own choice' rather too warmly and after some careful orchestration of street demonstrations, the Deputy Soviet Foreign Minister, Vyshinsky, arrived in Bucharest and gave the King a two-hour ultimatum to appoint a Communist-controlled government under Petru Groza or risk Romania's disappearance as a sovereign state for ever.

By November 1946, when elections finally took place, Maniu had become the principal leader of the anti-communist opposition in Romania, trying to stop his country being absorbed into the USSR as a Soviet satellite state. He was consequently arrested on 25 July 1947 and sentenced to life imprisonment on 11 November, aged seventy-five. He died in the notorious political prison at Sighet in 1953. The one person who now stood between Romania and a fully fledged Soviet satellite state was the King. On 30 December, Petru Groza, the Prime Minister, and Gheorghiu Dej, the Secretary General of the Communist Party, had an audience with the King and his mother. Surrounded by troops, his telephone lines cut and threatened with mass arrests of monarchists, the King had no option other than to abdicate.

Mackenzie, in his *Secret History of SOE*, sums up:

> Romania had been a disappointing story for SOE . . . a coup
> d'état to remove Antonescu, in the end worked perfectly, but

it was too late to be more than a recognition of a Russian fait accompli, of little use to either the Allies or to Romania. It might well have come sooner if luck had favoured SOE a little. The death of Captain Russell and the capture of de Chastelain were both disasters outside of its control. They showed how high the chance of failure was: SOE might perhaps have re-insured by doubling and redoubling the number of attempts, but there is a limit to the number of 'forlorn hopes' for which a commander can call, and it would have been a hard decision to put more brave men in peril for so uncertain a gain.

On 1 June 1944, Russell was posthumously 'Mentioned in Despatches', a somewhat insignificant and meagre award given the importance of his mission and his courage in carrying it out. His father, Captain E. Russell, corresponded with the War office about David's grave. His other son, George, had been killed at El Alamein with the 7th Battalion of the Rifle Brigade, but at least in his case his father had managed to visit his grave with its view over the Mediterranean.

Russell's grave, a wooden cross at Vărciorova, had been left unmarked – 'here lies an unknown' – since neither the Germans nor the Romanians would have countenanced it. Now that the area was under the control of the Allied Commission, a headstone was organized to replace the simple anonymous cross with the inscription 'Captain David Russell, a gallant gentleman who died in the battle for the liberty of Europe.'[81] His father wondered whether the MC could be added and offered to pay for the cost and upkeep of the grave. The advice of the British Commission was sanguine: best not as it could not guarantee that the mayor would use the funds for the purposes he intended.

De Chastelain remained convinced that if AUTONOMOUS had been dropped in the right place and had been able to make contact with Maniu as planned, the war could have been dramatically shortened. On 22 August 1944, General Tobescu, head of Romanian internal security, told de Chastelain that if the mission had not been picked up, 'Romania would have been out of the war six months earlier.'

Notes to Part Three

1. 1415 and 1498 respectively.
2. The final Act of the Congress of Berlin, the treaty recognized the complete independence of the principalities of Romania, Serbia and Montenegro and the autonomy of Bulgaria, though the latter remained under formal Ottoman overlordship. The three newly independent states subsequently proclaimed themselves kingdoms – Romania in 1881, Serbia in 1882 and Montenegro in 1910 – while Bulgaria proclaimed full independence in 1908.
3. England, France and Russia.
4. Germany, Austria-Hungary and Italy.
5. Treaty of Bucharest, 27 August 1916.
6. Treaty of Bucharest, 7 May 1918.
7. Formerly part of Hungary, the Maramureş region was split between Romania and Czechoslovakia with the Tiza River forming the boundary.
8. The eastern borderlands belonging to Hungary.
9. Formerly part of Hungary, the vast majority was ceded to Romania, with a small amount going to Serbia and some remaining with Hungary.
10. The statistic of 250,000 military dead is the figure reported by the Romanian government to the International Labour Office. The British War Office's 1922 estimate was higher at 335,706 killed and missing.
11. *Eastern Europe 1918–1941.*
12. Codreanu (1899–1938) had been an activist since 1919 and been arrested several times, including being tried and acquitted for the murder of an Iaşi judge.
13. During his short six-week period in government, Goga intensified anti-Semitic legislation and on 12 January 1938 his government stripped Romanian Jews of their citizenship.
14. For instance, the banker Aristide Blank and the industrialists Nicolae Malaxa and Max Auschnitt.
15. By this award, Germany and Italy compelled Czechoslovakia to return southern Slovakia and southern Subcarpathia (now in Ukraine) to Hungary on 2 November 1938.
16. In 1938, the top five oil exporting countries were Venezuela (19m tons), USA (15m tons), Persia (8.5m tons), Dutch East Indies (6.5m tons) and Romania (5.7m tons).
17. In 1916, British engineers under the direction of Colonel (later Lord) Thomson blew up most of the oil installations round Ploieşti, rendering production impossible for several months.
18. Porter, *Operation Autonomous.*
19. This act was reciprocated on 21 September 1939 by the Iron Guard when they assassinated PM Călinescu. While passing through the Eroilor area of Bucharest, Călinescu's car was ambushed by assassins, who gunned him down as he sat in the back seat. The assassins then stormed into the Radio Broadcasting Society; holding the employees at gunpoint they announced that they had killed the Premier. The message was never broadcast, as transmission had already been interrupted by staff.

20. In 1940 and 1941, Romania supplied 94 per cent and 75 per cent of German oil imports respectively.
21. By this award, Germany and Italy compelled Romania to cede half of Transylvania (an area henceforth known as Northern Transylvania) to Hungary on 30 August 1940.
22. 43,000 sq.kms and about 2.6 million people.
23. On 7 September 1940, southern Dobrudja, an area of 7,000 sqkms, was returned by Romania to Bulgaria under the Treaty of Craiova. It had been been part of Romania since 1913, after Bulgaria's defeat in the Second Balkan War.
24. The archives of the Centre of Oral History of the Romanian Radio Broadcasting Corporation.
25. Via the offices of Beneš and the Czech Government in exile.
26. Antonescu had been Military Attaché in both Paris and London in the 1920s.
27. The first of ten meetings with Hitler between 1940 and 1944.
28. The Abwehr had infiltrated over 250 members of the Brandenburg Regiment into Romania and Bulgaria to watch out for British skulduggery.
29. See Geoffrey Household's *Against the Wind*, pp. 106–8.
30. The Agency wanted Major Orde Wingate, later of Chindit fame, to lead the operations. The Army, whilst sympathetic, declined their request.
31. This was vested in Kontinentale Oel AG, a company founded to take over companies belonging to enemy and neutral powers in the countries occupied by Germany.
32. Taylor finally made it back to London in June 1941 somewhat overtaken by events.
33. The Principality of Transylvanian had been the first European state to promulgate an edict of religious tolerance in 1553.
34. By giving the same rights to Uniats as Roman Catholics, Leopold effectively gave them political emancipation as well.
35. Father of General de Chastelain, who oversaw the IRA weapons decommissioning programme.
36. With the exception of John Toyne, who remained in Bucharest reporting directly to London.
37. In turn owned by the Glico Petroleum Company, a subsidiary of the Anglo-American Oil Company (later Esso), and the Petroleum and Industrial Trust Ltd.
38. Leith-Ross delegation.
39. This was an underestimate. The Fourth Romanian Army, which had 4,821 officers before the operation, lost 4,599 during the three assaults on Odessa. 'Strategically,' King Michael was to comment, 'Odessa was possibly an important point on the war map, but not on our war map, on the German.'
40. Formally re-established as Romanian provinces on 4 September 1941.
41. The principles to be applied after the war would include the right of peoples to choose the form of government under which they would live.
42. SOE/3IG Cipher telegram to Cairo, 11.2.1942, No. 4094.
43. Deletant, *Hitler's Forgotten Ally*, p. 84.

44. Source: July 22 1943 Political Intelligence Department, FO Stockholm.
45. Deletant, *op. cit.*, p. 75.
46. Constantin Vulcan, the Romanian Cultural Attaché in Bern, was in contact with the OSS and Allen Dulles.
47. A colleague recalls how Russell took every occasion to visit Germany after school – 'he loved the country'. Source: letter George Bold to SG.
48. 'Natasha' married the English diplomat and accomplished poet and translator Charles (Hepburn) Johnston in 1944. Her presence in Cairo in 1943, where Charles was posted, supposedly caused David some discomfort.
49. Letter Pulteney to SG.
50. According to the testimony of a fellow officer, Russell was dining in the Officers' Mess when a bomb exploded nearby and blew in the windows and blackout curtains. He promptly pulled out his revolver and shot all the lights bulbs out to prevent the bombers overhead from targeting the now illuminated barracks!
51. Letter George Bold, SG archives.
52. Virginia Cowles writes that David Russell 'transferred from the SIG where he had been helping Captain Buck train his Palestinian German unit'.
53. Cowles, *The Phantom Major*, p. 222.
54. Stirling was deeply uneasy about how the original small-scale raid had escalated into a major combined arms operation.
55. Landsborough, *Tobruk Commando*, p. 35.
56. Afrika Korps motifs were painted on the trucks using captured German stencils; likewise identification marks were painted on the cab roofs to ward off marauding Stukas. Also across the bonnet was a wide white stripe, the sign of '*Bentezeichen*' or booty, which the Germans painted on captured Allied vehicles, and the divisional sign ER 372, which Intelligence had discovered was a real division stationed near Alamein.
57. Buck was killed near Chard in an air crash en route to Germany on 22 November 1945.
58. The other destroyer, HMS *Zulu*, was also hit by shore batteries and later damaged by a bomb. She sunk 100 miles west of Alexandria while under tow.
59. Russell was listed as 'reported missing' on 14 September and 'reported safe' on 2 December.
60. Commanded by Anthony Berry of the Lifeguards.
61. Letter to parents 1943.
62. A former Managing Director of Unirea.
63. On 22 July, an officer called David Thomas was dropped to the same Mission, with orders to proceed to Romania.
64. Strong Romanian plum brandy.
65. Țurcanu's debrief to SOE.
66. On Vodița River.
67. Their first radio messages reached Cairo on 12 and 13 August.
68. Russell wore his personal Longines as well as an army issue watch.
69. The word Petre Mihai used was 'Stai', usually associated with military patrols.

70. SOE report by Captain S.G. Mețianu, 23 March 1945.
71. Signal in SOE archives. One wonders what happened to the 'four machine pistols of German make which [Russell] had specially reserved before leaving North Africa' that were successfully dropped to him on the night of 22 July according to Jasper Rootham.
72. In a letter to Russell's sister dated 14 September 1945, Rootham amplifies this sentiment: 'What impressed me about him, though, was his extreme unselfishness and consideration for others in small matters, which became very important under guerrilla conditions.'
73. Porter recalls that they jumped into thick fog through which it was impossible see any lights at all.
74. MI9 had experienced a similar problem when Operation MANTILLA (an operation to assist the return of Allied aircrew on the run) was dropped very wide of its Romanian pinpoint on 1/2 October 1943. The two-man team of Sgt Liova and Sgt Fichman landed in the centre of a town and were immediately captured. Subjected to weeks of severe interrogation (one was sent to Germany for interrogation by the Gestapo), they were finally recognized as POWs. Both were repatriated in September 1944.
75. Ambassador to the Greek and Yugoslav governments in exile in Egypt.
76. Avram Zissu was Chairman of the Zionist Executive Committee.
77. Ivor Porter, *Michael of Romania*, p. 91.
78. Ivor Porter remained in Bucharest, running the SOE network until joining the British Legation, first as a press officer, then as Third Secretary. In 1947, he returned to London where he joined the FO.
79. Estimates of total actual reparations are US$2 billion.
80. As Nadia Gray, she later became a successful stage and screen actress and singer, starring in the Paris production of Noel Coward's *Present Laughter* and in Fellini's *La Dolce Vita*.
81. Another account says: 'Here lies Captain David Russell, The Scots Guards, killed August 1943'. Source: letter to SG from Nancy Holmes, 16 September 1946.

Epilogue

It is easy, especially in hindsight, to underestimate the effectiveness of SOE's operations in those countries of central and south-eastern Europe allied to the Axis powers. Compared to the results achieved in France and Yugoslavia, even Albania, there were few military or political laurels to emerge from Hungary, Romania or Bulgaria. Scantily resourced and diplomatically constrained by the need to defer to and consult with the USSR, SOE's ambitions, though laudable like those of Icarus, were brought to earth by the gravitational pull of insuperable political forces. Yet, when measured on the scale of the elephant and the flea, the catalytic impact of SOE's clandestine operations served as a persistent irritant, continuously undermining Germany's strategic and political assumptions about the loyalty of her allies.

The handful of SOE missions probing the Hungarian border and occasionally reaching Budapest, combined with German intelligence on the seditious antics of the Surrender Group and its many-tentacled representation in the Hungarian legations abroad, persuaded Hitler that Hungary was not to be trusted as an ally and thus brought about Plan *Margarethe I* on 17/18 March 1944 when eleven German divisions, including panzer troops equipped with the latest King Tigers, were deployed to seize it; troops who should have been much further east, defending the high passes of the Carpathian mountains against the approaching Russian invaders. For the Hungarian people, the reality of the horror of occupation had arrived, nullifying their Mephistophelean pact with Hitler.

The presence of the first SOE mission, RANJI, within the borders of Romanian was equally destabilizing to the planners of OKW in Berlin, for Romania was the prime supplier of petroleum products to the German war machine. By quickly following it up with the AUTONOMOUS Mission, which in turn prompted Prince Stirbey Romanian peace delegation to Cairo, SOE's comprehensively undermined Germany's trust in Romania's reliability as an ally. No fewer than 57,000 German troops were deployed in Romania in 1944. When the coup against Marshal Antonescu finally took place in August 1944, it was too late to alter the timetable of the war for the Russians were only days from Bucharest. If, as Colonel Chas de Chastelain later speculated, AUTONOMOUS had avoided capture and made its way successfully to Bucharest in December 1943, then there might have been a real possibility of extricating Romania from the war by the early spring. That in turn would have in all likelihood triggered a German invasion and drawn troops away from the defence of France and Italy.

In the case of Bulgaria, although exasperated by his ally's refusal to take up arms against the Russians, Hitler relied on King Boris to police Macedonia and Thrace, thereby keeping vulnerable supply routes to Greece open, and to provide a substantial military reserve in case of an Allied invasion through Turkey, or indeed Greece itself. Once it became known to the Gestapo and Abwehr that SOE missions were operating within Bulgaria's expanded borders and were planning to create a Yugoslavian-style Partisan movement with the communist-led Fatherland Front, thus threatening to tie down the Bulgarian Army in wide-scale anti-Partisan operations and jeopardize the security of the tenuous supply lines to Greece, their confidence in their most reliable and placid ally wilted.

These results, achieved by a handful of courageous and determined men, are remarkable by any measure, the more so since the conditions under which they were carried out were consistently adverse, with the odds stacked against success. It could be argued that, in the course of planning and executing these operations, SOE invented the concept and practice of asymmetric warfare in which the actions of a few disproportionally impact on the lives of the many. But there was no magic formula at work other than human ingenuity and heroism. Motivated by a desire to take the war to the Germans, the officers and men of SOE who made up the Missions were all exceptionally resourceful and brave, qualities reflected in the gallantry awards bestowed on many of them by the end of the war. The words from Verse 23 of the first chapter of the Second Book of Samuel inscribed on David Russell's headstone in the little Commonwealth War Graves cemetery outside Bucharest read: 'They were lovely and pleasant in their lives, and in their deaths they were not divided.' It is a fitting tribute to all the members of SOE who fought in Hungary, Bulgaria and Romania to recall the rest of the verse: 'They were swifter than eagles, they were stronger than lions.'

Select Bibliography

Amery, Julian, *Approach March*, Hutchinson, 1973.

Andrew, Christopher, *Secret Service*, William Heinemann, 1985.

Axworthy, Mark, *Third Axis, Fourth Ally*, Hailer Publishing, 2007.

——, *Axis Slovakia: Hitler's Slavic Wedge*, Europa Books, 2002.

Axworthy, Mark and Thomas, Nigel, *Balkan Battleground 1939–1945*, Aurum Press, 2002.

Barker, Elizabeth, *British Policy in South-East Europe in the Second World War*, Macmillan, 1975.

Beevor, J.G., *S.O.E.: Recollections and Reflections*, Bodley Head, 1981.

Bérenger, Jean, *History of the Habsburg Empire 1273–1700*, Pearson Education, 2002.

——, *History of the Habsburg Empire 1700–1918*, Pearson Education, 2002.

Bolitho, Hector, *Roumania under King Carol*, Eyre & Spottiswoode, 1939.

Callimachi, Anne-Marie, *Yesterday was Mine*, Falcon Press, 1952.

Conradi, Peter, *Iris Murdoch – A Life: The Authorized Biography*, Harper Collins, 2002.

Cowles, Virginia, *The Phantom Major*, Collins, 1964.

Crampton, Richard, *A Concise History of Bulgaria*, CUP, 1997.

Davidson, Basil, *Partisan Picture*, Bedford Books, 1946.

——, *Special Operations Europe*, Gollancz, 1980.

Davidson-Houston, James, *Armed Pilgrimage*, Hale, 1949.

Deletant, Dennis, *Hitler's Forgotten Ally*, Palgrave, 2006.

Deroc, M., *British Special Operatives Explored*, East European Monographs, 1988.

Dilks, David (ed.), *The Diaries of Sir Alexander Cadogan*, Cassell, 1971.

Downs, Jim, *O.S.S Tragedy in Slovakia*, Liefrinck Publishers, 2002.

Dulles, Allen, *From Hitler's Doorstep*, Pennsylvania State University, 1996.

Duke, Florimund, *Name, Rank and Serial Number*, Meredith Press, 1969.

Elsberry, Terence, *Marie of Romania*, Cassell, 1973.

Foot, M.R.D., *SOE: An Outline History of the Special Operations Executive*, Pimlico, 1999.

Footman, David, *Balkan Holiday*, William Heinemann, 1935.

Gardiner, Leslie, *Curtain Calls*, Duckworth, 1976.

Gladwyn, Lord, *Memoirs*, Weidenfeld & Nicolson, 1972.

Glantz, David, *Red Storm over the Balkans: The Failed Soviet Invasion of Romania in Spring 1944*, University of Kansas, 2007.

Glen, Alexander, *Footholds against a Whirlwind*, Hutchinson, 1975.

——, *Target Danube*, The Book Guild, 2002.

Hamilton-Hill, Donald, *S.O.E. Assignment*, William Kimber, 1973.

Hastings, Stephen, *The Drums of Memory*, Pen and Sword Books, 1994.

Hill, George, *Go Spy the Land*, Cassell & Co., 1932.

Hollingsworth, Clare, *There's a German Just Behind Me*, Right Book Club, 1943.

Horthy, Admiral, *Memoirs*, Hutchinson, 1956.

Household, Geoffrey, *Against the Wind*, Michael Joseph, 1958.

Howarth, Patrick, *Undercover, The Men and Women of the Special Operations Executive*, Routledge & Kegan Paul, 1980.

Howie, Claerwen, *Agent by Accident*, Thorold's Africana Books, 1997.

Johnson, Stowers, *Agents Extraordinary*, Robert Hale, 1975.

Jones, Francis Stephen, *Double Dutchman*, Hale, 1977.

Kállay, Nicholas, *Hungarian Premier: A Personal Account of a Nation's Struggle in the Second World War*, OUP, 1954.

Keyes, Elizabeth, *Geoffrey Keyes VC MC*, George Newnes, 1956.

Király, Bzla and Veszprémy László, *Millennium of Hungarian Military History*, Atlantic Research & Publications Inc., 2002.

Kirke, Maj-Gen W.M., *An Outline of the Rumanian Campaign 1916–18*, The Naval & Military Press, 2010.

Kontler, László, *Millenium in Central Europe: A History of Hungary*, Atlantisz Könyvkiadó, Budapest, 1999.

Kurapovna, Marcia Christoff, *Shadows on the Mountain*, John Wiley, 2010.

Landsborough, Gordon, *Tobruk Commando*, Corgi, 1957.

Lebor, Adam, *Surviving Hitler: Choices, Corruption and Compromise in the Third Reich*, Scribner, 2001.

Lees, Michael, *Special Operations Executed*, William Kimber, 1986.

Lendvai, Paul, *The Hungarians*, Hurst & Co., 1999.

Lesle, Henrietta, *Where East is West*, Jarrolds, 1993.

Lodge, Professor Sir Richard, *History of Modern Europe — from the Capture of Constantinople 1453 to the Treaty of Berlin 1878*, John Murray, 1906.

Londres, Albert, *Terror in the Balkans*, Constable, 1935.

MacDermott, Mercia, *The Apostle of Freedom*, Allen & Unwin, 1967.

Maclaren, Roy, *Canadians Behind Enemy Lines 1939–1945*, University of British Columbia Press, 1981.

Macmillan, Margaret, *Peacemakers*, John Murray, 2001.

Macpherson, Ian, *Blurred Recollections 1939–1946,*.

Magris, Claudio, *Danube*, Harvill Press, 2001.

Manning, Olivia, *The Balkan Trilogy*, Arrow Books, 1992.

Marriott, Sir J.A.R., *The Eastern Question: An Historical Study of European Diplomacy*, Clarendon Press, 1919.

Masson, Madeleine, *Christine, S.O.E Agent and Churchill's Favourite Spy*, Virago, 2005.

Mather, Carol, *When the Grass Stops Growing*, Pen and Sword Books, 1997.

Mazower, Mark, *Inside Hitler's Greece: The Experience of Occupation 1941–44*, Yale University Press, 1995.

Miller, Marshall Lee, *Bulgaria during the Second World War*, Stanford University Press, 1975.

Minshall, Merlin, *Guilt-Edged*, Bachman & Turner, 1975.

Napier, Lt Col the Hon H.D., *Experiences of a Military Attache in the Balkans*, The Military Press, 2010.

Neave, Airey, *Saturday at MI9*, Leo Cooper, 2004.

Newman, Bernard, *The Blue Danube*, Herbert Jenkins, 1935.

Nichol, John and Rennell, Tony, *Home Run: Escape from Nazi Europe*, Viking, 2007.

Nutting, David, *Attain by Surprise: Capturing Top Secret Information in World War Two*, David Colver, 2003.

O'Sullivan, Vincent, *Long Journey to the Border: A Life of John Mulgan*, Penguin, 2003.

Pakula, Hannah, *Queen of Roumania*, Simon and Schuster, 1984.

Palgi, Yoel, *Into the Inferno*, Rutgers University Press, 2003.

Pálóczi-Horváth, George, *The Undefeated*, Eland, 1993.

Pearton, Maurice, *Oil and the Romanian State*, OUP, 1971.

Porter, Ivor, *Operation Autonomous*, Chatto & Windus, 1989.

——, *Michael of Romania*, Sutton, 2005.

Quinlan, Paul, *The Playboy King*, Greenwood Press, 1995.

Richardson, General Sir Charles, *Flashback*, William Kimber, 1985.

Rootham, Jasper, *Miss Fire*, Chatto & Windus, 1946.

Rothschild, Joseph, *East Central Europe between the Two World Wars*, University of Washington Press, 1974.

Runciman, Sir Stephen, *A Traveller's Alphabet*, Thames and Hudson, 1991.

Schandl, Catherine Eva, *The London-Budapest Game*, Lulu, 2007.

Seaman, Mark, *Special Operations Executive: A New Instrument of War*, Routledge, 2006.

Senesh, Hannah, *Her Life and Diary*, Valentine Mitchell, 1971.

Seton-Watson, R.W., *History of the Roumanians*, Cambridge University Press, 1934.

Seton-Watson, Hugh, *Eastern Europe between the Wars 1918–1941*, Cambridge University Press, 1945.

Smith, Peter, *Massacre at Tobruk*, Stackpole Books, 2008.

Stafford, David, *Britain and European Resistance 1940–945*, John Murray, 1997.

Sutherland, Christina, *Enchantress*, John Murray, 1996.

Sweet-Escott, Bickham, *Baker Street Irregular*, Methuen, 1965.

Thompson, E.P., *Beyond the Frontier*, Merlin Press, 1997.

Thompson, Frank, *Selected Poems*, Kate Thompson (ed.), Trent Editions, 2003.

——, *There is a Spirit in Europe: A Memoir*, Gollancz, 1947.

Tomasevich, Jozo, *The Chetniks*, Stamford University Press, 1975.

Treptow, Kurt, *History of Romania*, The Center for Romanian Studies, 1996.

Ungvary, Krisztian, *Battle for Budapest*, I.B.Taurus, 2005.

Veress, Laura-Louise, *Clear the Line: Hungary's Struggle to Leave the Axis during the Second World War*, Prospero Publications, Cleveland, Ohio, 1995.

von Hassell, Agostino and MacRae, Sigrid, *Alliance of Enemies*, Macmillan, 2006.

von Rezzori, Gregor, *The Snows of Yesteryear*, Chatto & Windus, 1990.

von Waldeck, Countess Rosa, *Athenee Palace*, Constable, 1943.

Vukmanovic, Svetozar, *Struggle for the Balkans*, Merlin Press, 1990.

Walker David, *Death at my Heels*, Chapman & Hall, 1942.

Wilkinson, Sir Peter, *Foreign Fields*, I.B.Taurus, 2002.

Williams, Heather, *Parachutes, Patriots and Partisans*, University of Wisconsin Press, 2003.

Woodhouse, Christopher, *The Struggle for Greece 1941–1949*, Beekman Inc, 1971.

Index